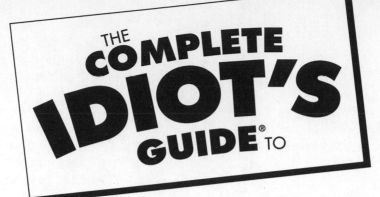

Meeting and Event Planning

Second Edition

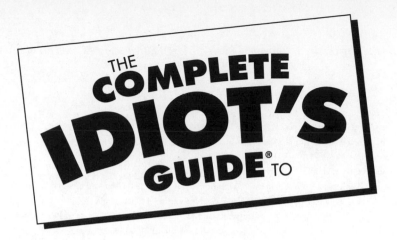

THE COMPLETE IDIOT'S GUIDE® TO

Meeting and Event Planning

Second Edition

by Robin E. Craven and Lynn Johnson Golabowski
with D'Etta Waldoch, CMP

ALPHA

A member of Penguin Group (USA) Inc.

This book is dedicated to our children, Clayton, Charley, Morgan, Taylor, Jared, and Andrew, who make it all worth the effort.

ALPHA BOOKS

Published by the Penguin Group

Penguin Group (USA) Inc., 375 Hudson Street, New York, New York 10014, U.S.A.

Penguin Group (Canada), 10 Alcorn Avenue, Toronto, Ontario, Canada M4V 3B2 (a division of Pearson Penguin Canada Inc.)

Penguin Books Ltd., 80 Strand, London WC2R 0RL, England

Penguin Ireland, 25 St Stephen's Green, Dublin 2, Ireland (a division of Penguin Books Ltd.)

Penguin Group (Australia), 250 Camberwell Road, Camberwell, Victoria 3124, Australia (a division of Pearson Australia Group Pty. Ltd.)

Penguin Books India Pvt. Ltd., 11 Community Centre, Panchsheel Park, New Delhi—110 017, India

Penguin Group (NZ), cnr Airborne and Rosedale Roads, Albany, Auckland 1310, New Zealand (a division of Pearson New Zealand Ltd.)

Penguin Books (South Africa) (Pty.) Ltd., 24 Sturdee Avenue, Rosebank, Johannesburg 2196, South Africa

Penguin Books Ltd., Registered Offices: 80 Strand, London WC2R 0RL, England

Publisher: *Marie Butler-Knight*
Editorial Director: *Mike Sanders*
Senior Managing Editor: *Jennifer Bowles*
Senior Acquisitions Editor: *Randy Ladenheim-Gil*
Development Editor: *Lynn Northrup*
Production Editor: *Megan Douglass*
Copy Editor: *Ross Patty*
Cartoonist: *Richard King*
Book Designer: *Trina Wurst*
Cover Designer: *Bill Thomas*
Indexer: *Angie Bess*
Layout: *Ayanna Lacey*

Contents at a Glance

Contents

Foreword

Dear Readers,

When this book was first released, we lived and planned in a different world. On 9.11.01 all that changed. In my meeting-planning seminars I always start with a disclaimer that meeting planning is complex and requires careful attention to detail and attention to the objectives around which the meeting is designed. In fact, I always say it's *more* than brain surgery: brain surgeons are responsible for one life at a time; we who plan meetings often are responsible for tens of thousands of people at a time. After 9.11.01, we had to look very differently at every aspect of how we planned and executed meetings—and we learned that what we did was truly more than brain surgery as we learned to cope in a new world of security and regulations.

Individuals who are responsible for a few or a multitude of people at a meeting have to plan and manage carefully. We are responsible for the education, care, feeding, and safety of all those who attend our meetings and events. If one detail is forgotten, such as checking to see if the meeting dates conflict with a holiday, we might not attract the right audience. The holidays with which we concern ourselves are greater in number as our world becomes more accessible to all. If the sessions are not designed to maximize interaction and education, people will walk out. If the entertainers or speakers we engage are not briefed about the audience (gender and age mix, ethnicity, level of experience, and so on), they may either fall flat or, worse, insult the audience. If the implications of alcohol consumption are not considered, we are liable for the consequences. The list goes on and on. And if we do not consider current events and their impact on our meetings, we have not adequately performed our jobs.

Those who plan meetings and events often don't understand the breadth of the industry in which we work. *The Complete Idiot's Guide to Meeting and Event Planning, Second Edition*, will help you understand the complexity of meeting and event planning. It is a great resource for learning about the meetings industry and provides a beginning view of meeting and event planning fundamentals. It also provides a multitude of resources including software, websites, associations, higher education, and much more.

This is also the perfect companion book to the texts and manuals already on the desks of seasoned meeting professionals. It is the consummate resource for those who think that "anyone can plan a meeting"—this book explains why it is a specialized profession that requires knowledge beyond brain surgery!

Suppliers who provide facilities and services for meetings and events should read this book, too, because the best way to market and sell is to know your customers and help them do their jobs better. Planners are most loyal to those who have empathy for their work.

After you've read this book, read it again. All the smartest people know that education is a lifelong process. Make lists of what you still need to learn and, with the resources in this book, determine where to turn for networking, assistance, and finding the right vendors.

Make a promise to me and others in our profession: do what you do with the skills of a brain surgeon, with the compassion of the kindest person you've ever known, with the curiosity of the child who has yet to be told that asking "why?" is not okay, and with the knowledge that when you stop learning how to do this job better, you will get out.

—Joan L. Eisenstodt

Joan L. Eisenstodt, Chief Strategist of Eisenstodt Associates, LLC, a meeting consulting, training, and facilitation company based in Washington, DC, has been in the meetings industry for 30+ years. Recognized for her expertise and contributions to the industry by numerous organizations, she has been on every list of "Most Influential People in the Meetings Industry," published by *Meeting News Magazine*, since the first list in 1992, and inducted into the Convention Industry Hall of Leaders, the industry's most prestigious honor. She continues to learn and work in an industry she loves.

Introduction

Did you know there is an entire industry dedicated to planning meetings and events? People we talk to are surprised to find out that there are professional industry associations, suppliers, and other resources available to make their lives easier when it comes to planning meetings and events. Maybe you plan one or two corporate meetings a year or are tasked with planning a volunteer event or an annual conference for an association in the near future. Are you aware of the myriad details and nuances needed to plan these kinds of events? How do you know where to turn for help?

Some of the meeting- and event-planning books available today are more like text-books or manuals than this book. We promise no in-depth mathematical equations and hard-to-follow formulas (well, maybe one or two). When it comes to finalizing your food and beverage, audio-visual equipment, sound, lighting, and stage production needs, we urge you to rely on professionals who make their living doing just that. This book will give you the basics so you can talk to the pros intelligently and with confidence throughout the process.

This book offers insightful tips and information gained by working many years in the industry. As with any endeavor, there are many ways to accomplish the same thing. Because we have experience from both sides—planner and supplier—of the industry, we are able to give you varied perspectives. You need your suppliers as partners in your meetings and events, not just as a contractual entity. On the flip side, suppliers should know what it is like to plan a meeting or special event to be better able to partner with planners.

We have tried to give you as many resources as possible in this book. The main challenge is keeping the information current as time elapses. A lot of that is up to you to stay informed about the industry. We wish you all the best!

How to Use This Book

This book is divided into four parts that are all designed to lead you step-by-step through the planning process:

Part 1, "Bird's-Eye View," sets the stage for understanding the meetings industry. You'll learn about setting meeting goals and objectives, determining a meeting's value, and discovering who's who in the industry, all of which are important in the planning process. We'll also take a look at technology and what it's like to book a meeting from the other side of the desk—the supplier side.

Part 2, "First Things First," explains what you need to do to get the planning process rolling: creating your timeline (roadmap) and budget, writing and distributing a request for proposal (RFP), and negotiating with vendors and venues. Then we have a guest author, an attorney, to walk you through the hotel contracting stage. Finally, we discuss marketing and exhibits—both very important components.

Part 3, "Care and Feeding," is all about taking care of your attendees. How should you set the meeting rooms? Where do you buy all the things you need to produce a meeting? How do you find and hire speakers? What about travel arrangements? What about registration and housing? How do you determine your audio-visual equipment and staffing needs? This part is the heart of the planning process—you'll want to pay close attention!

Part 4, "Center Stage and Beyond," addresses onsite meeting management issues and all the other "stuff" that needs to be done. You'll learn about being onsite, preparing for and managing glitches and crises, putting closure to a meeting (like paying the bills), preparing final meeting reports, and discussing ethical dilemmas. There is also a chapter for suppliers only that addresses what planners really want from suppliers. Also, you'll find a bit about certification and certificates/degrees in meeting and event management. Finally, there's a chapter on how to keep from becoming overwhelmed by all of your planning responsibilities.

Extras

You will find helpful tips and hints for survival in the fast-paced world of meeting planning. Look for these fun and useful features throughout the book:

Food for Thought
These are handy pieces of advice and helpful tips.

The Inside Scoop
Class is in session! Meet us here for the "inside scoop" on what every planner should know.

Meeting Speak
Planning a meeting or event calls for a new vocabulary. Here is where you will learn to speak the language. It's not really a foreign language, but it may seem like it on occasion.

Don't Drop the Ball
Meeting and event planners juggle many tasks. Pay attention here so you don't "drop the ball" and lose precious time and money in the process.

Acknowledgments

Writing this book was a huge and fun endeavor for us. It's one we wanted to write for many years and finally got the chance, but it wasn't written alone. We have had many wonderful experiences in our combined 75+ years in the business, and it is through those experiences that we are able to write about the meetings industry. Our careers have led us to many people and places, and all of these interactions play a part in what we know today. We are grateful for all of these experiences.

We have one special person who kept us on the right path in order to bring the first edition of the book to completion. Many thanks to Glenn Brill, who had an answer for just about any question and who was always there for us when we needed him. We also extend warm thanks to all the editors we worked with at Alpha Books. We appreciate their assistance and the opportunity to write this book. There are also the people who contributed to the book. These people include John S. Foster, Esq., CHME, who wrote the legal chapter; Corbin Ball, CMP, for www.corbinball.com, the world's most comprehensive site about meeting planning and events technology; Jeff Rasco, CMP, who provided invaluable information and research on meetings technology and Jim Lampert, who contributed his expertise on the ever-changing world of audio-visuals; Joe Guertin, who helped us with information on generation learning styles; Chris McMasters and Gene-Michael Addis from MeetingMatrix, who provided the room diagrams; Nick Topitzes, CMP, of PC/Nametag, for the nametag photo; and finally, Robert M. Eilers from the Meeting Professionals International Foundation and Donald Dea and Hugh K. Lee from Fusion Productions for giving us permission to share their return on investment (ROI) model with you.

Last and most important are our families who supported us when we worked until the wee hours of the morning for months on end. For Robin, this includes her husband, Charles Bonham, and her two sons, Clayton and Charley. For Lynn, it includes her husband, Barry Golabowski, her two daughters, Morgan and Taylor, and her in-laws, Nancy and Ray Golabowski, who are always available to take care of the kids when work duties call. And D'Etta cannot imagine what life would be like without 100 percent support from the two most independent men in her life—her sons, Jared and Andrew; and her growing-younger-every-day-parents, Ed and Marilyn Waldoch; all who have lovingly and patiently endured life in the background of many, many meetings.

Special Thanks to the Technical Reviewer

The Complete Idiot's Guide to Meeting and Event Planning, Second Edition, was reviewed, as was the first edition, by a leading industry expert and one of the 25 most influential people in the meetings industry, as named by *MeetingNews* magazine. Special thanks to Joan Eisenstodt of Eisenstodt Associates, LLC, for her time, expertise, and brain cells. We couldn't have done it without her.

Trademarks

All terms mentioned in this book that are known to be or are suspected of being trademarks or service marks have been appropriately capitalized. Alpha Books and Penguin Group (USA) Inc. cannot attest to the accuracy of this information. Use of a term in this book should not be regarded as affecting the validity of any trademark or service mark.

Part 1

Bird's-Eye View

You don't need to be a professional meeting or event planner to pull together a successful meeting or event. That said, before you start planning a meeting or event, you need to know a few things about the industry in general, and meetings and events in particular. You also need to know whom you can call to assist you in your planning journey to make your life a bit easier.

We'll also look at the big picture to set up your meetings and events for success, including processes such as creating goals and objectives, determining return on investment, and utilizing technology tools to get the job done. Finally, we'll take a look at what it is really like to sit on the other side of the desk when you call a facility to book your meetings or events. You'll learn how your business is evaluated and what you can do to make your program a better piece of business for the meeting facility or event venue.

What Is a Meeting or Event, Anyway?

In This Chapter

- Discover the sizeable economic impact made by the meetings industry
- Understand the definition of a meeting and event planner
- Learn about various types of meetings
- Learn what meetings and events have in common
- Understand the roles that for-profit and nonprofit organizations play when developing meetings and events

In the United States alone, there are thousands of individuals who plan meetings and events. Although it is impossible to count every one—even those who plan as part of their job or as volunteers—the number is huge, and the hotels, conference centers, and resorts know it. They have meetings in their facilities practically every day of the year. If you include the planners of events, such as festivals, parades, weddings, sports competitions, concerts, and fundraisers, the number of planners is even higher.

Yet most people do not even know that the meeting planning profession even exists. We often hear, "Oh, that sounds like fun. You must be a party planner!" As most professional meeting planners will tell you, planning a meeting or event (or even a really great party!) can be one of the most challenging things you will ever do. No matter what you call it, meetings and events require careful planning in an organized, detailed, step-by-step fashion. This book will walk you through the myriad details, so that your next get-together, meeting, or event is a success.

Meetings Are Big Business

According to the 2004 Economic Impact Study from the Convention Industry Council (CIC), the meetings, conventions, exhibitions, and incentive travel industry accounted for $122.3 billion in annual spending. This makes the meetings industry the twenty-ninth largest contributor to the U.S. Gross National Product, as it supported more than 1.7 million American jobs and generated more than $21.4 billion in annual taxes. Hotels and other meeting venues reaped the greatest share of attendee expenditures, and the airline and restaurant industries were the next greatest benefactors of this spending.

The CIC is currently made up of 30 member organizations that represent over 100,000 individuals, and some 15,000 facilities and firms in the meetings industry. They provide a forum for member organizations to exchange economic and logistic information and resources in order to advance the professionalism and success of the meetings industry. The CIC's Accepted Practices Exchange (APEX) initiative was developed to enhance planner and supplier efficiency through implementation of industry-wide accepted practices, systems, and processes. While we do not go into a lot of detail regarding APEX in this book, it is well worth the time to keep an eye on APEX as it continues to evolve, and make use of its many tools. More information is available on the CIC website: www.conventionindustry.org.

Who Are These Planning Professionals?

Meeting management has only become a recognized profession since the 1990s. Meeting planning job titles may include Director of Meetings, Meeting Coordinator, Meeting Planner, Conference Manager, or Special Events Manager. Oddly, many meeting planners do not carry a job title with the words "meeting planner" in it at all. Some individuals do not even know they are meeting planners! Administrative assistants, executive secretaries, and managers at all levels and in different areas (marketing, sales, and so on) frequently hold a prominent and time-consuming role in planning meetings and events for their organizations. Most are not recognized for their planning skills, despite their diligence and successful achievements.

Meeting and event planners should proudly stand together. We get to create, organize, manage, implement, and improve upon an essential communications tool—meetings. We can use cutting-edge technology, use our creativity, and we can make a strong impact. What we do has real and tangible value. The bottom line is that all of the players in our industry need to be champions of it.

The U.S. meetings industry puts planners into distinct categories: *corporate planners, association planners, government planners, independent planners, and planners for not-for-profit organizations.* It is hard to pinpoint exactly how many planners exist in the United States. However, if we look at the membership breakdown from the industry associations, we estimate that corporate planners make up the largest segment, at just over 50 percent. Association planners make up close to 30 percent, and independents come in around a little more than 20 percent. Many corporations and associations are large enough or have enough meetings to warrant full-time, in-house planning personnel. However, many organizations do not have these resources and look to their administrative or management staff. In other cases, they outsource some of their meeting needs to independent planners. Independent planners may work alone, partner with other planners, or become part of a meeting management firm.

> **The Inside Scoop**
>
> There are many professional organizations dedicated to the education and professionalism of the meeting and event industry. One very helpful website is www.corbinball.com. This site includes articles and spreadsheets for planners and has the most complete listing of meetings industry websites, bar none. It is a valuable resource for every planner.

So how do meeting and event planners learn about the meetings industry and meet other planners? Here are four of the key professional organizations within the meetings industry:

- ◆ **Meeting Professionals International (MPI).** Since 1972 MPI has held the distinction of being the largest association of planners and suppliers in the meetings industry. With more than 20,000 members representing 66 worldwide chapters and clubs, MPI provides educational opportunities to enhance career pathways and growth opportunities for businesses. You can find them at www.mpiweb.org.

♦ **Professional Convention Management Association (PCMA).** Begun in 1957 as a network of association executives in the health care industry, PCMA today has 16 regional chapters and more than 5,000 members in the United States and Canada. Its mission has expanded to include educational opportunities for all who work in the professional convention management and meetings industries. Their website is www.pcma.org.

♦ **American Society of Association Executives (ASAE).** Founded in 1920 with 67 charter members as the American Trade Association Executives, today ASAE has more than 25,000 members representing 10,000 associations. As an advocate for the nonprofit sector, ASAE dedicates itself to strengthening professionalism within the association community. Their website is www.asaenet.org.

♦ **Society of Government Meeting Professionals (SGMP), founded in 1981.** With more than 4,000 members in 26 chapters throughout the United States, this national organization is dedicated to improving quality and promoting cost effectiveness of federal, state, and local government meetings through education and training of the planners who manage them, and the suppliers who provide support and services. More information is available at www.sgmp.org.

Two other organizations for event planners to consider are:

♦ **International Festivals and Events Association (IFEA).** Celebrating its fiftieth year in 2005, IFEA membership extends to 38 countries through IFEA North America, IFEA Europe, IFEA Asia, IFEA Australia, and IFEA Africa/Middle East. IFEA supports professional standards, educational programs, and certifications in the festivals and events industry worldwide. More information is available at www.ifea.com.

♦ **International Special Events Society (ISES).** Represented by more than 4,000 special event professionals in over 12 countries, ISES offers the CSEP (certified special events professional) designation for professional achievement in the industry. For more information, check out their website at www.ises.com.

And there's more. Meetings and events don't just happen because planners make it so. There is an entire flip side of the industry—the suppliers. Suppliers are all of the people, vendors, and organizations that supply products and services for meetings and events. They are very important, and their role is addressed in Chapters 7 and 11.

Determining the Purpose of a Meeting or Event

When you begin to plan your meeting or event, the first question you should ask yourself is "why?" What are you trying to accomplish? How does this meeting or event support the goals and objectives or strategic plan of the meeting host? The primary reasons that meetings are held are to inform, teach, exchange ideas, discuss problems, make decisions, and communicate issues and strategies. Of course, there are other reasons to have a meeting, such as to raise money for a good cause or to make money for the organization. Getting acquainted, team-building, or good old-fashioned public relations are other valid motives. Events can exist for a whole host of reasons, from celebrations to commemorations. It's important to recognize why your meeting or event is being held and to set the agenda to accomplish the most important goals and objectives.

Why do people attend meetings or events? In most cases, the answer is to obtain information—to walk out of the room knowing more than when they came in. Another important reason is to network or develop and enhance professional relationships. Many people spend so much time focusing on work that they don't have a lot of time for—dare we say it?—fun. Meeting new people and catching up with colleagues, old friends, and acquaintances is a key reason people actually want to go to a meeting or event.

> **The Inside Scoop**
>
> The MPI Foundation offers two excellent publications well worth reading from their "Making Meetings Work" research series. Both are available via the website (www.mpifoundation.org): "Making Meetings Work: An Analysis of Corporate Meetings" and "Who Attends Association Annual Meetings … and Why?"

What Are Meetings, and What Are Events?

Board meetings, staff meetings, technical and scientific conferences, product launches, annual conferences, training seminars, fundraisers, galas, conventions, tradeshows, and incentive programs are just some of the meetings and events that make up the meetings industry. Because one of our biggest challenges is to categorize and differentiate between meetings and events, let's focus on some of the more widely held definitions:

- *Conferences* generally bring together people who have a shared discipline or industry, usually for educational reasons.

- *Conventions* (or *Congresses*, as they are known in Europe) are assemblies of delegates to formulate a platform, select candidates, and sometimes take legal action.

They also focus on a common topic or issue and tend to be larger than conferences.

◆ *Expositions* (open to the general public) and *tradeshows* (by invitation only, usually to members of a organization) are designed to communicate services and products to consumers and members.

◆ *Special events* can cover a wide variety of areas such as awards banquets, community programs, concerts, fairs and festivals, fund raisers, gala dinners, hosted parties, parades, political rallies, public shows, road shows, sporting events, tradeshows, tributes, and weddings. (More in Chapter 6.)

◆ *Corporate* or *institutional meetings* are for those from the same company or organization. They include board, staff, and sales meetings and focus on information exchange, problem solving, and decision making.

Before we go any further, you should know that meetings and events are not interchangeable. Although meetings and events have many similar components such as security, decorations, alcohol, big-name speakers, and so on, they are still different things. An event tends to have a higher profile or focus on a unique special occasion. It can be by invitation only or open to the general public.

> **Food for Thought**
>
> Consider outsourcing some parts of your meeting or event to an independent meeting or special events planner or a meetings management company. Hiring a seasoned and reputable meeting manager can save you time and money in the long run. (See Chapter 4 for more information.)

For all kinds of organizations, a meeting and an event can occur during their annual conference. For instance, an educational meeting may take place for three days, and end with an elaborate gala awards program. The overall program would be categorized as a meeting, but one with a final event.

Throughout this book we will focus a bit more on meetings than events; however, you'll learn plenty about the skills you need to plan both. (Chapter 6 focuses specifically on events.)

For-Profit and Not-for-Profit Perspectives

It's helpful to understand the roles that corporate, association, government, and not-for-profit organizations play when developing meetings and events, as their perspectives and the rules and regulations that guide them will vary.

For-profit organizations such as corporations have employees who attend mandatory training, sales, motivational, and other meetings. The key word here is "mandatory." Their boards of directors usually meet several times each year, and their marketing departments have product launches and strategic-planning meetings. These meetings are almost always paid for by the corporation. Special events may include a tradeshow, a fundraiser for a charitable cause, a company picnic, or a holiday party.

Associations, professional societies, and *not-for-profit* organizations typically hold meetings for their members that are not mandatory. Members have the option to attend an annual meeting, educational conference, convention, exposition, congress, tradeshow, or workshop. Participants usually pay a registration fee and are often responsible for their own expenses. Their employer may or may not reimburse them for the cost. To be successful, it is critical that these meetings are perceived as valuable to their attendees; otherwise, attendance will be low and the organization hosting the meeting may lose money. Events may include a fundraising or awards dinner, a holiday or other themed gala, or a thank-you dinner for sponsors.

What distinguishes federal, state, and local government meetings from others is a rigid adherence to rules and regulations governing contracting and expenditures. As an example, planners need to obtain special government hotel room rates that are available only to those traveling with government-issued ID cards, and travel expenses must stay well within government-mandated per diems. This specialized group of planning professionals requires specialize training and experience to work effectively within tight guidelines. The first government planners to receive CGMP certification, offered by the Society of Government Meeting Professionals, graduated as recently as September 2005 (more information at www.sgmp.org).

Meeting Speak

For-profit organizations (such as companies and corporations) typically pay for meetings out of their own pocket. **Not-for-profit** organizations (such as some but not all associations and professional societies) ordinarily charge attendees a registration fee for their meetings and/or solicit external financial sponsorship to cover their costs.

The Sarbanes-Oxley Act (SOX)

Meeting planners, particularly those who work with incentive programs within publicly traded companies, have recently had to learn how to comply with the Sarbanes-Oxley (SOX) Act as an added part of their job description. SOX was created in 2002 as an after-effect of scandals such as Enron, WorldCom, and Tyco to protect investors from a rampage of accounting abuse in the corporate world. Today, companies must not only have external auditors review income and expense reports, but also demonstrate compliance with internal policies and procedures that govern the accountability for these numbers.

For meeting planners, this means increased scrutiny of typical duties such as managing the RFP process, site selection and contracting with facilities, supplier rebates and discounts, travel policies, employee per diems, tracking of funds, awards and rewards, and all other onsite and pre- or post-conference activities where even the perception of risk in accountability and compliance exists. Planners who plan to survive this new wave of checks and balances need to become fully educated regarding SOX rules and regulations, and continue to stay abreast of any updates to the Act.

Least Common Denominators

Whether you are planning a meeting, an event, or other gathering, there are several key factors all have in common.

The Right Timing: Date and Time

Deciding when to hold a meeting or event is a critical factor in its success. Be wary of competing with major holidays or other significant dates such as elections or major sporting events, which can decrease overall attendance and make travel hectic and difficult. Check out www.aglobalworld.com for holiday information in every country and every major religion around the world.

Before selecting dates, research other industry- or company-related meeting and event dates and keep a master calendar of potential conflicts. It is also wise to check the dates of other industry functions during your selected timeframe. A quick way to do this is to check the websites of your industry's associations.

The Right Place: Venue

Location is everything. One of the most important decisions in the planning process is the venue. Although this may not seem like a big deal, it sets the tone for your attendees' entire experience. You are responsible for providing participants with an environment that reinforces why they are there in the first place.

There are a wide variety of venue options to choose from, and figuring out how to select a site is the focus of Chapter 10. For example, a resort or conference center setting is used to foster a relaxed, laid-back meeting atmosphere. A downtown facility (hotel, conference center, or in-house meeting room) sets the tone for a serious business meeting and keeps the pace moving. An airport facility is the perfect place for a meeting for busy people who have to fly in and out quickly. An all-inclusive conference center may be the place for training workshops where the attendees need a professional atmosphere in a comfortable, quiet setting. To find valuable information about conference centers, check out www.iacconline.org, the website of the International Association of Conference Centers. This book mostly addresses what you need to know about planning meetings in hotels, but many alternate venues are wonderful options and should be considered.

Alternative meeting and event sites are places such as museums, zoos, aquariums, gardens, restaurants, and other facilities with meeting space. Consider these venues for a change of pace. Alternative venues do not always have in-house providers of food and beverage and audio-visual equipment. Sometimes you even have to rent tables, chairs, dishware, and so on. However, usually these services can be contracted and brought in to an alternative facility through an outside vendor. (There's more information at www.uniquevenues.com.)

The Right People: Attendees

Keep in mind you are planning this meeting (or this event) for your attendees. If you don't identify and reach the right people, then why hold the meeting or event? Create a target attendee list and add to it when appropriate. Take time to consider where your attendees come from. Naturally, if you are working for an association, then most of the attendees will be members, but what about potential members? If you work in a company, you have a defined attendee list. If you are raising money, you need to decide whose checkbooks to go after. Decisions, decisions.

The Right Message: Speakers

Having the right speaker or speakers deliver your message is critical to a meeting or event's success. A big factor in drawing attendance to a meeting or event can be the *keynote speaker*, or headliner, and some organizations spend upward of $50,000 to $125,000 for a sought-after speaker. (There's more information on finding and hiring speakers in Chapter 17.) There are many speakers available, and you

Meeting Speak

A **keynote speaker** is someone with a wealth of expertise who is a respected authority on the subject at hand. He or she is often a celebrity or a well-known personality from the industry.

need to decide what message you want to get across to your audience. Larger meetings typically have a general session with at least one keynote speaker and numerous breakout sessions.

To find a keynote presenter who will provide a good audience draw, first think carefully about the goals of the meeting or event, topics to be covered, and the level of expertise and sophistication of your attendees. An executive from a prominent company—one that stands above the rest in your industry—might serve you well. If you are hosting a city-wide arts council event, your keynote might be the mayor or head of the arts commission.

Also consider contacting the National Speakers Association at www.nsaspeaker.org, to research the numerous speakers bureaus on the web, or tap into your own network. Another organization to check out is the International Association of Speakers Bureaus at www.iasbweb.org. Be prepared to pay a speaker fee (some are negotiable) in addition to travel expenses.

Breakout sessions are back-to-back shorter sessions ranging from 45 minutes to 2 hours. The speakers for these are often people from within a given industry, who are considered experts. If your budget is tight—and whose isn't?—you can probably find good speakers among colleagues and industry peers for free if you take care of their travel expenses.

Consider also whether you need a master of ceremonies to provide continuity between speakers and to tie the program together.

The Right Scoop: Agenda

A well-thought-out and well-formatted agenda or schedule is critical to staying on track and to providing an atmosphere in which adults learn. Whether it is a meeting or event for 2 or 2,000, every program needs an agenda to accomplish its objectives.

Don't Drop the Ball

Meetings should support the organization's goals, mission, and strategic plan. Don't get so caught up in the logistics that you lose sight of your meeting's purpose. Read Chapter 2 for more on this topic.

Always start with an overview of the program and the key people. You should set the tone and direction of the meeting or event from the beginning.

The agenda is the road map for a successful meeting. Allowing adequate time for attendees to interact at breaks, meals, and social events will help fulfill the participants' needs of peer-to-peer learning. A good agenda not only will take care of business, it will make a positive, lasting impression.

The Least You Need to Know

- The meetings industry is a multibillion dollar business that continues to grow every year.

- Meeting and event planning is a recognized profession.

- Meetings and events are not the same thing, often differing in terms of size and number of attendees, and profile.

- For-profit and not-for-profit organizations have different perspectives, as well as rules and regulations to comply with, regarding meeting and event planning.

- In planning a meeting or event, you need to consider time, venue, attendees, speakers, and agenda.

- Meeting and event planning is very involved—and a lot of fun!

Chapter 2

Goals and Objectives: Critical from the Start

In This Chapter

◆ Understand the importance of setting goals and objectives

◆ Learn how to create goals and objectives

◆ Develop a goals and objectives worksheet

◆ Define what makes a meeting successful

Meetings should be held with purpose. Too many times, meetings are held because one person thought the meeting was necessary. Knowing why the meeting is to be held sets the tone and framework for all that is planned. How often have you attended a meeting and walked away feeling like it was a big waste of your time? You are busy, and going to another meeting just takes time away from getting things crossed off your ever-growing to-do list.

Goals and objectives define your entire meeting or event. In this chapter, we'll discover how to set goals and objectives and how to communicate them to the stakeholders: meeting sponsor, participants, vendor partners, press, and others as appropriate.

Why Bother with Goals and Objectives?

Imagine that you receive two brochures in the mail for different meetings. One is black and white, and one has splashes of color all over it. Immediately, you recognize a difference. Upon reading the material, you find that the black-and-white brochure has only a basic agenda, location, and registration form. The colorful brochure describes the reasons why you need to attend the meeting, how you will learn several new techniques, network with your peers, and go home with helpful tips. Of course, this is Marketing 101, but the colorful, descriptive brochure illustrates the *goals* and *objectives* of the meeting. The basic brochure just gives you the logistical details. Which meeting are you more likely to attend?

> **Meeting Speak**
>
> A **goal** is the foundation of a meeting. It explains why the meeting is being held and provides a road map for the planning process. An **objective** is a measurable, attainable target that, when completed, contributes to the accomplishment of the goal. A meeting can have one or more goals. Usually, there are multiple objectives supporting the goal(s).

Setting specific goals and objectives should be the very first step in planning every meeting. Establishing goals and objectives with assistance from *stakeholders* in the early stages of the planning process is a critical component of successful meeting planning. When the meeting is over, the planner and stakeholders will determine whether the meeting was a success based on a review of whether the goals and objectives were met.

Meeting stakeholders are under constant pressure to justify every dollar spent, and they need to clearly define why they are holding a meeting. It is critical that stakeholders have an opportunity early on in the planning process to provide very specific input regarding goals and objectives. From that point on, it becomes the meeting planner's job to make sure they are achieved.

> **Meeting Speak**
>
> A **stakeholder** is someone who has a vested interest in the success of the meeting. In the corporate (for-profit) world this could be the vice president of the company who is paying the bill. For association (nonprofit) meetings, often the board of directors, financial sponsors, and/or planning committee members have a vested interest in a successful outcome.

All stakeholders have their own objectives. Make sure they agree with the primary meeting objectives, and that they are written from the attendees' perspective. Your meeting can't accomplish all things for all people.

The Big Picture: Goals

To determine what goals need to be achieved, think big picture. Goals should be strategic in nature, setting the stage for creating objectives to support them. When the question is asked whether a meeting was necessary, the answer will be found in the goal(s). Ponder the following questions to get your creative juices flowing:

◆ What is the meeting's primary emphasis? Recognition, education, networking, training, reward, entertainment, to conduct business, teambuilding, or to display products?

◆ Will the emphasis be focused more on the organization or the attendee? Is the purpose to reinforce the company's/organization's mission? Is the purpose to train attendees or employees?

◆ How much new information will be communicated? Or will the meeting reemphasize current information and procedures?

◆ How will financial success be determined and how important is the financial outcome, as compared to other goals?

Here are some sample goals:

◆ To introduce cutting-edge technology advancements for seasoned banking professionals

◆ To teach new hotel sales managers how to increase their sales and establish loyal customers

◆ To foster an atmosphere for networking within the meetings industry

◆ To provide hands-on instruction for establishing a strong website presence within the pet-food industry

◆ To celebrate a milestone; for example, the twenty-fifth anniversary of a company

◆ To communicate the company's new direction and business plan for the next year

◆ To turn a profit from meeting registration fees and sponsorships, which will contribute to the organization's operating budget

The Inside Scoop

Some meeting planners are required by continuing education accreditation boards to set goals and define measurable objectives for the overall meeting, as well as each individual session presented. Detailed evaluation forms based on the goals and objectives are collected at the end of the meeting, which provide clear indications of the meeting's success. (Learn more about post-meeting evaluations in Chapter 3.)

Goals are not task oriented. They do not tell you how they will be accomplished; they only tell you why the meeting is being held. In some cases, your goals will be the same from year to year. If you have past goals, determine whether it is appropriate to start with them. If you are starting from scratch, brainstorm with key people. In either case, make sure the goals are in line with your organization's mission.

When starting the planning process, the most difficult thing to do is to figure out your goals and objectives. It's far easier to start on the logistical planning such as booking the hotel, hiring the speakers, and doing other detail work. If you resist this temptation, you will be rewarded with a meeting that is worth the time, effort, and money.

The Smaller Picture: Objectives

After you have determined your big picture—the goals, it's time to look at the little picture—the objectives. Does the thought of writing objectives send shivers up your spine? Well, help is on the way. Create objectives that mean something and that answer the following SMART questions:

- Are the objectives **Specific?**
- Are they written in such a way that they are **Measurable?**
- Can they be **Attained** within the time constraints of your meeting or event?
- Are they **Relevant** to the information presented?
- Can they be achieved in a realistic **Timeframe?**

SMART is an easy-to-remember set of rules that is frequently used to create objectives. By using the SMART criteria, you create solid objectives that support your overall goals.

Getting Down to Work

There are many ways to get started setting goals and objectives. Take a look at the following scenarios, the first from a for-profit perspective and the second from an association perspective.

Scenario #1: Happy Camper Company

You work for a Fortune 500 company that produces camping equipment, and the vice president of sales asks you to help plan the annual sales meeting. It is scheduled for September, which is six months away. You begin by meeting with some of the stakeholders (the vice president and other management staff) to discuss the meeting. The first question is, why is this meeting being held? A typical answer could be, because we always have it and the sales managers get a chance to have fun. So the goal is to have fun. Right?

Wrong! Asking the key people at Happy Camper what they want their salespeople to take away from the meeting is the real question. Ahhh, now they get it. They may answer that an increase in sales would be a great outcome. Okay, now we're making progress.

Having fun could be an objective on everyone's list. But let's face it. Who wants to pay for fun with no other benefit? It isn't going to happen in corporate America. Finally, you and the other Happy Campers decide that the goal is to motivate and train the sales managers, so they can get out there and increase sales. When finalizing your goals and objectives, you also want to think about the following:

♦ What is the most important message you need to convey to your sales team?

♦ What works best to motivate your salespeople? Has something worked well in the past, or do you need to try new methods?

♦ Are there new processes and techniques you could teach your salespeople? Do you need to train them on any new software?

♦ How does this meeting fit into the overall company goals and objectives? How can this meeting support them?

Food for Thought

Be diligent when establishing goals and objectives. Resist the temptation to skip this step. This will be especially hard if your boss or other decision-makers do not want to participate in this process. Insist they do it anyway. Without this, you will not have a basis to make key decisions as the planning proceeds.

To help you in your task, you may want to draft a worksheet that lists the meeting's name, goal, and objectives. For example:

Meeting Name: Happy Camper Company—Annual Sales Meeting

Goal: To motivate the Happy Camper sales team by providing fun and interactive education, so that the sales team can leave the meeting enthused to go out and exceed all revenue projections for the company this year

Objectives:

- ◆ Increase sales by 25 percent over last year.
- ◆ Teach how to prospect for business in the new economy.
- ◆ Provide training on how to use the Internet as a sales tool.
- ◆ Motivate the sales team so they are excited about selling our products.
- ◆ Hire a motivational speaker to entertain at the final dinner.
- ◆ Emphasize the new strategic plan and how the sales department is an integral part of its success.
- ◆ Roll out the new company logo and branding initiative.

What do you think? Are these good objectives? Do they seem reasonable and logical? Do they help reach the company's goal(s) and support the company's mission? Actually, there are two important things wrong with them. First, they do not meet the SMART criteria. Read each one and apply SMART. Some are not specific enough or measurable. How, for instance, will you know you have motivated the sales team?

The second thing is that they are written in the wrong perspective. They are written from the planner's perspective. It may be the aim of the organizers to roll out the new company logo or to hire a motivational speaker, but how does that benefit the attendee? The real issue is what will the sales team be able to "do" once they go back to work?

If we rewrite the objectives using SMART rules *and* keeping the attendee in mind, they might end up like this:

Revised Objectives:

By attending the annual sales meeting, the Happy Camper sales team will do the following:

♦ Increase all product sales by 25 percent in the next six months.

♦ Learn five ways to prospect for new business.

♦ Pass a 35-question test covering the five customer service links on the company website.

♦ Identify three ways the sales team contributes to the company's new strategic plan.

Now these objectives are definitely specific, measurable, attainable, relevant, and time based. They will keep everyone on track for achieving the overall goal of the meeting.

Scenario #2: Big Association of Rare Cat Owners (BARCO)

You are an employee at a nonprofit association that provides resources for owners of rare cats. Because there is not a dedicated meeting planner on staff, everyone helps with the BARCO annual conference. There is a lot of competition for attendees in this specialized market, so your meeting has to be the best to attract the right audience. You need a detailed plan.

The first thing you do is have a meeting to plan your meeting. You schedule a meeting with the conference committee, association officers, and those who will assist as meeting staff—one year in advance of the conference is a good rule of thumb. This first meeting will determine the goals and objectives and define everyone's role. When determining goals and objectives, take into consideration the following:

♦ Attendees' comments from last year: What did they like? Dislike? What do they need that they aren't getting elsewhere?

♦ What are the current hot topics in your industry?

♦ Do the attendees need networking time?

- Is there a recognition program to reward members? Does this need to be incorporated into the program?

- Will there be governance meetings—board of directors, committees, or councils?

- Do you need a formal business meeting?

- Are there any burning issues to resolve?

Let's take a look at a worksheet:

Meeting Name: BARCO Annual Educational Conference and Tradeshow

Goal: To introduce new products and services and to provide industry education and networking opportunities to our members

Objectives:

By attending the BARCO conference and tradeshow, attendees will do the following:

- Meet at least 10 new members who share their interest.

- Learn three new ways to prolong a rare cat's life.

- Understand the latest technology in rare cat breeding procedures.

- Meet vendors who sell products and services to meet members' needs.

- Learn how to join the online discussion group and how it helps you take care of your rare cat.

A side benefit from establishing objectives is that you can use them in your marketing collateral. Attendees will be interested to know that they will meet at least 10 new members who share their interests and see vendors who sell products and services for BARCO attendees. These objectives explain what they will get out of attending the meeting.

Roll Up Your Sleeves

Now it's time to roll up your sleeves and put your goals and objectives in writing to make sure all the players, including the top decision-makers, understand and embrace them. Keep in mind, although you may report to a person or a group of decision-makers, *you* also have a vested interest in the outcome and need to take ownership of the meeting.

Begin by creating a worksheet with the goals and objectives, similar to the examples in Scenarios 1 and 2.

What? More Objectives?

The objectives we have focused on so far are based on outcomes for the attendee. Outcome objectives are primary and should identify what the attendees will learn at the meeting. However, it is perfectly okay and maybe even necessary for you, the planner, to develop an additional set of objectives. These objectives are called *process objectives* and they will give you direction or a "how-to" approach on how to accomplish your primary objectives.

You will make better decisions about the meeting location, speaker selection, program agenda, marketing strategies, and other important details if you continuously ask yourself what impact they have on your goals and objectives.

The Preliminary Agenda

Now you are ready to create an agenda to support the objectives and incorporate them into a schedule. This process will get you ready to create your timeline in Chapter 8. Take a look at a sample agenda for the preceding BARCO scenario. The agenda states only the day, time, general schedule, and any special events associated with the 2-day/2-night meeting. This is a very basic agenda just to get you started. It will be modified over time, as you delve deeper into the planning process.

Overall theme: "Cats Are the Purrfect Companion"

Wednesday/Date	Agenda
Evening	Check-in
8:00 P.M.–10:00 P.M.	Hospitality suite open

Thursday/Date	Agenda
7:00 A.M.–4 P.M.	Registration
7:30 A.M.–8:00 A.M.	Breakfast
8:00 A.M.–10:00 A.M.	Opening session
10:00 A.M.–10:30 A.M.	Refreshment break
10:30 A.M.–12:00 P.M.	Three breakouts
12:15 P.M.–1:00 P.M.	Lunch
1:15 P.M.–3:00 P.M.	Tradeshow opens
3:15 P.M.–4:45 P.M.	Three breakouts
5:45 P.M.	Reception/dinner

Friday/Date	Agenda
7:00 A.M.–4 P.M.	Registration
7:30 A.M.–8:00 A.M.	Breakfast
8:00 A.M.–9:45 A.M.	Tradeshow open
10:00 A.M.–10:30 A.M.	Refreshment break
10:30 A.M.–12:00 P.M.	General session
12:15 P.M.–1:00 P.M.	Lunch
1:15 P.M.–2:45 P.M.	Three breakouts
2:45 P.M.–3:15 P.M.	Refreshment break
3:15 P.M.–4:30 P.M.	Closing session

Food for Thought

Send a note to each member of the conference planning committee thanking them for assistance in creating the meeting goals and objectives, and mention that you look forward to a successful meeting as a result of their critical input.

Continued Support from the Planning Committee

After your goals and objectives are agreed on, distribute the goals and objectives worksheet and tentative agenda to the people who attended the planning meeting(s). Ask them for updates, changes, or additional input. Explain that planning efforts are underway and that every part of the meeting will be designed to support the goals and objectives.

Now it is time to address who is responsible for making ongoing decisions and getting all of this work done.

Who's the Boss?

The lead meeting planner is really the boss. In meeting planning, many things can go wrong or slip through the cracks. Sloppy decisions, or ones that stray from your objectives, will ultimately result in more work and cost more money. Someone needs to manage the entire program. In most cases, it's the lead meeting planner because this person understands the big picture and is also close to the details. This ensures that the goals and objectives are met during every step of the planning process.

In today's industry, more seasoned planners are taking on the responsibility of program planning and strategic meeting planning as well as "just" the logistics. This is a welcomed trend and one that is frequently discussed in trade publications, educational programs, and networking forums.

The Least You Need to Know

- ◆ Goals and objectives are the critical first step of planning a meeting or event.
- ◆ Create SMART (Specific, Measurable, Attainable, Relevant, Time-based) objectives, which support established goals.
- ◆ Stakeholders must be involved in setting the goals and objectives.
- ◆ Goals and objectives should support the organization's overall mission and strategic plan.

Time to Evaluate: Was It Worth It?

In This Chapter

- ◆ Discover who has a vested interest in your meeting
- ◆ Explore the return on investment (ROI) process
- ◆ Learn how to measure the success of your meeting
- ◆ Use it, don't lose it

This chapter is about evaluating your meeting. Why hold a meeting if you don't take the time to make sure it was worth it? All organizations look for ways to save money, scrutinize their expenditures and improve the bottom line, meetings included.

In Chapter 2 we discussed how meetings should be held with purpose, and that goals and objectives are key in the overall meeting-planning process. In this chapter you will learn how to use your goals and objectives to determine the value of your meeting.

Who Cares?

You might just be surprised. Meetings take a lot of time, effort, and money. Attendees, sponsors, exhibitors, senior management and other stakeholders, and planners care. Each has an interest in the success of any meeting with which they are associated.

> **Food for Thought**
>
> Be creative. Incorporate the meeting's message (goals and objectives) into the meeting theme, agenda, collateral/ marketing material, website and other e-communication, organization letterhead and envelopes, fax cover sheets, and so on. Continue the message onsite with the content presented in general and breakout sessions, signage, meal functions, trade-show, and handouts.

An organization producing a meeting has to decide whether its message was effectively communicated. If not, what other ways could the information have been delivered? Would a manual have given the salespeople the same information? Was an expensive motivational speaker necessary to deliver the message? Could a video have taught the same thing? These are all examples of questions that could be answered to determine whether the meeting was a success.

Your exhibitors and sponsors have an interest, too. Did they see an increase in sales as a result of their participation or financial support in the meeting? Do they have more potential customers? Did they gain the valuable exposure to the market share that they anticipated? Did they walk away feeling that the time and money spent was worth it?

The Attendee: I've Gotta *Attend* Another Meeting?

Attendees are motivated to attend meetings for a variety of reasons:

- Education
- Networking
- New product information
- Force of habit
- Recognition
- Job requirement
- Entertainment
- Just because

From their perspective, attending a meeting should fulfill specific goals and make it worth participants' time and money. In Chapter 2, you learned about the SMART process for writing meeting objectives. This is where the objectives are put to the test. Clearly written objectives will help attract attendees.

The Planner: I've Gotta *Plan* Another Meeting?

Meeting planners have their own subset of motivators. Once the goals and objectives are set, you are charged with the responsibility of producing the meeting according to those goals and objectives. You also have to deal with these contingencies:

- ◆ Budgets
- ◆ Staffing
- ◆ Office politics
- ◆ Economic climate
- ◆ Contracting issues
- ◆ Working with vendors
- ◆ Deadlines
- ◆ Attendee issues
- ◆ Unforeseen circumstances

As mentioned in Chapter 2, you are the master communicator to all meeting stakeholders. It is your job to implement and monitor the planning process and to make sure the stakeholders stay advised on relevant issues. In most situations, you will need to interact with and motivate senior management as well as committee members and peers to make decisions and get tasks completed on time. Keep in mind that, as long as you keep people on track in a nonconfrontational and professional manner, they will respect and in most cases adhere to your schedules.

The Inside Scoop

During the past several years, a push for measuring the return on investment (ROI) of meetings has moved planners into a more strategic role. In many instances, the professional corporate and association meeting planners hold senior/vice president and executive-level positions.

The Sponsor: I've Gotta *Fund* Another Meeting?

Financial outlay is an important part of any meeting. Someone pays, whether it is the company, association, attendee, sponsor, or all of the above. The people writing the checks have their own set of motivators for doing so:

- ◆ Educate staff/attendees
- ◆ Introduce a new product or service, or increase existing sales and collect sales leads
- ◆ Public relations/advertising
- ◆ Roll out a new strategic plan
- ◆ Motivate staff or customers
- ◆ Customer appreciation

Exhibitors from sponsoring companies attend a conference to show their products and services within the tradeshow arena or in sessions designed to showcase their products or services. They are there to gain exposure for their company or organization.

Sponsors participate in a conference for the same reasons but on a different level. They give money or in-kind products or services (meaning that the product or service is donated) to the meeting's host organization.

Make sure your organization's accountant is aware of sponsorships. He or she will determine the tax implications regarding the goods, services, and cash given to your organization.

After the meeting, both sponsors and exhibitors will need hard and fast evidence to take back to their management, showing that the meeting's goals and objectives were accomplished. A summary of post-meeting evaluations can be just the ticket.

Measuring Return on Investment (ROI)

Some meetings have been a ritual for so long that the reasons behind having them either have changed or are forgotten. Today, organizations want to know if the resources spent on a meeting brought a return on the investment. Industry leaders

are defining the value that meetings bring
back to their stakeholders. In other words,
the meeting was a success because the goals
and objectives were achieved and ultimately
provided a positive *return on investment (ROI)*.

Meeting Speak

Return on investment
(ROI) is the process of evaluating
a meeting in terms of value to the
stakeholders involved in it.

A company called Fusion Productions created
an ROI Series for Meeting Professionals
International. It is based on Fusion's approach
to meetings and benchmarking of leading meetings and conventions worldwide.
Their ROI model can be found at www.fusionproductions.com/tools/roi/index.cfm.
For a meeting or event, the ROI process can make it easier to justify your next meeting and focuses you to …

- ◆ Identify and prioritize your stakeholders and gain their input.

- ◆ Establish measurable meeting objectives and review them with your stakeholders.

- ◆ Design measurements for success.

- ◆ Design, develop, and deliver meeting content based on the objectives.

- ◆ Demonstrate your ROI by using the measurement results and by reporting
  those results to management.

Although this process is fairly time consuming, it is becoming increasingly more important to know and understand your ROI. The
process gets easier once you are familiar with it,
and it makes the difference between bringing
value to what you do and just winging it.
Consider discussing this further with management, or your stakeholders, particularly for
high-end or high-volume meetings.

Don't Drop the Ball

CAUTION

The meeting's budget
compared to actual expenditures
is how you measure the financial
success of a meeting. Did you
make money, lose money, or
break even? That answer is the
bottom line.

There are many ways to measure the return on investment of a meeting. In most
cases, a combination of measuring tools is used in ROI. It is best to customize the
process for each meeting based on the goals and objectives.

Hard Dollars and Sense

Did the meeting make or lose money? This is an easy answer to obtain once the bills
are paid and the revenue is accounted for. Many association meetings need to make

money to support the organization; some are member-services and are not designed to make money; some are designed to break even. The tool for measuring this is the budget.

Has your sales meeting ever been postponed or cancelled because company revenue was down? In many for-profit organizations, meetings are looked at as cost centers. The attendees do not pay a registration fee, and there is little or no income associated with the meeting. When companies look at cutting costs, meetings are usually one of the first items to be eliminated. Many times, this decision is made without analyzing the real value of a meeting. That's when understanding the ROI is key.

When Losing Money Makes Cents

But wait, earlier you learned that objectives are based on many things besides money. What if your sales team needs to learn about new products or become more motivated? In that case, the cost of the meeting may be an investment in the company's future. It is easier to keep the meeting from being eliminated if it is presented to senior management from this perspective. In the long run, holding the meeting, despite an initial financial loss, could actually increase sales. Imagine that!

Food for Thought

The time to think about your ROI is in the beginning. You need to understand from the start what represents a positive return on investment to collect and measure the appropriate outcome data.

If your objective is to increase sales by 25 percent during the next six months, then your sales report is the measurement tool used to determine whether the goal was achieved. Create a review system and share the sales figures on a monthly basis with the team. It keeps the goal in front of everyone and is less likely to be forgotten.

In summary, it's important to remember that ROI is not just about money. An increase in productivity, efficiency, motivation, and education are just some of the outcomes a positive ROI can achieve.

Measure the Success of Your Meeting

Measuring attendees' ROI takes more time than an internal ROI process. Sometimes you will never know what actually motivated someone to attend your meeting.

There are several tools for measuring attendee return on investment. The first, an evaluation, is a questionnaire designed to measure satisfaction after having attended a meeting. Be consistent with the questions and the format of your evaluations, especially if you want to compare results from different meetings. Retain a history of meeting evaluations to consider when planning for the future.

Here are some sample categories for questions:

◆ Whether an individual's and organization's written goals and objectives were met.

◆ The overall quality program content and educational value.

◆ Speakers' delivery styles and expertise.

◆ Attendee level of understanding about key parts of the meeting—did they learn what they needed to enhance their work?

◆ A place to provide comments or questions.

◆ Suggestions for improvement.

◆ Whether they will return next year.

◆ The facility, including meeting space, guest rooms, public areas, and recreational opportunities.

◆ The food and beverage.

◆ Audio-visual and/or meeting hand-out materials.

◆ Meeting location—existing air and ground transportation options.

Food for Thought

Offer an incentive for returning the meeting evaluation. Either give everyone a small trinket or enter their name in a drawing for a larger prize. People love prizes!

Evaluation Forms

Written evaluation forms usually use a rating system for each question on a numerical scale or from excellent to poor. They are collated, tabulated, and summarized after the meeting. Planners who typically manage large groups often make use of electronic scanning equipment to make tabulating quicker and easier. Software and hardware options can vary widely in cost and complexity, and should be evaluated depending on volume of evaluations processed.

Always provide written instructions on how to return the completed evaluation. Ask that forms be returned at the end of the conference for the best response, or better, e-mail them to the participants when they return from the conference.

Registration-supply companies sell large, free-standing boxes for just that purpose. Strategically placed evaluation boxes at the entrance of a room or in areas of high traffic, perhaps near the meeting registration desk, will serve as a reminder to attendees to return forms promptly. In case attendees opt to take evaluations with them to complete later (or simply forget), have an address or a fax number for them to return the forms later, within a given deadline.

If you have a lot of breakout sessions, consider a separate evaluation form for each. Distribute forms at each breakout session or with meeting registration materials. Ask questions about the speaker's delivery and content and if the program was relevant to the participant. Consider asking what one "take-away" idea is from the session. Evaluations can be short or long and as quick or detailed as you want. Your chances of a higher return lay with the shorter forms. The longer and more involved they are, the fewer will be returned. See Appendix A for sample evaluations for attendees, exhibitors, and breakout sessions.

Audience Response System

Another way to poll attendees is an audience response system. A moderator asks questions, and the audience provides immediate answers via an electronic keyboard. The results are available before the participants leave the room. This is also a great lead-in to asking the audience open-ended questions about the meeting and about specific issues being addressed. You'd be surprised at how many people will voice their opinions if you ask them. So ask!

Keeping Up with History

You can also use statistical data to evaluate your meeting. Is attendance up or down compared to the past two to three years? If you work with an association, how do those numbers compare to membership statistics? How many participants each year are first-timers? If your registration numbers are really different, make sure you take into consideration any changes to your fee structure, agenda, meeting location, and program content.

Exhibitor Perspective

There are several ways to measure the success of your meeting from the exhibitor perspective. First, a written evaluation is important. Ask them to rate the following:

◆ Networking with attendees

◆ The cost of the exhibit booth

◆ Material received from the organizer prior to the event

◆ The overall exhibit schedule

Also ask why they attended and if their objectives were met and what they liked best and least about the conference. Don't forget to invite them to return to exhibit at your next meeting. Let them know that their comments are valuable and that they will be used in making future decisions.

In addition, during the meeting or tradeshow, visit the exhibit booths and ask how things are going. Talk to them. Did they obtain qualified leads? After all, that's why they are there. Solicit feedback on the entire agenda. Exhibitors attend many meetings each year and can give you some of the most valuable suggestions you will ever receive!

Food for Thought _____

Spend time talking with your exhibitors. This extra attention goes a long way. All too often, we hear about the forgotten exhibitors and how their needs go unnoticed. They should be considered "expert meeting attendees" and can provide great insight. Most will appreciate receiving copies of post-meeting evaluation summaries, from which to base their decision to continue exhibiting at your meeting in the future. Consider establishing an exhibitor advisory committee to provide year-round feedback.

Place the summary of your evaluations in your meeting binder. This information needs to be readily accessible, and will be valuable to you for years to come.

Use the Information!

Too often, organizations go to great lengths to evaluate the meeting from all angles, and then the report grows dust on the shelf.

Once the results are tabulated, distribute them to the stakeholders and schedule a wrap-up meeting. Discuss all aspects of the evaluations. Brainstorm ways to improve for next year. Write it all down. This is one of the best places to start reviewing, when planning your next meeting.

The Least You Need to Know

◆ A meeting stakeholder is any person who has a vested interest in the successful outcome of a meeting.

◆ Return on investment is not just about money; it determines the real reason(s) you should hold a meeting.

◆ Evaluation forms are one important tool to find out if attendees' objectives were met.

◆ The information you learn from evaluations and ROI is essential. Use it for your future meetings and events.

Chapter 4

Meeting Industry Resources: Who Ya Gonna Call?

In This Chapter

◆ Identify valuable resources for meeting and event planners

◆ Discover how to find and contact industry resources

◆ Understand what industry resources can and cannot do for you

◆ Create your own resource network

The meetings industry has a multitude of organizations that supply a product or service for professional planners and novices alike, but how do you know where to find them?

Beyond contacting colleagues and industry experts for advice, resources can be tapped from contacting websites, associations, trade publications, convention and visitors bureaus, destinations, management companies, national sales offices, meeting management companies, and more. This chapter is all about who they are, what they do, where to find them, and how to use them.

Websites

The Internet provides a tremendous opportunity for meetings-industry players to research, gather, and use information they have never had access to before. But wading through thousands of websites can be a daunting experience. There are many solutions to your particular issue, but you have to pick and choose what is right for you. You can't use them all! Understanding what is available on the web is a good start to finding what you might need later on in the planning process (see Appendix B for information on meeting-related websites). In this chapter, we will discuss meeting-planning tools available on the web. You will be amazed at what is out there.

> **CAUTION**
>
> **Don't Drop the Ball**
>
> The industry's most comprehensive listing of meeting-related websites is found at www.corbinball.com, and it is updated regularly.

Associations

Just like any industry, there are a variety of trade associations dedicated to providing education, conferences, books, magazines, newsletters, and other services. The meetings industry is no different.

In Chapter 1 we discussed some key meeting industry associations: Meeting Professionals International (MPI), Professional Convention Management Association (PCMA), and American Society of Association Executives (ASAE), Society of Government Meeting Professionals (SGMP) and two industry associations for event planners: International Festivals and Events Association (IFEA) and International Special Events Society (ISES). Each is an excellent resource because it is on the cutting edge of our industry. All have excellent meetings and conferences designed to help educate meeting and event planners on the how-tos and what's new in the industry.

Depending on what type of planner you are, you might want to join additional associations. Each discipline (corporate, association, government, special event, medical, insurance, and so on) has its own association and focuses on industry-specific issues. They are there for you. However, don't just join for the heck of it. Really investigate what they can bring to the table and make sure it is of value to you. Membership dues can be costly—especially if you join more than one association.

One thing to keep in mind is *why* you are joining. The following is a list of things you should ask yourself before signing up:

1. Are you joining for one or more of the following?

   ◆ Education

   ◆ Networking

   ◆ Access to publications

   ◆ A members-only website

   ◆ Conferences and events

   ◆ Certification

   ◆ Access to a resource library

   ◆ Dedication to your profession

   ◆ Credibility

   ◆ Job/employee search

   ◆ Contacts in other cities

2. Will this association help you in your job? How?

3. Will you be an active participant? How?

4. Do you plan to attend conferences and events? Which ones?

Food for Thought

The common thread for getting the most out of an industry or trade association is involvement. People who are actively involved in one way or another feel that the time and money are worth it. Before joining, think about why you wish to be affiliated with the group. Write down what you expect to gain from being a member and review the benefits available. Then, when your renewal notice arrives in the mail, you can make an educated decision whether or not to renew.

When polling planners who are members of associations, we heard some great reasons to join. The number one reason was networking. It is great to have access to other people who do what you do, especially if you do not work with others who plan meetings in your organization.

Even if you only attend a few meetings, are involved in a committee, or just read the trade publications for information, use your association as a resource. It is worth the money only if you take advantage of its benefits.

Trade and Other Publications

Trade pubs are your vehicle for current news about your industry. Keeping up with local news is hard enough, but the meetings and events industry is so global that these publications are an essential tool for keeping abreast of pertinent industry news. Why, you ask, should you read them? These publications often contain articles on meeting and event planning how-tos, salary surveys, destination information, hotel and resort information, best practices, contracting issues, job opportunities, and information on products and services.

The list is endless, but our point is that industry publications are a great resource. Some are free to planners, so you have nothing to lose. Try the following: MeetingsNet.com is a great place to start. Primedia Business Magazines & Media publishes a half-dozen publications with special focus on various industries including *Association Meetings*, *Corporate Meetings and Incentives*, *Insurance Conference Planner*, *Medical Meetings*, *Religious Conference Manager*, and *Technology Meetings*. Go to the company's website (www. meetingsnet.com) and click Contact Us for subscription information.

Here are some other excellent and more broad-based publications:

- *Business Travel News* (www.btnonline.com)
- *Corporate & Incentive Travel* (www.corporate-inc-travel.com)
- *Meetings & Conventions* (www.meetings-conventions.com)
- MeetingNews (www.meetingnews.com)
- Successful Meetings (www.successmtgs.com)

In addition, you'll discover publications designed for special markets or regions. Here is a sampling:

- *Midwest Meetings* (www.midwestmeetings.com)
- *Meetings West, Meetings South, Meetings East, and Meetings Mid-America* (www.meetings411.com)
- *Small Market Meetings* (www.smallmarketmeetings.com)
- *Event Solutions* (www.event-solutions.com)
- *Where Magazine* (www.wheremagazine.com)

> **CAUTION**
>
> **Don't Drop the Ball**
>
> Once you subscribe to the applicable trade publications, you could have well over a half-dozen magazines and newspapers rolling in each month. Don't let them pile up. If there is no time to read them all, skim through them, tear out the applicable articles, and recycle them. File the articles for future reference. Don't stop there! Read general business publications for a wealth of information that is applicable to your work.

Convention and Visitor Bureaus (CVBs)

Convention and visitor bureaus (CVBs) are typically nonprofit membership organizations that are available to meeting and event planners to provide information on a host city or destination. They are typically funded by a combination of membership dues and room taxes. Their members are organizations that provide products and services to planners, such as hotels, restaurants, and attractions and they exist to draw people to their cities and support meeting planners. They are a valuable resource both before selecting a location and after a decision is made. They help you locate products and services available in the area and will work to make sure your experience in their city or destination is a successful one. Smaller communities may not have a CVB, in which case the local Chamber of Commerce serves this role.

Here are some services that CVBs provide at no or low cost to meeting planners:

- Site inspection of the destination
- Meeting guides about the destination
- Lead referrals to appropriate facilities with your meeting specifications
- Supplier contacts
- Attendee name badges
- Registration assistance
- Promotional brochures
- Arranging a welcome from the mayor or another official
- Assistance in wading through city red tape
- Welcome signage at the airport

- ◆ Spouse and guest program coordination

- ◆ Press releases about the meeting

- ◆ Promotion material such as photographs

Just ask—you may be surprised. (One CVB we know ordered and delivered 500 balloons for a client's awards luncheon because the client was so busy. They often will go above and beyond the call of duty!) They are a great resource for just about any question or dilemma.

<table>
<tr><td>

The Inside Scoop

All CVBs have websites, but the umbrella organization is Destination Marketing Association International. This organization can be found at www.iacvb.org. From their consumer site, www. OfficialTravelGuide.com, you can find most CVBs worldwide.

</td></tr>
</table>

Keep in mind that the meeting guides produced by CVBs are sales tools for the city or destination. They are not intended to be recommendations. Always be on the lookout for ways to garner recommendations from colleagues (join those associations!) before signing vendor contracts. CVBs have to be fair and equitable to all of their members, so you need to do some research on your own, too.

Destination Management Companies (DMCs)

Destination management companies (DMCs) are fee-based companies that provide general information and assistance in a city.

Need a tour arranged? A special event venue? Theme ideas and event coordination/management? Spouse tours? Someone to meet and greet your VIPs at the airport? Special gifts? A DMC is a second pair of hands at your meeting location. They know the city well and can recommend suppliers based on unbiased firsthand experience. You can find one at the website for the Association of Destination Management Executives: www.adme.org.

To CVB or DMC?

What's the difference between a CVB and DMC? A CVB is usually a nonprofit entity available to guide you in what a city or destination has to offer. They provide a range of services to assist you before meeting and onsite. They know the press, government officials, and other important people. They can tout your group as the best thing to hit the area since sliced bread.

A DMC is a for-profit company with expertise in most aspects of meeting and event planning. They arrange airport transportation for VIPs and others, create themed dinners, take spouses and guests on city tours, and hire motor coaches for the delegates' opening reception. They are hired by you and report to you, whereas a CVB would act on your behalf in taking care of requested tasks and projects.

Look at it this way: a DMC takes on a contractual responsibility with your organization, and a CVB provides general overall needed services. If you require assistance above and beyond what a CVB will provide for you, a DMC may be your next phone call. Feel comfortable asking the CVB for a list of recommended DMCs in the area, or ask your hotel salesperson.

The Inside Scoop

If you are considering using a CVB, it is key to investigate what they can and cannot do for you. Their services will vary depending on location and the size of the city. If you are visiting a small town, you are like the big fish in the little pond and may get more services and attention. If you are meeting in a large city, you are like the small fish in a very big ocean and may receive limited services. CVBs will do what they can, based on the size of your meeting, your needs, and their resources.

National or Global Sales Offices (NSOs/GSOs)

Most hotel chains have national or global sales offices (NSOs/GSOs). An NSO/GSO is a sales office for one hotel company that represents all of their properties and facilities. If you book a lot of meetings, the advantage of establishing a strong contact with an NSO/GSO is having one centrally located, knowledgeable person to deal with, rather than one at each facility. For example, if you had to book 20 meetings throughout the United States, without an NSO, you would be calling 20 different hotels within the same company.

If you work with an NSO/GSO, one person can help you book all 20 meetings, saving you a lot of time.

Another advantage in using an NSO/GSO for booking multiple meetings is that you generate greater buying power. The NSO understands the value of your collective meetings and can help you get better rates and other concessions.

Today, there is a growing consolidation of many hotel chains within the same company; therefore, you may even be able to book more than one chain with a single call to an NSO. Do your homework and see what works best for you.

Industry Experts

Industry experts are a must-have resource for every planner. At first glance, you may think you could not possibly have access to them. You have no clue who they are! Read on and we'll show you the way. Then you can hob-nob with the experts!

MeetingsCoach

MeetingsCoach is an innovative service developed by Robin Craven and Lynn Johnson Golabowski (yours truly) of Alliance LLC based in Menomonee Falls, Wisconsin. Robin and Lynn are veteran meeting professionals who provide constructive, balanced feedback on your unique meetings-industry issues. You simply select one of the coaching options (cyber, telecoaching, or in-person), and they'll be there to answer your questions. By using MeetingsCoach, you will …

- Be able to ask questions to a seasoned meeting professional.

- Gain a quick second opinion on an important, pending decision.

- Have someone help you through challenging situations.

- Have assistance weeding through the many issues you face daily.

- Discover ways to make the most of your opportunities.

- Learn how to set better goals so you can accomplish more.

Coaching topics include planner/supplier relationships, meeting-planning form and process review, meeting and event planning 101, career development, website development, technology in the meetings industry, and all of the topics covered in this book.

MIMlist Meeting Matters

The MIMlist is an online discussion group moderated by Joan Eisenstodt, a well-known, leading educator and expert in the meetings industry. It's a place to learn, discuss, ask, get information, and build your network of industry peers. It is a moderated discussion group where you can actively participate by asking and answering questions, or you can just lurk in the background and read the e-mails as they whiz by. This is a tremendous resource because you learn from your peers. Chances are, if you post a question, someone has an answer to it. Their website is www.meetingnews.com.

Weblogs ("Blogs")

A blog is a web-based online journal made up of postings and links usually about a specific topic. There are hundreds of thousands on the Internet, and the numbers are growing. Many blogs allow visitors to post feedback. They may be interactive or non-interactive and most make use of date- and time-stamping to individual entries, with the most recent appearing at the top of the page.

Blogs can be informative and quite interesting; however, comments and feedback tend to be gut-level honest and opinionated. At the very least they are certainly entertaining. As blogs become more commonplace, expect to see more meetings industry blogs pop up.

A few examples of current meeting and event industry blogs include:

- http://blog.meetingsnet.com/face2face
- www.misoapbox.com
- www.tech3partners.com/blog
- www.hotelchatter.com
- www.tradeshowstartup.com

Meeting Management Companies (MMCs)

If you are a planner who does not work directly with a company or an association, chances are you work for a meeting-management company (MMC) or are an independent planner. MMCs are companies who will provide a single component or do the entire planning and management of an event or meeting for an organization. Some call themselves meeting resource firms. They bring to the table experience, know-how, and a host of time-tested resources. If you just want consulting services, they can provide objective opinions and fresh ideas. Fee structures vary from company to company. Some charge a flat fee, and some work solely for the hotel commission, others on an hourly and daily basis. A major benefit of working with a large MMC is that some of them have prenegotiated contracts with larger hotel companies and book millions of dollars in rooms revenue. Many smaller organizations benefit from working with an MMC because they get the advantage of being part of a larger group.

Many organizations do not have the resources to handle all their meetings and special events in-house, so they hire professional help to get the work done. If you don't have time to find a meeting site, calling an MMC may be just the ticket to getting it done in an expeditious manner.

You can find these companies by asking CVBs, peers, or suppliers; through trade associations and trade publications; or just by looking in the phone book. The big three are www.conferencedirect.com, www.conferon.com, and www.helmsbriscoe.com.

The Least You Need to Know

- ◆ Many industry or trade publications offer free subscriptions to meeting planners.

- ◆ Convention and visitor bureaus (CVBs) will help you find the suppliers, products, and services you need at no charge.

- ◆ Destination management companies (DMCs) are for-profit firms with expertise in most aspects of meeting and event planning.

- ◆ A national or global sales office (NSO/GSO) is a central sales office for a single hotel company or chain that represents all of their properties and facilities.

- ◆ You have easy access to a multitude of industry experts online.

- ◆ Meeting-management companies can help you with any aspect of your meeting.

Chapter 5

Planning and Technology: Soft-Where? World-Wide-What?

In This Chapter

◆ Discover how planners manage meeting and event data

◆ Get tips on online registration, diagramming, name badges, site selection, and more

◆ Learn where to find answers to planning questions online

◆ Understand how valuable the web is to meeting planning

Data. A significant portion of meeting and event management revolves around managing data—and there are *a lot* of data. You have data about your attendees, facilities, vendors, speakers, and on and on. In the old days, meaning before the web, there were limited resources available for meeting and event management. Fortunately, today there is a plethora of software and web tools available to help you track and manage your data.

This chapter just scratches the surface of what's out there, both online and in the ever-evolving field of meeting-management software. We could not possibly provide an accurate or up-to-the-minute review of all meeting software, or even address all the different categories of online services for planners—there is just too much available and it seems to be changing every day. We will, however, point you in the right direction and give you the lowdown on how to find a complete software review—just read on.

Do It Yourself

In the do-it-yourself toolbox, there are three key pieces of software that every planner should have: a word-processing program, a spreadsheet program, and a relational database. Let's elaborate.

It's a no-brainer that everyone uses a word-processing program. Planners need to correspond, right? It's also a given that, if you need to manipulate numbers—and we all have budgets—then you need a spreadsheet, too. But what is this relational database thing?

A database is a collection of information using records. A record is a unique collection of information about a specific thing. For example, you might develop a new database for all the attendees of your upcoming meeting—BARCO 2 (the second annual meeting of the Big Association of Rare Cat Owners). The database consists of records about all your attendees. A record is the specific information about one attendee.

If you use a relational database (which allows you to access groups of related data within a database or even different databases), when you input a name, the database checks last year's database (BARCO 1) to see if the name exists. If it does, the record can be accessed and input into your BARCO 2 database— no retyping! That's the beauty of a relational database; you can manage, update, and use data (records) from other databases, making your work a lot easier.

Food for Thought

Give each attendee in your registration database a unique identification number. You just might have two people with the same name attending or people registering multiple times, and you need to keep their records straight.

Don't Drop the Ball

Be sure to save your files and back them up frequently and in multiple locations. Also, keep hard copies of everything important. Databases do crash and data is lost. Be prepared!

For planners just starting out, those on a limited budget, or working on small meetings, all you really need are the three basic software applications. However, if you generate your own marketing collateral or need a polished look, desktop-publishing software makes a nice addition. You can also purchase stand-alone specialty software packages for name badges, floor diagrams, and other specific tasks. The following table gives you a sampling of the documents generated in the planning process and the software you need to do the job.

Document Type	Word Processing	Spreadsheet	Database	Desktop Publishing	Specialty Software
Budgets		X			
Calendars	X	X			
Diagrams	X			X	X
Evaluations	X			X	X
Floor plans				X	X
Forms	X			X	
Letters	X		X	X	
Lists	X		X	X	
Memos	X				
Name badges	X		X	X	X
Name tents	X			X	X
Outlines	X	X			
Place cards	X				X
Postcards	X				
Posters				X	
Press releases	X			X	
Receipts	X		X		
Reports	X		X		X
Schedules	X	X			
Signage	X			X	X
Thank you notes	X				
Tickets	X		X	X	X
Timelines	X	X			X

As you can see, you can do a lot with just three or four programs. However, as your meetings and their respective budgets grow, you may find it more advantageous to invest in specially designed meeting-management software.

Meeting and Event Management Packages

Just a few years ago, there were not a lot of meeting- and event-management programs available. Today the number is soaring as more and more are being developed. You now can opt to purchase individual software packages to handle specific tasks or you can integrate all your essential tasks such as budgeting, registration, housing management, session scheduling and room layouts, travel arrangements, tours, and more in a meeting management package. Packages may also provide attendance tracking (from past meetings); allow complex registration processes and payment options; track food and beverage and audiovisual sets; handle exhibitor and vendor details; design and produce correspondence, confirmations, mailing labels, receipts, name badges, certificates, confirmations and tickets; and often produce a dizzying array of reports.

> **The Inside Scoop**
>
> An excellent compendium of descriptions and analyses of meeting-management software is *The Ultimate Technology Guide for Meeting Professionals* by Corbin Ball, CMP. It contains more than 1,200 product listings and is available from the MPI Foundation (www.mpifoundation.org) or www.corbinball.com.

The upside of these types of meeting and event management packages is that, much of the time, they really *do* everything you need. The real advantage of these packages is that the infrastructure has been built so you can focus on managing meetings and events, not building tables and reports.

The downside is that they can be pricey and may take time to learn and become comfortable with. Most packages allow for customization, but if you have significant or unique requirements, you may need to work with an experienced programmer. Here we highlight three popular categories, just to whet your whistle.

Registration and a Whole Lot More

Registering your attendees can be one of the most challenging and time-consuming parts of your job. You need to decide what information to collect, how to store it, and how you want to use it. Also, factor in the lost time spent trying to read handwriting, contacting someone who did not answer key questions, or solving payment problems. ARGHH!

What about housing and transportation? Even if your attendees are responsible for their own, they still need to know what is available in terms of dates, rates, location, directions, discounts, and payment options. They will also have questions about attire, food choices, disability access, family programs, social events, and on and on. Look at it from their perspective. It's your responsibility to select vendors, determine services offered, and clearly communicate this information. Attendees today often prefer to consider a variety of options (with or without your recommendations), so they can make their own educated decisions about travel decisions.

Do yourself a favor—check out existing meeting- and event-management packages. Not all provide the same services across the board and fees vary widely, so you will have to do some research to determine what features best meet your needs for the money you have to spend. Some come as simple downloadable software that reside on your computer's hard drive, however, more comprehensive meeting and event registration programs are provided through online application service providers (ASPs). While some allow basic customization to your meeting specifications, others are more programmable. A good package will generate up-to-date, accurate reports, offer password protection, and allow attendees to register 24 hours a day, 7 days a week. The following examples offer of a variety of what's available out there at the time of this writing—your job is to decide what will work best to manage your meeting or event:

- cvent.com (www.cvent.com)

- Exposoft Solutions (www.exposoft.com)

- GetThere (www.getthere.com)

- goMembers (www.gomembers.com)

- onVantage (www.onvantage.com)

- Passkey (www.passkey.com)

- PeoplewarePro (www.peopleware.com)

- Pro X (www.pcnametag.com)

- Register123 & Meeting Planner Plus (www.certain.com)

- Starcite (www.starcite.com)

- ViewCentral (www.viewcentral.com)

The Inside Scoop

Full-scale custom design could cost thousands and thousands of dollars, and still not work right. We've heard dozens of horror stories. The best advice is to do your homework when you're reviewing software, and make sure you get the best fit in the first place. Understand that it is probably easier and cheaper to adapt your procedures to the software than the other way around.

Many planners are moving away from trying to manage online meeting and attendee management software and are working with service bureaus like Attendee Management, Inc. (www.attendeenet.com). These companies license leading software from major providers and provide all the access you need to attendee data and reports. It's like adding your own meetings technology department.

Room Diagramming

Imagine sitting down with a pencil, a diagram of your meeting space, and the property's specification sheet (a list of meeting rooms and the number of people they can hold). You need to figure out if the room will hold your extra-large stage with rear screen projection, the four motorcycles (giveaways) on the side, and an extra-wide center aisle (for the marching band). Can you do it accurately? Probably not. This is where meeting and exhibition design software comes in.

Room diagramming or design software helps you create accurate floor plans, seating arrangements, exhibits layout, staging, and any other component you need to "fit in." These programs are fairly easy to use and provide an accurate layout of how you want your room to be set up.

Room design software allows you to ...

- ◆ Quickly modify layouts (over and over, if need be).
- ◆ Provide clear instructions to venue staff.
- ◆ Work with the venue to be more creative.
- ◆ Update diagrams from prior meetings quickly and easily.

You can change your specifications, and the diagrams immediately update. They allow for customized shapes (to draw tables, chairs, stages) and are printable so that all users can have a copy. Some also create a detailed inventory report that keeps track of how many tables, chairs, podiums, and so on that you need. Wow!

Want to learn more? Check out these programs as a few examples:

- ◆ MeetingMatrix (www.meetingmatrix.com)
- ◆ Delphi Diagrams (www.newmarketinc.com)
- ◆ Room Viewer (www.timesaversoftware.com)
- ◆ A2Z (www.a2zinc.net)
- ◆ Expocad (www.expocad.com) (for exhibit diagrams)

Name Badges

Because meeting people, both formally and informally, is one of the most important parts of the meeting ritual, it's important to have name badges that stand out and can be read easily from a distance. This is one area where everyone seems to have a different gimmick, so have fun with it!

If you are handy with database and word-processing software, you can design and format customized name badges quickly and easily. If not, to the rescue are stand-alone name badge software programs, such as BadgePro (www.badgepro.com) or *pc/nametag* (www.pcnametag.com). These applications import registrant data from your source (word processing, spreadsheets, or even certain databases) or let you input data directly. They produce badges that are easy to read and very professional looking. They allow you to use different fonts, manipulate text, and add logos. Because they use a database structure, you can print all, one, or a subset of badges as well as find, sort, and update records. The applications also have templates for certificates, place cards, name tents, and tickets.

It's also nice to be able to take the software onsite and print badges for new attendees or redo existing ones. Attendees appreciate it, and it promotes a higher level of service and professionalism to your meeting than handwritten name badges.

Looking to add a little fun and some glitz to your name badges for a party or special event? How about having your name scrolling along in lights? Individually programmable L.E.D. name badges can be purchased through www.streettags.com (however, at more than $25 each, these are not for your everyday, budget-conscious event).

Here's a different twist to printing name badges onsite. Instead of asking a registrant to fill out a form, ask for his or her business card. Using a special scanner that will export business card information into electronic address software, such as CardScan, you can download information into your existing software and print badges lickety-split. What a time-saver! CardScan claims it can be incorporated into any software application, so you can export business card information directly into your

> **The Inside Scoop**
>
> If you want high-quality name badges but don't want to purchase the software, contact *pc/nametag* toll-free at 1-877-626-3824 or www.pcnametag.com. For very reasonable fees, they will prepare great-looking name badges, alphabetized and assembled. Hate the way the plastic holders bend out of shape? Consider getting the sturdy and shippable carrying case as well. Done!

registration database, too. Find them at www.cardscan.com. Or you can simply take a DYMO LabelWriter (www.dymo.com) and print labels that you can stick onto blank name badge stock. This is a fast and easy way to make just one badge.

Site Selection Online

One of the hottest areas in online meeting resources is site selection. First, let's point out that there are thousands of venues: hotels, resorts, conference centers, convention centers, and numerous unique venues. Because these facilities are in the business of selling space, they always need to have available specific and accurate information about their venues, and the Internet is the perfect mechanism to communicate this information.

Enter online search engines, such as mpoint.com (www.mpoint.com) and starcite (www.starcite.com), that extensive searchable databases of meeting and event venues and facilities, as well as other industry suppliers. In addition, Unique Venues (www.uniquevenues.com) references more than 7,000 non-traditional facilities in the United States, United Kingdom, and Canada. These companies want you to use their resources to find the right location for your meeting. Some even go beyond just providing venue listings; they have developed an online *request for proposal* (*RFP*) feature that makes it easy for you to outline your specifications. The RFP process makes sure you don't forget important details when communicating your needs to a venue. Many companies will track the status of your RFP and offer assistance in the booking process if you want it.

> **Meeting Speak**
>
> A **request for proposal** (RFP) is an outline of all pertinent meeting or event specifications. Its purpose and intent is to locate the perfect venue. An RFP includes contact info, dates, tentative agenda, description, history, special needs and requests, and the date of decision.

Also, don't forget hotel chains. Most of the major hotel chains, and many of the smaller ones, have powerful search engines built in to their websites, as well. To stay competitive, the major players are adding free customized meeting websites for clients, and other special features for meeting planners. Many of the hotel search engines are powered by companies like mpoint.com, so it can be the best of both worlds.

When using an online RFP website, stick with just one. Sending your RFP using several online RFP services can create extra work for venues (and you) because they could easily receive two or more of the same proposal and not realize it. It's also good professional manners to let the venues know that they were not selected and why.

Other Online Resources

There are a ton of other online resources to choose from, and we can't possibly cover them all, nor will all of this information remain up-to-date by the time you read it. As you investigate the websites listed in this chapter, you will discover links to many other valuable websites.

Here's just a sampling of some additional interesting and useful web resources for the planning professional in all of us:

- **all-hotels.com (www.all-hotels.com).** A compendium of more than 80,000 hotels worldwide. Also includes availability checks and discounts.

- **Mimlist Meeting Matters (www.mim.com).** The meetings industry's leading e-mail–based discussion group.

- **MeetingsNet (www.meetingsnet.com).** A meeting industry portal for information and resources related to planning meetings and events.

- **OfficialTravelInfo.com (www.officialtravelinfo.com).** Contains more than 1,200 official tourism organizations worldwide.

- **Successful Exhibiting (www.tradeshowresearch.com).** A good resource for tradeshow trends, reports, and tips.

Current Trends of the Trade

With all the technology tools available, planners have oodles of choices. How is this technology improving the meeting and event-planning process? Let's take a look at some of the trends.

The Registration Process

Old way: Collect hard-copy registration forms and input (retype) information into a spreadsheet or database. Communicate lists to interested parties (venues, decision-makers, speakers, and so on). This process is labor intensive and does not lend itself to providing timely information.

New way: Attendees register electronically with an online, full-service, registration-management program. No retyping! Their data is instantly downloaded into a customized database. The group's housing inventory, sessions, and social event counts are automatically updated. Interested parties have online access to real-time data on demand. (More on this in Chapter 21.)

Site Inspections

Old way: Pour through directories and hotel brochures. Call venues to arrange for a site visit. Get on a plane. Get off a plane. Tour the site with a sales representative. Collect lots of material about the site. Possibly do this for several sites in different locations.

New way: Get on the Internet. Use one of several online site-selection companies and submit an electronic RFP. From your desk, do virtual site inspections on the Internet. More and more venues have web cams that provide 360-degree views of their facilities. Pick a site, or at least narrow it down to a few based on an educated decision. If you then want to visit, you'll have a better understanding of the whole picture before you arrive.

Templates and Toolsets

Old way: A few scattered websites have a few templates for budgeting, site inspections, evaluations, and more, but they are hard to find and don't necessarily use industry standards.

New way: Enter the Convention Industry Council and the APEX OfficeReady product. APEX (Accepted Practices Exchange—voluntary standards designed by the meetings, conventions, and exhibitions industry) now offers a new resource containing more than 200 meeting, event-management and business templates. It interfaces with Microsoft Office (especially, Word, Excel and PowerPoint). OfficeReady is available at a minimal cost and can be purchased at the Convention Industry website (www.conventionindustry.org).

Meetings That Are Not Face to Face

Old way: Initially it was a matter of a phone call. Then three-way and multiple-user conference calls pretty much summed it up. Participants would need to be faxed or e-mailed handouts in advance to refer to. With luck those who chose to make distracting noises in the background would make use of their mute button. The advent of folks using mobile phones to participate in conference calls added a new level of distracting background noise. Not being able to see the face of the person speaking lent itself to confusion, not only as to being able to identify who said what, but making sure of the intent. A statement made with a smile can be interpreted in person as positive, while that same statement without the smiling face can have a whole other meaning. In support of conference calls, a lot of work can get done quickly if you can weed out the chaos.

New way: Meetings online. More and more web-conferencing services are available, allowing a group of users to experience simultaneous, virtual audio and visual participation. Here are just a few:

- www.gotomeeting.com
- www.saveonconferences.com
- www.imconferencing.com
- www.webex.com

The Least You Need to Know

- For the most comprehensive listing of meetings industry websites, we recommend you start your search at www.corbinball.com.
- Meeting and event technology software makes planning more efficient.
- Save time by using online, full-service, meeting and event-management packages.
- The Internet will continue to change the way planners and suppliers do business; don't be afraid to browse around to find out what works best for you!

6

Focus on the Special Event

In This Chapter

- ◆ Identify some of the features that make up an event

- ◆ Understand how a theme can make your event more appealing and memorable

- ◆ Understand the merits of fund-raising and sponsorships

- ◆ Learn what you need to prepare for before an event and how to have a backup plan

Quick, what's the difference between a meeting and an event? Give up? It's a difficult question, and there is no right answer. For the most part, meetings are congregations of individuals gathered together for a specific purpose—usually educational or business-related. The word "meeting" implies work or seriousness. An "event," on the other hand, is a collection of people who come together for a variety of purposes. Events (often referred to as "special events") are intended to be fun, social, entertaining, and interesting.

There are many planning components that meetings and events have in common. These can include setting goals and objectives, selecting a site, marketing, food and beverage, timelines, staffing, and working with vendors. However, event planning also includes considerations that meetings usually do not have to deal with. Because the line between meetings and events can get blurry, you'll need to evaluate your needs based on each situation. In fact, some of the following information applies to meetings as well as events.

A Smorgasbord of Events

We touched on the various kinds of events in Chapter 1, including anniversaries, award ceremonies, auctions, bar/bat mitzvahs, birthday parties, concerts, fairs, festivals, fundraisers, galas, golf outings, ground-breaking ceremonies, graduations, holiday parties, parades, political rallies, reunions, road shows, school functions, sports competitions, theme parties, tradeshows, and weddings—and even funerals.

Think about what these events have in common. Many are festive, special occasions that last a day or maybe just a few hours. Of course, there are special events like the Olympics or county fairs that last several days. Even events like concerts, expositions, and festivals can span more than one day. However, one thing is certain: No matter what your event size, it takes a lot of time and resources to organize it!

Who are the people that create and produce events? Meeting planners plan meetings and events; event planners plan events and meetings. Often administrative staff is asked to plan and execute smaller corporate events. Large festivals, fairs, and parades, to name a few, often have executive directors and additional staff members who do the planning on an ongoing or annual basis.

> **The Inside Scoop**
>
> Events can be private or public, large or small, lavish or frugal. Just like meetings, they have goals and objectives, budgets, agendas, and many of the other components that a meeting has.

You will find some professional planning companies that specialize in either meeting planning or event planning. They may define their specialization one step further by specializing in corporate events. Don't get frustrated trying to define the difference between meetings and events. You'll know an event when you see one.

Making the Event Memorable

One of the first things to think about when planning an event is its event identity. After you establish goals and objectives, the next step is to create a memorable identity. Think of a popular event in your area. Does it have its own personality? A logo? A catch phrase? Could you recognize the event just by its colors, logo, or jingle?

If you can, then it has a recognizable brand, or an identity. Also consider whether the event is a one-time occurrence or if it will be held again in the future.

For example, your company may decide to hold a one-time golf tournament as a fundraiser. Your event's identity may be as simple as putting your corporate logo on all promotional pieces and marketing it as a community fundraiser. This works for some events. Others need a true identity to survive and ensure longevity. Even the consistent use of color or themed artwork appropriate to the event can add a creative touch to promotional pieces. Consider something like firecrackers for an anniversary celebration ... you get the idea.

Think about the future. Is there the possibility that this one-time event could be held again? If there is, get the creative heads together to develop an identity for the event, which will provide a consistent and quickly recognizable message to your audience for at least the next few years. Even smaller events and parties can benefit from having their own identity. You may find a talented local freelancer by talking to other organizations in your area.

Food for Thought

Big events often have professional event planners managing them. Sometimes this is also important for smaller events, if they are very upscale or high profile. If you have a large or complex event, consider hiring an event planner or destination management company (DMC) to help. Initially, their fees may seem like an added expense, but in the long run, their contacts in the industry can save you money on props, food, and other supplies. As well, their experience and professionalism are always more than welcome in the event of time crunch or a true crisis. See Chapter 4 for more information on how to find these organizations.

More Than Little Drink Umbrellas: The Theme

This is the fun part. Events often need to deliver a festive, fun, and unique experience. Events need to motivate and engage your participants as well. For example, an annual event can have the same theme every year, or you can change it depending on the message you want to convey. Even dinner parties are more fun when planned with an underlying theme in mind. Here are some of the more popular themes:

- ◆ Carnival
- ◆ Casino night

- Celebration
- Color (for example, "black and white")
- Ethnic, regional, or country (for example, Italian)
- Festival
- Game show or reality show
- Island adventure, beach party, or Hawaiian theme
- Jailbreak
- Mardi Gras
- Picnic in the park
- Sports
- Western BBQ
- Zoo or safari
- 1950s or any other era

Think Outside the Box

This is where you can really get your creative juices flowing. Themes can be tied to current events, popular movies, or historical events. You might even come up with a new theme idea that ties into your organization's mission. Keep your theme simple, relate it to your message, and weave it throughout the entire event. If your theme involves activities, try to include those that appeal to a broad range of people. Incorporate entertainment and a variety of related food choices, if appropriate. Even the follow-up correspondence after the event should tie into the theme.

Checklist for Events at Alternative Venues

Events are often held at locations other than hotels, conference centers, convention centers, and self-contained facilities. If you hold events in parks, festival or company grounds, churches, or other alternative locations, you may need to bring in all the equipment and food for the events. You may also need to comply with city/county ordinances and other local and municipal laws. Listed below (in alphabetical order, not ranked in order by importance) are items that may need to be considered in your planning process; there may be others:

- ❏ Accessible services
- ❏ Alcohol sales (permits)
- ❏ Ambulance/medical aid
- ❏ ATMs
- ❏ Band
- ❏ Carpeting, sub-flooring, or artificial grass
- ❏ Cooking equipment
- ❏ Dance floor
- ❏ Decorations
- ❏ Delivery and shipping procedures
- ❏ Eating utensils
- ❏ Electrical outlets and backup power sources
- ❏ Emergency and evacuation procedures
- ❏ Exhibit/display areas
- ❏ Fencing
- ❏ Fire safety and fire marshal approval
- ❏ Fireworks
- ❏ Flowers
- ❏ Food/beverage (including special commemorative items, such as a themed cake)
- ❏ Green room (for speakers and entertainers)
- ❏ Insurance (both for you, the event sponsor, and all contractors)
- ❏ Internet connections
- ❏ Kids area/games for family events
- ❏ Lighting
- ❏ Local public relations
- ❏ Logo item sales
- ❏ Lost and found

❏ Lost children

❏ Master of ceremonies

❏ Music (and licensing)

❏ Name badges

❏ Overnight or other time restrictions

❏ Parking permits

❏ Pedestrian walkways

❏ Permits

❏ Photography

❏ Press coverage

❏ Pricing

❏ Protection from inclement weather

❏ Public transportation stops and schedules

❏ Re-admission procedure

❏ Refund procedure

❏ Registration area

❏ "Reserved" signs

❏ Restroom facilities

❏ Security

❏ Sleeping rooms

❏ Sound/video equipment

❏ Staging

❏ Street closures

❏ Tables (including linens) and chairs

❏ Telephones and wireless device access

❏ Temperature-controlled areas (heat, air conditioning/fans)

❏ Tents

- ❑ Ticket sales
- ❑ Traffic control
- ❑ Uniforms, costumes, or formal wear
- ❑ Vendors
- ❑ Volunteer staffing
- ❑ Waste/trash removal
- ❑ Water
- ❑ Wheelchairs and strollers, and ramps
- ❑ Other: _____
- ❑ Other: _____
- ❑ Other: _____

An alternative event facility may provide some of these components. Before you sit down with the site manager(s), prepare a list of questions or develop your own checklist using the previous one as a guide. Be sure to get full contact information for all individuals who provide services you need. Some venues have lists of vendors that they prefer to work with or with which they have exclusive contracts. You can either work directly with these vendors or ask the site manager to handle arrangements for you. In either case, stay on top of the details because, ultimately, it's your responsibility.

If the site does not have a preferred or exclusive vendor list, look into catering companies first. Obtain at least three proposals. Ask them for references, and referrals to other vendors, such as florists, DJs, bands, and so on. Hiring contractors who frequently work together can make things easier and run smoother. Find out what permits and any other contractors the catering company (and others) will be responsible for.

Staging big outdoor events (as opposed to smaller events or indoor events) takes a different set of knowledge and skills. How do you know the rules? The best resources are the Convention and Visitor Bureaus (CVBs), city

> **CAUTION** **Don't Drop the Ball**
>
> Make sure all contractors you hire have adequate insurance. Get a copy of their policy and ask them to add you as an additional insured for the event. Look for a minimum of $1 million to $2 million in liability coverage, more if appropriate.

officials, and other companies with whom you contract. Many cities have an instruction handbook for holding public events. They may have requirements for everything from crowd control and the number of portable toilets to liquor licensing restrictions and noise control.

A Marriage Made in Sponsorship Heaven

Sponsorships are in. They are big business. Companies spend billions of dollars each year sponsoring meetings and events. If you find the right sponsors, it is a huge opportunity for both of you because it gives them exposure to a targeted audience and gives you additional resources to produce your event. Often times, the CVB directory of contractors and services is an excellent place to begin your search.

Sponsors should understand the event's goals and objectives and should be approached from the standpoint of creating a long-term strategic partnership. Don't approach them just because they have something you want. Understand what they need from the relationship and then build a sponsorship package.

Before you begin, you need to understand what you need from your sponsors. Sponsorships often are a way to defray costs. What do you currently buy that could be donated "in kind"? Make a list and target these first. Here are some items to consider:

- Airline or train tickets
- Audio-visual equipment and technicians' time
- Bus/motorcoach transportation
- Entertainment
- Food and beverage
- Flowers and linens
- Giveaway items
- Hotel rooms
- Kids games
- Phones/communication equipment

- Receptions/specific meal functions
- Security
- Signage
- Speakers
- T-shirts
- Tote bags

Don't Drop the Ball

Consult your accountant before you start soliciting sponsorships. He or she will tell you how it affects your tax situation and what verbiage to include in your sponsor correspondence.

In addition to in-kind donations, your organization obviously will accept cash donations. You need to decide whether sponsorship items will support your current budget and defray costs or enhance your event by providing items that weren't initially in your budget.

The best way to find sponsorship dollars is to match the opportunity with the sponsor. Do your homework. What organizations are potential sponsors? First, look at exhibitors and other organizations that do business with you.

Next, look at your audience and determine what companies are looking for the same audience. Create sponsorship opportunities that meet the needs of the sponsoring organization. Are they looking for recognition? Access to participants onsite? Marketing opportunities before, during, and after the event?

In other words, *customize*. Sponsorship is a give and take deal. Each company gives something in exchange for a benefit. Some companies want their name out in public, or at least in front of your participants. Others want more direct interaction with participants. Here are some ideas to give your sponsors exposure:

- Recognition in front of participants onsite
- Pre-event mailings, flyers, and invitations
- Logo on items such as hats and T-shirts
- Website banner ads or links to their websites from yours
- Promotional materials
- Prominent signage before, during, and after
- Fax cover sheets

The Inside Scoop

The tax-deductible portion of a ticket is the difference between the ticket price and the fair market value of the ticket. The event organizer determines the fair market value and communicates the tax-deductible amount in writing to the participant.

◆ Mailing list

◆ A booth at the event to promote the company or to sell products or services

Don't just create one sponsorship brochure with stock benefits. Personally contact potential sponsors and ask them to be a part of your event. Then send a letter outlining your discussion and confirming participation.

"Fun"-Raising

Events are also frequently used to raise funds for a charity, organization, person, or a multitude of other reasons. These are different from sponsorships because the monies you collect at a fundraiser are donated to a pre-selected cause.

Meeting Speak

A **silent auction** raises funds through the sale of (typically donated) items displayed for bid. The participants wander through the display area, indicating what they will pay for an item on a bid sheet in front of the item. Minimum bids usually start below market value to entice bidding. At the end of a specified time period, the person with the highest bid buys the item. All proceeds go to your cause.

Ways to raise funds include designating that a portion of ticket sales will go to the cause, staging a *silent auction*, selling raffle tickets, auctioning off donated items, you name it. Brainstorm. Anything (legal, that is) that people will pay for can be used to raise money.

Your target audience are those who hold your *cause du jour* near and dear to their hearts. Match the right audience with the right cause and half the battle is won—resulting in high attendance, great exposure for your sponsors, and money raised for the cause.

A good resource for fundraising questions is the Association of Fundraising Professionals (AFP, formerly the National Society of Fund Raising Executives or NSFRE). They are a professional association of individuals responsible for generating philanthropic support for a wide variety of nonprofit, charitable organizations. The AFP has a resource center available to members (for free) and nonmembers (a fee applies) to answer your questions and will send information to you regarding your topic of interest. They also hold an annual conference on fundraising, workshops nationwide, and periodic audio conferences. Located in Alexandria, Virginia, they can be reached at 703-684-0410 or on the web at www.nsfre.org.

You will need to solicit giveaways or prizes if you sell raffle tickets (don't forget the raffle license) or if you hold a silent auction. Giveaways are solicited the same way as sponsors. Decide who can benefit from an affiliation with the event and ask for a donation. Give them what they need in return, such as recognition or access to your participants in some way.

Four Key Considerations

There are many things to consider when organizing an event. The following sections discuss four key areas that require special attention.

Master Schedule

As every meeting needs an agenda, every event needs a master plan. This should be a written document with all the details for the event, including a complete diagram of the site with placement of all activities, a list of contractors, a list of responsible parties, any required permits, staff training and work schedules, an event schedule, emergency phone numbers, security procedures, and all other pertinent details.

During the event you will need to be mobile, so carrying around binders or folders is not practical. If you consolidate the important event information onto a few sheets of paper and keep them on a clipboard, you'll have the right info at your fingertips when you need it.

Contingency Plans: Risk Management and Safety

Contingency plans provide the details of what to do in an emergency. Emergencies can include, but are not limited to, the following: earthquakes, tornadoes, floods, hurricanes, fires, medical emergencies, inclement weather or excessive heat or cold, electrical/power outages, labor strikes, terrorist attacks, and violence. Training for all volunteers and staff is a must. They should know who to notify and what to do in case of any emergency. Work with your site managers and vendors and with local emergency personnel (fire, police, medical, and others) in preparing this document. They probably have one in place and can help you customize contingency plans for your unique event. There are some

Meeting Speak

Contingency planning is a process to plan for and implement decisions to avoid or control undesirable events.

Contingency plans must be written documents, prepared in advance, that address every conceivable contingency, emergency, and other urgent issues.

very good books available regarding event risk management and safety; it is your responsibility to read them *before* you need them. A potential lawsuit could be the *least* of your problems if your contingency plans fall short. We recommend *Event Risk Management and Safety* by Peter E. Tarlow. There's more about contingency planning in Chapter 24.

Joe Q. Public can also be a huge challenge when you consider all the things human beings are capable of. Potential onsite problems include disorderly conduct, drunkenness, theft, medical problems, and littering. Include dealing with these situations in your contingency plan.

Another consideration with regard to weather is what you will do if your outdoor event is curtailed by inclement weather. Will it be cancelled or postponed, or do you have a backup site? For a large event, you may consider contracting with a convention center or other indoor venue as an inclement-weather backup. Think of the rental fee as a kind of insurance policy. Be sure to have a plan in place to change venues at the last minute. This includes keeping your vendors in the loop, too.

Entertainment

If your event includes entertainment, and most do, you are responsible for the care and feeding of the entertainers and their entourage. Many will request a "green room" in their contract, which is a secure area where they can rest and stay when backstage, throughout the event. You may also need to provide private dressing rooms, showers, and other special accommodations. If you hire a really big name, he or she will very likely require even more services and amenities. Read your entertainment contracts thoroughly to make sure you can accommodate any requests.

Volunteers

Most events require a large number of staff, and many of them will be volunteers. They may be volunteers from within the company or organization planning the event, or they may be drawn from the local community, or both. Some volunteers have experience working on events; others do not. The best thing you can do for your volunteer staff is provide solid training and clear lines of communication. The goal is to avoid any accidents or other unfortunate incidents involving untrained or "under"-trained volunteers. And don't forget to thank them before, during, and after the event.

You also need to establish procedures for volunteers to eat, take breaks, and have some fun. Provide an area stocked with food, beverages, and a place to rest. Remember, they are volunteering their time. If you take care of them, they will take care of your event.

The Least You Need to Know

♦ Events may take on a broader array of details and considerations than meetings.

♦ Give your event a theme, and use that theme throughout—in marketing, food and beverage, décor, giveaways, and so on.

♦ Sponsorship packages should be customized to each organization.

♦ Raising funds needs to appeal to the emotions of both the participants and sponsors.

Chapter **7**

Supplier Secrets No More: Where Communication Is Key

In This Chapter

- ◆ Understand in advance what happens when you contact a hotel, resort, or conference center sales office regarding a meeting or event
- ◆ Establish good communication with the sales manager
- ◆ View your meeting or event under a supplier's microscope
- ◆ Understand the "passing off" of your business
- ◆ Focus on understanding what makes your meeting profitable to a hotel

Suppliers and vendors are the folks who provide you with the products, places, and services necessary to plan and execute a meeting or event. They include, but are not limited to, the following: venues (hotels, convention centers, conference centers), airlines, ground-transportation companies, decorators, florists, destination management companies (DMCs), name badge and other meeting and event supply companies, registration companies, software suppliers, speakers, and entertainers.

In this chapter, we explore the sales process and how your meeting or event is evaluated and booked, primarily from the perspective of a hotel or similar facility. Just because you contact a hotel and request meeting space and sleeping rooms doesn't mean you'll get it. The facility booking process is really a business decision based on experience and predetermined calculations. The process will vary depending on the type of facility and the business plan of the owners. This chapter primarily addresses hotels and similar facilities. Your meeting will be carefully evaluated, and a decision made about whether it is a viable "piece of business" for the property.

Initial Contact

One of your first tasks is to contact the hotel sales office to book space. This is called an inquiry call. Some offices assign a person each day to be dedicated to handling these inquiries, or your first contact could be with an administrative assistant who is trained to ask you initial qualifying questions. Be sure to ask whom your sales contact will be before you end the call. You will then be directed to the appropriate sales manager, based on his or her assigned sales territories or market segments. If you prefer, you can contact a national sales office or global sales office for the hotel brand and they can assist you in contacting individual hotels.

Here are some typical assignments:

- Corporate
- Association
- SMERF (social, military, entertainment, religious, fraternal)
- Small meetings (for example, each hotel defines a small meeting based on the hotel size; in some hotels it could be fewer than 10 guest rooms while in others it could be 50 to 100 guest rooms)
- Territories by state or region

Most hotels have booking parameters for assigning inquiries to salespeople. A typical standard is that all inquiries with 10 or more sleeping rooms are booked by the sales department. Inquiries with less than 10 sleeping rooms are booked by the catering department.

When you make the inquiry call, there are some relatively standard questions you will be asked about your meeting or event. If these questions are not asked, you should provide the information anyway. You may also choose to put your meeting specifications in writing and send a request for proposal to the hotel. Either way, the same information needs to be provided so the hotel can effectively analyze your business.

- What are your goals and objectives for the meeting/event?
- Who are your attendees?
- Where do they come from?
- What are your preferred dates?
- Are the dates and arrival/departure pattern flexible?
- Is the agenda set? Can you provide a copy of (at least) a provisional agenda?
- What food and beverage functions will be held?
- What is the required guestroom block?
- What reservation method will you use?
- What is your guestroom and food budget?
- Where was the meeting/event held the past three years?
- What did you spend last year for guestrooms?
- What did you spend last year for food and beverage?
- What mode of transportation will attendees use to get to the city?
- Will attendees have any free time?
- Will you be planning any outside activities?
- Do you plan on having all the functions at this hotel?
- Is this a required or optional meeting?
- What other facilities are you looking at?
- What will your location and facility decision be based on?
- When will your decision be made?
- Who makes the location and facility decision?

- What did you like best about last year's meeting/event?

- What is one thing you would change about last year's meeting/event?

These are all important questions that help the sales manager qualify and learn about your business. The more he or she knows about you and your meeting/event history, the better he or she can service your group. It is a good sign if you are asked a lot of questions.

Once the sales manager understands the details, he or she checks availability. The sales manager then analyzes whether or not it is good business for the hotel. Many hotels and other facilities now use computer programs that calculate, based on projections, whether an event fits their projected profit for that period of time. For example, if you ask for a really low rate in peak season, some properties may not book your meeting. If you are not getting the space and dates you want, start asking questions. These work well:

- What space *is* available over those dates? At what rate?

- What could I do with my program to fit it into your facility? Change the agenda? Change the dates?

Food for Thought

If you are not making progress with a facility, ask the sales manager what would make it a better piece of business for them. Groups that are flexible on their check-in and check-out have a better chance of getting the room rates and space they are looking for. The hotel can then fill the "holes" in their bookings, possibly with transient (individuals reserving rooms) or other group business. It's a win-win situation.

- How many group rooms can you give me over those dates? At what rate?

- Is this business you want to book into your hotel during this timeframe?

- What other business is in the hotel or the city at that time?

These questions will, at the very least, start a dialogue about space availability and your needs.

Most hotels have a group target rate that they aim for on any given date. The revenue manager will typically calculate a target rate based on the hotel's budget and supply and demand. Your meeting will also be evaluated for total room revenue, food and beverage revenue, and the amount of meeting space required. Groups are often allotted a specific amount of meeting space based on the number of rooms reserved/room revenue and food and beverage revenue. Every hotel is different based on the number of guestrooms in its inventory and the amount of meeting space available, so there is no standard calculation figure. This will also vary according to season, the day of check-in, and group history.

Do a little research about the destination (city) before setting your budget. Don't go to a city in October if you want a downtown hotel for $75 a night and the going rate is $250. You can call the reservation department and see what rates it is quoting during your dates. Ask for their best corporate rate, even if you don't qualify for it. This will at least give you a ballpark figure. Be aware of the business climate and know what is reasonable and what is not.

Hotels know when they need group business. For example, groups that meet on Sunday through Tuesday, Thursday through Sunday, and holiday periods may be the perfect group for hotel X and not so good for hotel Y. These are called booking patterns. The booking patterns vary at each property because of *transient demand.*

Why don't hotels sell all their rooms to groups? You will find that most hotels have a maximum group block or ceiling. Transient (individual) customers pay a higher rate, so hotels are careful about not turning them away too many times because they may never return. Every night has a transient-demand, guestroom-usage projection. The difference between transient demand and the total hotel room inventory is the group room inventory available to sell to groups.

Meeting Speak

A **booking pattern** is the arrival and departure days for a group or individual. All meeting facilities determine what pattern they need for groups during each week of the year. Booking patterns vary depending on **transient demand,** which is the demand of the individual traveler. When transient demand is high, group blocks are kept to a minimum. When transient demand is low, groups are needed to fill the hotel.

Hotels have an annual budget and marketing plan. These documents serve as the road map for selling group, transient, and catering business. From these documents, sales and catering managers create their own goals and objectives for selling to their market segment.

It's important to keep your own meeting history. Track all statistics including revenue and expenses associated with each of your meetings and events. Ask the hotel to supply this data after you have checked out. With this information, you have more bargaining power when you book your next meeting or event. See Appendix A for a sample history form.

Your Business Under a Microscope

Not only will you be asked about every single meeting detail, the hotel salesperson will also do a history check. Unless it is a first-time meeting, your meeting already has an established meeting history. The sales manager will contact meeting facilities you have contracted with previously and inquire about the dates, the number of guestrooms used each night, the agenda, food and beverage functions, and any other pertinent issues and statistics about previous meeting(s). The only thing he or she can't ask about is your room rate (because of anti-trust laws). Meeting history information is frequently shared among hotels and is a requirement at most hotels before a contract is sent to a client.

If the sales manager finds any discrepancies in the meeting history and the space you are trying to book, he or she will ask more questions. Be prepared with details to support the space you need. If your room pickup last year was 90 rooms for three nights and this year you are asking for 150 rooms for three nights, the hotel will want to know why there's such a big difference. Support the difference with a solid reason, such as you hired more salespeople or experienced a big increase in membership.

Be aware that hotels may internally cut your block (called blind cutting). For example, if you are holding 100 rooms for one night, the hotel may internally only hold 85 rooms. They will take a look at your meeting history before making the decision on how much to blind cut your block, if any. Not all groups will sell their entire block, so blind cutting usually works in their favor. When your *cutoff date* appears, rooms that have not sold in your block (if any) are turned back over to the hotel's general inventory to sell. Request that any rooms sold after your cutoff date to your attendees are booked at the group rate and counted in your block. If the hotel agrees, make sure this is written specifically into the contract. Also consider adding a damage clause to your contract that protects you from blind cutting. This clause should state what you get if the hotel cannot fulfill their room block commitment prior to the cutoff date.

Meeting Speak

A **cutoff date** is the date on which the hotel releases your room block back to general inventory. It is typically 21 to 30 days prior to arrival and is negotiable at most properties.

The following is an example of room pickup statistics. Let's take a look at some important calculations.

Group Pickup Report

Pickup Timeframe	Day 1	Day 2	Day 3	Total
Contracted room block	90	95	85	270
Room pickup five weeks out	40	44	39	123
Room pickup three weeks out	85	88	84	257
Room pickup one week out	89	90	87	266
Room pickup two days out	88	89	88	265
Room pickup arrival day	88	89	88	265
Actual room pickup	85	87	86	258

The time increments for tracking room pickup can vary depending on your situation. Some larger conventions start tracking a year or more prior to the arrival date. Smaller (typically corporate) meetings may only track pickup three to four weeks out. Ask the hotel to provide you with weekly pickup reports as your meeting draws near so you can stay informed about your group and handle any potential problems proactively. Ask who will be providing these reports and set a schedule for when you will get them.

Assuming we are working with the preceding report, you would know the following:

◆ The contracted room block is 270 room nights.

◆ The room pickup one week out is 266 room nights.

◆ The room pickup on the day of check-in is 265 room nights.

◆ The actual room pickup after group checks out is 258 room nights.

◆ The peak night is the second night (the night with the most rooms picked up).

◆ If you qualify for one complimentary guestroom for every 50 paid for on a cumulative basis, then $258 \div 50 = 5.16$. Five complimentary (comp) room nights will be given to your group.

◆ Calculate total room revenue by multiplying the actual room pickup minus comps by the room rate: $258 - 5$ comps $= 253$; $253 \times \$110 = \$27,830$.

- ◆ Your room pickup percentage is the total number of rooms picked up divided by the contracted room block: $258 \div 270 = 95.5$ percent. You picked up 95.5 percent of your group block.

- ◆ The difference between the room pickup for the day of check-in and the actual room pickup is the number of *no-shows* or cancellations you had on the day of check-in: $265 - 258 = 7$ rooms. Ask the hotel if these were cancellations or no-shows.

Meeting Speak

A **no-show** is a person who has a reservation for a guestroom and does not show up. There are two kinds of no-shows. One is someone who has a reservation guaranteed until a specific time, for example, 4 or 6 P.M. the day of arrival or 24 to 72 hours prior to arrival. If a person does not show up or guarantee the room, the room is released and is available for sale again. The second type of no-show has a guaranteed reservation. This means the person has guaranteed to the hotel that he or she will pay for the room. If the person is a no-show, the hotel charges his or her credit card or keeps the deposit, or if the group is paying for the room, charges the group.

You need to know how many no-shows and cancellations your group typically has because it helps you block properly in the future. You also should know whether anyone on your rooming list that you are paying for was a no-show. This will have an effect on your meeting budget.

A form for tracking your meetings is located in Appendix A. Make copies and start today. You may want to expand and customize this form so it fits your specific needs.

Hotel Tag Teams

After you've booked your meeting with the sales manager at a facility, your file is "turned over" to the convention services and catering department. Either a catering manager (CM) or a convention services manager (CSM)—or both—will handle the details from this point forward. A CSM typically handles the meeting details such as meeting room setups and meeting production. A CM generally handles only the food and beverage arrangements. Sometimes a catering manager or a convention services manager does both.

Put meeting specifications in writing to the catering and/or convention services manager. When you discuss the details, a written document provides a place to take additional notes and is a reference when the actual hotel documents are written. It also provides a record of what you requested, and makes it easier to review the hotel banquet and event orders and meeting/event resume for possible errors or omissions.

The Details, Please

Once your file is assigned to a catering and/or convention services manager, you should schedule an appointment to discuss the details. If possible, visit the hotel again; however, sometimes you'll have to do this over the phone or via e-mail. Before the appointment, ask for an updated packet with menus, AV price lists, and other applicable information. Make sure the information is consistent with what is in your contract (for example, if you are contracted in at last year's food and beverage prices, make sure you aren't ordering from this year's menus with this year's pricing).

> **The Inside Scoop**
>
> If you have a very small meeting (fewer than 50 people), some hotels have what they call a "one stop shop." The sales manager actually keeps the file and services the meeting or event, rather than turning it over to another services manager. Usually this applies to contracts with 10 to 50 total guestrooms or less, but this varies by property. Ask if the hotel has this program. It will save you time to work with just one individual throughout.

The catering and/or convention services manager will take the meeting details and create internal documents for staff members. You'll learn more about this in Chapter 19.

Use your sales and catering managers as a resource. They see hundreds of meetings each year and know what works. Ask them for ideas and suggestions that might work for your meeting.

Sales Managers Just Wine and Dine—Not!

Once your meeting has been passed off, your sales manager is still a contact for you; however, his or her job is to move on and keep booking business. This person should check in with you occasionally to find out how things are progressing and to see if there is anything else you need. In some hotels, it is his or her responsibility to get the rooming list from you.

One of the best ways to have a successful meeting is if both the sales manager and the meeting planner take the time to continually communicate with each other about the meeting. This is a two-way street. It is their job to help you have a successful meeting, and you need to give them the information they need to do just that. One of the biggest pet peeves of sales and catering managers is not being kept in the loop on changes. Don't need all the meeting space? Release it back to the hotel. Did your dinner drop from 500 to 250? Tell them, so they block space and order food accordingly. The time to tell them about changes is not right before the meeting. It is an ongoing process. This kind of reputation gives you big points when you work with them on a consistent basis. They will know your information is timely and accurate and that your word can be trusted. Excellence in communication will not go unnoticed, and will very likely spill over to when you book your next meeting at the same property.

The Least You Need to Know

- Know the value of your business and track your own meeting history to help you with contract negotiations and future planning.
- Never underestimate the importance of good communication between the planner and supplier.
- Pay attention to the venue's business climate to negotiate better deals.
- Flexibility with your meeting specifications can save you money.
- Always keep the hotel informed about changes to your meeting or event.

Part 2

First Things First

Okay, so you're ready to start planning. Before you can get into the details, however, you need a timeline, a budget, and a request for proposal (RFP) to distribute to potential meeting facilities.

Once that's out of the way, you can begin negotiations with vendors, and then you will be expected to sign a contract. Whoa! But are you ready? Especially with hotel contracts, where there are tons of things you need to know and understand. Don't worry, we've got the scoop on hotel contracts from one of the leading meeting-industry attorneys. He is a guest author and is here to share tips you need to have and to hold to stay out of trouble. (Thank heaven for lawyers!)

Will exhibits be part of your next meeting? Are exhibits right for your meeting? You will learn about exhibits and a bit about marketing and how to find the right people to market to. It's a never-ending battle. You will need to know what to tell people, so they will want to come to your meeting. We are here to help you—stay tuned and read all about these topics and more.

THE PLANNER FOR MY BIRTHDAY NEEDS A FIRM BUDGET FIGURE.

Chapter 8

Creating and Following a Timeline

In This Chapter

- ◆ Create your meeting road map
- ◆ Understand the importance of milestones
- ◆ Identify important tasks for any timeline
- ◆ Discover that a timeline is one place to capture many of your details

Developing a timeline for your meeting is an important early step in the planning process. You already know that planning a meeting or an event involves scads of details, and most planners are married to their to-do lists for good reason. However, a timeline is not just one big to-do list. In fact, it's quite different. A good timeline will identify key tasks and dates and keep your priorities straight. Most importantly, it will factor in the time you need to make sound decisions.

Timelines are as unique to an individual meeting as the people who create them. Your planning tasks differ from meeting to meeting. They are also different depending on whether you are planning a corporate, association, nonprofit, or business meeting or event, and so on. Effective timelines must be customized to each unique situation. This chapter looks at what goes into a timeline and offers suggestions for using timelines efficiently.

Timeline Types

Timelines, just like every component in meeting planning, will vary depending on your special circumstances. When thinking about your timeline, consider these questions:

- Who is the timeline for? The planner? Staff? Committees?

- Who will be the keeper/modifier/checker of the timeline?

- How frequently will the timeline be looked at?

- Do you need specific task due dates?

- Do you need specific task completion dates?

- Do you need to assign responsibility for tasks?

- What type of software, if any, will be used to manage the timeline (word processing/spreadsheet/project management)?

Some people prefer timelines that list only key dates or milestones. Examples of milestones are room block review dates, deposits due, publication dates, mailing dates, registration deadlines, housing cutoff dates, and meeting start dates. Missing a milestone usually has significant consequences. Because this type of timeline focuses on hard dates, it is usually short. Planners who use this type of timeline just want to make sure they don't miss a critical date or decision.

Other planners like an exhaustive listing of every task including who is responsible for the tasks, the dates by which tasks should be completed, and even the actual completion dates (for future planning purposes). These timelines resemble long to-do lists and that's okay—they still identify milestones and can be useful tools when working with large events or staff.

Still others like a combination of the two. Some planners find that creating a timeline that outlines the milestones plus some of the major tasks works best. They use a modified timeline to focus on major planning activities and use their own methods to handle specific action items.

Key Elements, Key Dates

One important question is "When do I begin working on my timeline?" The answer is "When you have a confirmed site." This is because your dates and location determine almost all of your other decisions such as marketing, selecting speakers, budgets, and so on. Before we go any further, however, realize that there are instances when you know for a fact you are doing a meeting, you just don't know the exact dates or location. You can and should develop a timeline that includes your RFP process, site selection, and the associated decisions. This is especially important for annual meetings, when you are preparing for them years in advance.

The Inside Scoop

Don't underestimate the value of a timeline. It keeps everyone on track, and most importantly, deadlines are not missed if the timeline is accurate. A good place to look for can't-miss dates is in your vendor contracts. Don't be afraid to spend a full day detailing and perfecting your timeline for an important meeting. Your ability to stay organized when others around you are floundering will dazzle the best of them! As you gain planning experience, timelines become second nature.

Whether you are developing a milestone timeline or a lengthy timeline, you need to incorporate the key tasks and key dates. The following is a (far from complete) task listing of timeline items to get you started:

- ◆ Develop meeting goals and objectives.
- ◆ Determine decision-makers and chain of command.
- ◆ Assign responsible parties.
- ◆ Determine calendar dates for future organizing committee meetings.
- ◆ Determine overall theme and title, if appropriate.
- ◆ Determine overall format—lecture, workshop, reception, etc. (Example: Consider best use of adult teaching methods based on educational needs of this particular audience.)
- ◆ Draft program topics and agenda.
- ◆ Prepare the budget.
- ◆ Determine policies and procedures.

- Do venue research (sites, weather, social activities).

- Prepare a site request for proposal (RFP).

- Establish site contacts (host committee, CVBs, and so on).

- Conduct site visits.

- Negotiate site contracts (hotel, convention center, other meeting rooms, or event location and guest rooms).

- Research, select, and invite speakers.

- Negotiate speaker contracts.

- Apply for continuing education accreditation, if applicable.

- Prepare RFPs for other vendors (audio-visual production, exhibition, airline and ground transportation, exhibit company, and so on).

- Negotiate vendor(s) contracts.

- Obtain insurance coverage.

- Determine whether you need music licenses and if so, apply for them.

- Develop a marketing plan.

- Determine/order promotional materials and any giveaway items.

- Create communication/marketing pieces.

- Finalize mailing lists or other avenues of distribution for invitations, hold-the-date flyers, and/or registration brochures.

- Create a meeting website with essential information; update it regularly.

- Decide on a registration process (in-house, outsource, and so on).

- Implement the registration process and fee-handling procedures.

- Send out letters of confirmation to attendees, if appropriate.

- Assign meeting rooms and ancillary space.

- Reconfirm speaker travel, housing, and other needs.

- Make VIP housing/staffing sleeping room assignments.

- Determine needs and create onsite materials (program guide, welcome letters, signage, etc.).

◆ Print materials for onsite use and distribution.

◆ Meet with convention services or catering managers face to face if possible; alternatively schedule conference call to discuss agenda, overall expectations, and details.

◆ Decide on food and beverage.

◆ Decide on audio-visual (AV) equipment.

◆ Determine and communicate meeting room sets.

◆ Determine needs for flowers, photographers, etc; arrange.

◆ Review ADA needs, including those for special dietary requests with catering and convention services contacts.

◆ Review banquet event orders (BEOs)/meeting resumé.

◆ Handle VIP requests.

◆ Receive and review copies of audio-visual presentations in advance, if applicable. Share with AV manager.

◆ Prepare evaluations for use by attendees and the distribution method (onsite, via e-mail, or other method).

◆ Order name badge stock/holders/ribbons based on anticipated attendance (if appropriate).

◆ Print and organize name badges.

◆ Prepare contingency/emergency plans and communicate with and train all staff and volunteers.

◆ Train staff members.

◆ Determine/order onsite supplies.

◆ Determine onsite office needs (setup, communication, security, and so on).

◆ Review the rooming list (on a periodic basis).

◆ Prepare registration packets; stuff registration bags with giveaways or other items (if appropriate).

◆ Ship materials to the site.

◆ Meet with hotel staff regarding final headcounts, etc., just before ("precon") and immediately after ("postcon") meeting/event.

◆ Meet and greet speakers and VIPs; monitor their rooms and travel arrangements to keep them on track.

◆ Get a good night's sleep the night before the meeting/event.

◆ Keep a running list of housekeeping announcements to keep things flowing smoothly onsite.

◆ Meet daily with accounting to review master account charges, with front office manager to know your house count, and with catering and convention services to keep the meeting running smoothly.

◆ Collect evaluations from attendees while onsite, if applicable.

◆ For your files, retain copies of handouts provided onsite that were not available previously.

◆ Distribute tips and honoraria.

◆ Send thank you letters to all vendors.

◆ Compare final invoices to budget.

◆ Review and approve all vendor invoices for payment.

◆ Summarize final attendee list (include walk-ins), if applicable.

◆ Summarize evaluations received from attendees.

◆ Evaluate the meeting with organizing committee, including return on investment (ROI).

◆ Plan next year's meeting/event while this year's is still fresh in everyone's mind (perhaps while still onsite).

The Inside Scoop

When prioritizing your timeline, there are many items where there are no hard and fast rules about the order in which they will be listed. Sometimes the venue is selected first and sometimes the venue is determined according to its availability, which must coincide with that of your keynote or other VIP speaker(s). Sometimes the budget drives the decisions (particularly true in a nonprofit environment) and sometimes the decisions drive the budget (generally this is reserved for high-end corporate programs).

Clearly, the previous list does not cover all components of a meeting or special event. In fact, some of the tasks really are a group of tasks. For example, before you print materials to be provided at onsite registration, you must know what the materials are. Tickets, name badges, agendas, programs, attendee lists, and maps all are important items for considerations. You may decide to add each of these items as individual tasks with a due date as part of your timeline.

When you want (or need) more breadth in your timeline and have many details, it is a good idea to apply a category to each of your tasks. Here is a sampling of categories:

- Audio-visual
- Budget
- Communications
- Exhibits
- Hotel or site
- Mailings
- Marketing
- Printing
- Programming
- Public relations
- Registration
- Speakers
- Supplies
- Transportation
- Vendors

The use of categories makes it much easier for you to view similar tasks (by using a sort function) and to delegate responsibilities for specific categories. For large timelines, categorized tasks are easier to understand and manage. Here are examples of timeline tasks that fall under the registration category:

- Develop a registration procedure.
- Create registration policies (cancellations, name changes, no-shows, and so on).
- Decide on registration deadlines.

- Decide on in-house or web-based registration.

- Develop registration forms (paper version).

- Develop registration forms (website).

- Develop accompanying registration documents (housing info, travel info, session selection, confirmations, receipts).

- Print accompanying registration documents.

- Put accompanying registration info on website (if appropriate).

- Hire/train registration coordinators.

- Test the registration procedure.

- Milestone: Registration system ready [date].

Remember that your milestones need a specific date that should be fairly fixed. Dates for other tasks are optional but recommended. You can identify important dates by talking with your vendors. Find out from them when they need something from you. Take a look at products you need to order and factor in enough lead time. Also look to internal organizational criteria for deadlines or decisions. The end of your fiscal year, a change in management, or even a maternity leave by a key staff member may impact your timeline.

Begin at the End

A good technique for developing a timeline is to use your meeting date as a starting point and work backward. To do this, prepare a list of the major tasks (refer to the list provided above) and pencil in due dates. If you are unsure how much time is needed for a task, use your best judgment—which is what even the pros do.

Food for Thought

Identify hard versus soft deadlines on your timeline. Many deadlines have some wiggle room, but the hard deadlines do not. It's a good idea to be able to tell the difference when looking at your timeline.

Here's an example. The annual In The Know (ITK) management conference is one year away in August. The three-day conference is for 120 people. There are general sessions and breakouts but no exhibits. A sample timeline (created backward) listing just the milestones might look like this:

August 23 to 26	ITK Meeting
August 18	Ship materials to site
July 30	Banquet event orders (BEOs)/resumé due
July 23	Housing cutoff date (hard date)
July 15	Program mailed to attendees
June 30	Early bird registration deadline (hard date)
June 18	Final program to printer (hard date)
June 15	Make staff/VIP housing reservations
June 15	Meeting room sets, food & beverage (F&B) requests, A/V needs to property
May 30	Deadline for ordering giveaways (hard date)
May 15	Room block review (hard date)
April 30	Second meeting brochure out
January 15	Registration open (hard date)
January 15	First meeting brochure out
December 15	Speakers hired
November 15	Site decision due
October 23 to 29	Site visits—three sites (hard date)
October 11	Site RFPs due back (hard date)
October 1	Finalize budget/agenda Prepare site RFP
September 15	Initial meeting to determine goals and objectives Tentative agenda Tentative budget

As you can see, the closer you are to the time of your meeting, the more deadlines you have and the more work you must do. This is true for all meetings and events. When working backward, consider the task and ask yourself whether you can schedule it further from the meeting start date. If so, do it. Every meeting has last-minute changes, problems, or unexpected issues. You are likely to be swamped with requests, questions, and "fire drills" that only you can handle, and time and energy—your time and energy—will be limited. It is essential that you schedule tasks away from the meeting due date whenever you can.

Another timeline-development suggestion is to identify a milestone first and then add the specific tasks about that milestone. For example, decide when your first promotional marketing piece needs to be mailed. Then determine what kind of mailer it is, what it says, what it looks like (logos, colors, printing), how many other promotional pieces you need, their mailing dates, and so on. By placing the critical element on the timeline before scheduling the associated details, you can ensure that you have allowed enough time to get them all done.

A timeline does not end with the start of your program. There will be important details to follow up on after your program is completed. You must write thank you letters to all vendors, helpful site staff, sponsors, committee members, planning staff, and many more in a timely manner. You will need to review all invoices, see that they are paid, and review/tabulate your meeting evaluation(s). Be sure to schedule these tasks so they are completed as soon as possible after your meeting.

Never consider your timeline complete. Just as you add new tasks as they are identified, be sure to delete unimportant or irrelevant tasks.

Stay on Track

Now you have a great timeline. You've covered every detail and identified every deadline. You've left no stone unturned. Now what? Well, make sure it is in a format that you understand and can easily modify. A timeline is a work in progress, and you will change it as your situation changes.

> **Don't Drop the Ball**
>
> Look at milestones at least one week before their deadline, especially if you have a deadline that requires a decision. Your decision-makers may be busy, out of town, or need time to make an informed decision.

Sometimes, how a timeline visually looks is important. If you have several pages of items and they all look alike, it may be hard to identify key tasks at a glance. Use colors, check boxes, bold, larger fonts, whatever makes it easy for you to identify the key tasks. Maybe your milestones are red, your less important tasks are blue, and your supporting tasks are black. Some people like to cross items off their timeline or leave a space to write in the date the task is completed.

Still others like to use software products that offer scheduling features. These products integrate many planning components such as contact management, budgeting, and to-do lists. They cross-reference tasks and allow prioritization. Many are web based, too.

Last but not least, meet with your staff or colleagues who are working on your meeting fairly regularly. Follow up, ask questions, and make sure they are getting their work done. Having a written document to which you can refer not only helps you see the big picture, but if you have to rattle some cages to get things done, you can reference the timeline to reinforce the importance of your deadlines.

The Least You Need to Know

- ◆ Successful planners use a timeline to stay focused.
- ◆ Schedule your to-do tasks around your can't-miss milestones.
- ◆ Your timeline is an important planning tool. Share it with all appropriate stakeholders.
- ◆ Updating your timeline is a must; it will help you improve future meetings.

Chapter 9

Budgeting: Dollars and Common Sense

In This Chapter

- ◆ Find out why a budget is so important
- ◆ Identify what goes into a budget
- ◆ Understand the value of fixed versus variable costs
- ◆ Check out useful cost-saving tips

One of the first things to do after outlining your meeting or event's goals and objectives is to prepare a budget. This is a key step because your budget is an essential tool that guides expenditures, and one to which you will refer frequently. Once prepared and approved, your budget, along with your goals and objectives, is your blueprint for planning your meeting. It will provide you with opportunities as well as restrictions, and allow you to make educated decisions to ensure you don't lose sight of your meeting or event's purpose.

In this chapter, we take a look at budget components, discuss the importance of fixed versus variable costs, and review some nifty cost-saving budgeting tips. Are you ready?

Everything Has a Price

Exactly what should you include in your budget? Answer: everything. Meetings and events cost money—much more than many people realize—so putting down every anticipated expense (and all revenues) is essential. Try not to use a "miscellaneous" category in your budget. Unless you clearly define in writing what is deemed as miscellaneous, you will always wonder exactly what it includes. To give you an idea, take a look at the following list of items frequently found in budgets:

- Activity fees (golf, theater, and so on)
- Ad hoc committees and board meeting expenses
- Administrative overhead
- Audio taping (sessions)
- Audio-visual equipment
- Audio-visual production and engineering services
- Communications (cell phones, copiers, pagers, radios)
- Complimentary registrations
- Computing onsite (data lines, equipment, licenses, personnel, supplies)
- Contingency fund for possible attrition or cancellation fees
- Credit card processing and bank fees
- Decorations
- Destination management companies (DMCs)
- E-mail kiosks for attendee use
- Entertainment
- Equipment
- Flowers
- Food and beverage
- Freight, shipping, and receiving charges
- Gifts (speakers, sponsors, VIPs, others)
- Giveaways (to attendees)

- Gratuities
- Insurance (liability, dramshop, meeting cancellation)
- Labor costs (including overtime)
- Marketing and promotion
- Meeting room rental
- Meeting supplies (ads, envelopes, letterhead, posters, materials)
- Notary services
- Office/meeting room furniture rentals
- Personnel (salaries, benefits)
- Phone and fax
- Photography
- Plaques and awards
- Postage and overnight services
- Poster presentations and abstract processing
- Printing (including layout and design work)
- Public relations
- Registration (online and manual, including credit card fees)
- Registration materials and software or Internet providers
- Rental cars/vans (for staff)
- Security
- Service fees, gratuities, and taxes
- Signs (banners and posters)
- Speaker costs (fees, expenses, travel)
- Staff costs (travel, lodging, and per diem)
- Supplies
- Temporary help
- Tent rentals

- Tickets (for social activities)

- Tote bags for attendee registration materials

- Transportation (prepaid airfares, shuttles to/from airport, other)

- Travel grants

- Venue rental (for other sites)

- Website (design, maintenance)

When you look at this list, you see that these are really expense categories and that each category can and should be broken down to describe specific budget line items. You may have additional expenses that fit into these categories or become their own category.

> **The Inside Scoop**
>
> For first-time budgets, many planners will take the time to get pricing for most categories. Once you have a feel for the general costs, you can estimate them for future meetings. However, do bid out high-ticket items every time for more accurate estimates.

When developing your budget, also consider current industry trends and how they impact your meeting costs. Tap into your industry's publications, your colleagues via the MIMList (www.mim.com) or elsewhere, the newspaper, TV, and so on. For example, just a few short years ago, no one even knew what the World Wide Web was. Today, online website registration is very common. This trend impacts your budget because eventually you may decide to move the majority of your registration resources to your website and only offer paper registration upon request. Think ahead.

Big Ticket Items: Up for Bid

Developing a budget takes quite a bit of work, and you probably won't be able to do it in one sitting. After you develop a list of anticipated expenses, figure out which categories will benefit from obtaining competitive bids. For example:

- Audio-visual

- Catering

- Decorators

- Destination management companies

- ◆ Equipment and furniture rentals

- ◆ Meeting venue (primary and additional venues)

- ◆ Printing costs

- ◆ Online registration services

- ◆ Speakers and entertainment (especially keynoters)

- ◆ Transportation (bus companies, shuttles)

These are major categories, but you can get bids for any expense, no matter how minimal. Whenever you are selecting vendors, also consider the quality of their product or service, their ability to meet your deadlines, and their willingness to make good if there is a problem.

Where do you find vendors once you have selected a meeting or event site? The best place to start is at the venue. They usually have in-house audio-visual and food and beverage services; many even require that you use them. Otherwise, ask the venue for a list of preferred vendors. Also contact the local area CVB, do web searches, or tap into your meeting- or event-planning network for recommendations.

> **Food for Thought**
>
> Unless you have extraordinary audio-visual or food and beverage requirements, it usually makes sense to use the in-house services. They have the experience at the facility, know the staff, and have the resources readily available onsite.

Don't be afraid to negotiate with vendors. In most cases, their bids are not cast in stone. Most vendors welcome the opportunity to work with you. There may be long-term business in store for them.

Building a Budget

Every meeting or event has a financial objective. Are you trying to make a profit? Will the sponsors and organizing body pay all the bills? Or, will your meeting just break even? Or is it a member service that may lose money?

Your financial objective plays an important role in how your budget is structured. If you are trying to make a profit, then you should be very cost conscious and need to get the most bang for your buck. You will also want to work hard to bring in revenue from sponsors or ticket sales. If your corporation or organization is footing the bill, let's say for an extravagant awards banquet, you will want high-end, excellent-quality (read: more expensive) products and services.

Expenses

When preparing a budget, we recommend that you first figure out what your expenses will be before you tackle the process of generating revenues. This is especially important if you need to determine a registration fee (not an issue for corporate meeting planers), but you'll learn more about that later.

To help illustrate the budgeting thought process, let's look at an example of a first-time meeting.

Meeting name:	The Toofers Conference
Meeting sponsor:	Toofers—Dentistry for Toddlers
Dates:	March 11 to 13 (3 days)
Location:	Dallas
Estimated attendance:	100
Goal:	To promote advancements in toddler dentistry
Planning/host objectives:	Get press coverage in at least three dental journals
	Develop a core attendance that will attend next year's meeting
	Raise $30,000 as seed money for next year
Program agenda:	Day 1: Keynote in A.M., three breakouts in P.M., reception
	Day 2: Breakouts in A.M., lunch, poster session (30 posters) in P.M., reception
	Day 3: Breakouts in A.M., lunch with keynote, end

Wow, even with this information you may still have a ton of questions. Where do you start? Well, based on your goal and objectives, you will have to make some assumptions that will impact your spending:

◆ **The quality of your program is key.** Identify well-known and respected industry speakers who are good at speaking and teaching, as well as being subject matter experts.

◆ **You want this to be an annual conference.** Don't skimp on food. Offer breakfasts and break food but remember that your audience is a group of dentists.

◆ **End on a high note.** Shoot for a whiz-bang capnote, maybe from outside the field. Make the Day 3 lunch fun and memorable.

◆ **People like to talk.** Give them opportunities to network, meet new colleagues, and engage in peer-to-peer learning.

◆ **As a new conference, you will be looking for an audience.** Brainstorm creative ways to market and promote your meeting.

> **The Inside Scoop**
>
> It's a good idea to generate a draft budget before you sit down with others to hammer out details. It's much easier for a group to work from an existing document than to prepare it from scratch. Plus, when working with the decision-makers, it is always easier to take something out than to add it in after the meeting or event is over.

It's a natural part of the process to guess and make assumptions. The important thing is to get your budget on paper. You'll be able to modify it as your program develops so that it truly meets your needs.

What are your anticipated expenses? Start with the expense categories previously listed. Ask yourself if you will have any expenses in these categories, or if there are other categories you need to add. You will be surprised to see how things add up.

If possible, prepare your budget using a spreadsheet; it will change several times before it's all over, and you won't want to do it by hand. Learn how to set up your budget so that most of your numbers are automatically calculated when you add raw information.

When calculating the amounts for any expense or income, show the formula used to arrive at the number. Always provide as much detail as possible so that others will understand your thought process if you are not there to explain it.

Fixed vs. Variable Costs

Understanding the difference between fixed and variable costs is useful. With any meeting, there are some expenses you will incur regardless of the attendance. Those are known as fixed costs (FC). There are also costs that will vary according to the number of attendees. These are variable costs (VC). Most items that are consumable would be considered a variable expense.

You could argue that some of the fixed expenses are variable and vice versa—and you would be right. If your attendance soared and you needed more space, your meeting room rental might increase (turning it from a fixed to a variable cost). And you still have to ship all of your stuff whether you have 10 or 100 people (fixed cost).

The following table compares some common expenses. Almost any fixed cost can turn into a variable cost, if the meeting grows substantially or there are add-ons.

Expense	Fixed	Variable
Audio-visual equipment		X
Food and beverage		X
Giveaways		X
Ground transportation		X
Insurance	X	
Labor		X
Lodging		X
Marketing	X	
Meeting room rental	X	
Office equipment	X	
Registration materials		X
Signage	X	
Speakers	X	
Shipping and freight		X
Staff travel and expenses	X	

Meeting Speak

A **break-even point** is the point at which your meeting neither makes nor loses money.

But now, the big question: Why should you care about fixed or variable costs? Well, if you need to calculate a *break-even point*, you need to know what your fixed and variable costs are.

If your meeting needs to turn a profit and you are deriving much of your income from registration fees, you need to know how many attendees you need to break even. Then, for all attendees above that number, your meeting will make money. Using the Toofers Conference as an example, we need to calculate the break-even number of attendees if we want to fund the conference strictly using registration fees.

First, determine the fixed cost (FC). Add up these costs, including meeting room rental, speaker fees and expenses, marketing costs, audio-visual costs, and so on, for a total expense number. Let's assume the Toofers Conference has its total fixed costs set at $75,000.

Then determine the variable cost (VC) on a per-person basis. Remember, like all association meetings (but rarely a problem for the corporate planner), we don't know how many people will attend. We can determine how much we'll need to spend per person on food and beverage, registration materials, giveaways, and so on. Let's assume the Toofers Conference has a variable cost of $200 per person.

To do the break-even attendee calculation, we must assume a registration fee (RF), so let's estimate we want to charge a registration fee of $500 per person. Now, to calculate the break-even number of attendees, use this formula:

$$FC \div (RF - VC) = \text{Number of attendees}$$

Let's run the numbers:

$$\$75{,}000 \div (\$500 - \$200) = 250 \text{ attendees}$$

We will need 250 attendees paying $500 to cover all of the meeting costs. Don't believe us? Let's reverse the calculation.

The fixed cost ($75,000) plus the variable cost (250 × $200 = $50,000) brings the total cost of the Toofers Conference to $125,000. If we charge all 250 attendees $500, we get a revenue of $125,000. Bingo!

Doing a break-even calculation is beneficial. Initially, the Toofers Conference anticipated 100 people. Now that we know the total costs, we see that keeping the registration fee at $500 requires an attendance of 250 people. If we really just want 100 people, the registration fee will have to be $950 just to break even. Take a look:

$$100 \text{ people} \times \$200 = \$20{,}000 \text{ (VC)}$$

$$\$20{,}000 + \$75{,}000 = \$95{,}000 \div 100 = \$950 \text{ (RF)}$$

Remember, however, that one of the planning/host objectives was to make $30,000 profit. So to do that, the registration fee for 100 people would need to be a whopping $1,250!

$$\$95,000 + \$30,000 = \$125,000 \div 100 = \$1,250 \text{ (RF)}$$

Don't Drop the Ball

Be sure to factor in the cost of complimentary and reduced-fee registrations from speakers, sponsors, VIPs, and staff. These are expenses for the meeting.

Armed with this information, we can choose to do some or all of the following:

♦ Increase the attendance (not necessarily within our control)

♦ Increase the registration fee (will it exceed current market fees?)

♦ Solicit sponsorships or in-kind donations (option is within our control)

♦ Reduce expenses (both fixed and variable—may be difficult)

Each individual situation will dictate which option(s) you choose. Registration fees may not matter, and the attendees will pay whatever is asked of them. (You are lucky!) Or sponsorships may be a natural solution to your budget issues. Discuss the options with the appropriate stakeholders and make the decision that is best for you.

Revenue

Up to now we have discussed expense and cost, but there are two sides to every budget and the other is revenue.

How are you paying for your meeting or event? This usually depends on the type of organization sponsoring it, as well as your financial objectives. In most cases, corporations will use internal funds from one or several budgets.

Associations and other nonprofit organizations depend on a combination of registration fees, grants, sponsorships, exhibition fees, product or ticket sales, host underwriting, and in-kind donations.

Cost-Saving Ideas

This topic could take up a chapter in itself, but alas, we've come to the end of this chapter. We leave you with 10 tips to help you stretch your meeting dollar:

1. Negotiate complimentary services when selecting a site (such as free parking, airport shuttles, free local calls, free freight storage, and so on). If it comes out of your budget, try to get the venue to provide it for free.

2. Order food and beverages in quantity, not per person.

3. When appropriate, order *on-consumption*. You won't pay for unused/uneaten food and beverage (sodas, packaged food such as granola bars, and so on).

   Meeting Speak

   On-consumption means you will only be charged for the items you consumed; this mostly applies to food and beverage items.

4. Bring your own data projectors and laser pointers if possible. Big savings! Address security and labor issues.

5. Reconfirm your speaker's audio-visual needs at least one week prior to the program.

6. If you are tax-exempt and are reimbursing certain attendees anyway, put their housing on your master bill to avoid taxes.

7. Ask the venue if it charges a service fee for taking care of special requests (offsite tours, purchasing supplies). If it does, handle the details yourself.

8. Look into entertainment booked by other groups at your venue or in town. Try to piggyback with another group to get reduced fees or travel.

9. Use your general session room as a breakout room to save on audio-visual or meeting room fees.

10. Ask for a cash discount if you pay your bill immediately after the meeting.

Keep your eye on expenses at all times and never lose sight of your budget. Meeting expenses add up quickly.

The Least You Need to Know

◆ A realistic budget says a lot about the feasibility of your meeting.

◆ Use a spreadsheet's formula functions. Let the spreadsheet do the math and calculations.

◆ Put every expense and revenue item into your budget and keep it updated.

◆ There are hundreds of ways to stretch your meeting dollar. Be creative and negotiate.

Chapter 10

Site Selection and RFPs

In This Chapter

- Discover how site selection contributes to achieving goals and objectives
- Learn how to write a request for proposal (RFP)
- Know what information to provide and ask for in your RFPs
- Explore the important aspects of a site inspection

Selecting the right location for your next meeting or event sounds easy, doesn't it? It is, if you do it right. Picking a location because it looks good or sounds like fun is not the best way to make a decision.

In this chapter, you will learn how to determine which is the very best site and the reasons behind the selection process. You will also learn how to write a request for proposal (RFP) and the correct way to conduct a site inspection.

It's All About Location

You've heard the cliché—location, location, location. Just as a retail store needs the right real estate to sell its wares, a meeting or event requires the right venue to be ultimately successful.

CAUTION

Don't Drop the Ball

No matter what type of meeting you are planning, the attendees have to get there. Is transportation abundant and reasonably priced? Is it convenient for participants to use? Keep these things in mind during the initial planning stage.

When you select a site, you are really buying service and an experience for meeting/event attendees. It is critical that the final decision is made in support of your established goals and objectives.

The location sets the tone for the entire meeting or event. Common meeting venue types include airport hotels, conference centers, convention centers, cruise ships, downtown hotels, gaming casino hotels, resorts, suburban hotels, and universities. Events may be held in any number of conventional or unconventional locations (refer to Chapter 6).

Is the main purpose business, pleasure, or both? There are no definitive rules for matching sites with meetings and events, but think about the goals and objectives before you begin the process of site selection. Book business meetings at facilities that cater to business travelers and meetings. Book pleasure-related groups (who may travel with partners or families) at resorts and other places that offer activities and lots to do. Book larger meetings and events at convention centers and large convention hotels. Conference centers are designed for smaller, educational meetings and retreats. Most festivals and fairs require outdoor locations. Depending on your budget, parties and celebrations can be held just about anywhere the theme of the event and the invitees fit best. Make sense?

Here are some questions you need to think about when selecting a site:

- What kind of facility and venue will help you achieve your meeting or event's goals and objectives?

- What type of facility has the services and accommodations you need?

- Which location and facility would best fit your meeting budget and the budgets of those who will attend?

- Is the space sufficient or flexible enough to accommodate everything on your agenda?

- Does weather matter?

- What are the average airfares and travel times to the site?

- Are there plenty of flights to and from the attendees' points of origin?

- What is the distance to the facility from the airport?

- Is there transportation from the airport to the meeting facility? What is the cost?

- Is the facility easily accessible for people driving to the meeting?

- Are there nearby area attractions and restaurants for attendees and their guests?

- What activities and services are available onsite?

- What other groups or activities will be in the city or using the facility when your meting is there?

Make sure you book the facility or location for the right reasons because it plays an important role in everyone's overall meeting/event experience.

A word about international meetings and events—this is *not* territory for a novice planner and we will not address issues of site selection, multicultural and language issues, and trends in international contract negotiations within the context of this book. Suffice it to say, international meetings can be defined 1) in terms of location, as those held in countries outside the United States, or 2) in terms of attendees, as those held within the United States with a high number of international attendees.

Don't Drop the Ball

Don't pick a venue just because you think you got the best deal. If a site is a mismatch (inappropriate space, poor service, too difficult to get to), it will ultimately reflect on the outcome and the success of your meeting or event.

Write the Right RFP

Once you have determined your goals and objectives and have outlined your agenda, you are ready to write a request for proposal (RFP), in which you determine what you need from a meeting/event facility and ask for bids based on your requirements. Your RFPs should be concise, detailed, and include everything you need from the facility. Making changes after the facility has sent a proposal can actually change the bottom line on the final contract, regardless of their original proposal.

We recommend putting your meeting/event needs in writing. For smaller programs, a call to a facility is probably okay, but a written document serves as a reminder of what you need and ensures that you (and they) don't forget anything. With a phone call, there is no record of what was discussed. Putting it in writing can actually save time because facilities can assign a sales manager and check space before the initial conversation takes place.

An RFP can be as basic or as detailed as you deem necessary, but generally speaking, the more detailed the better. Why? Because the meeting/event facility can only help you if it understands your requirements. The more a facility knows about your requirements, the better service you will get in the long run.

Meeting/Event Scoop

An RFP covers many aspects. Good RFPs should identify the following components:

♦ The name of the meeting or event

♦ Its preferred dates, days of the week, and times

♦ The flexibility of the dates/times (with alternatives presented)

♦ The goals and objectives of the meeting/event

♦ An attendee profile (who the attendees are, including an estimate of the percentage of men and women and their age ranges, where they are coming from, and their transportation methods)

♦ The sleeping room block (your estimate)

♦ *Commissionable* or *net* guestroom rates

♦ A meeting/event agenda with exact space needs (start/stop times, number of people, and room setup style)

♦ A meeting/event history, if any (total attendance, guestroom pickup, number of people served/meal function and rooms, and food/beverage revenue)

♦ The meeting/event budget (only share what you are comfortable with; you will be asked this question so be prepared)

Meeting Speak

A **commissionable** rate is a guestroom rate on which the hotel agrees to pay a specific percentage back to a designated organization (typically 10 percent). A **net** rate is void of any commissions.

♦ Food and beverage requirements

♦ ADA requirements, including diet and accessibility

♦ High-tech needs such as Internet access in the meeting rooms

♦ The proposal due date, decision date, and process

♦ Request that space be held on a tentative basis if applicable

◆ Where to send the proposal and what collateral to include (meeting room layout, menus, audio-visual price lists, and so on)

Include the date a decision will be made and consider letting facilities know how the decision will be made (by you, committee, supervisor, and so on). This information helps the facility understand the process.

You should also have a list of questions for the facility to answer in your RFP. The following are some sample questions:

◆ What is the guest room tax? Are there other taxes or a chance that taxes may be raised before your meeting?

◆ What are your taxes on rooms and food and beverage, service fees, or resort or other fees, such as porterage and housekeeping?

◆ Does the facility provide airport transportation? What is the cost? How long does it take, during rush hour and outside of rush hour? What are the transportation alternatives?

◆ Is there a business center on property? What are the hours of operation?

◆ Ask for a set of banquet menus, and an audio-visual price list.

◆ What company provides the audio-visual equipment? Does the company have an exclusive contract? Can outside audio-visual companies be brought in? Is there a cost to bring in an outside company?

◆ Do you have any exclusive agreement with outside vendors?

Food for Thought

If you are looking for a meeting or event venue other than a hotel, try www.uniquevenues.com. They list thousands of venues such as theaters, state parks, mansions, zoos, dude ranches, conference centers, inns, lodges, wineries, entertainment venues, and a plethora of locations that can make your program ... well, unique!

◆ What are the self- and valet-parking fees? Are there in-out privileges for overnight guests?

◆ What are room service hours?

◆ Do you have a health club? What is the cost and what are the hours and days of operation?

◆ How is the facility in compliance with the Americans with Disabilities Act, and the local or federal fire safety codes?

The questions you ask will depend on the needs of your group, so adjust them accordingly. Also, be sure to take notes as you receive responses to your RFPs. When suppliers call to get clarification on your requirements, you should update your RFP accordingly. You might need to send it out a second time.

You may wish to refer to the APEX Event Specifications Guide (www.conventionindustry.org), approved by the Convention Industry Council in September 2004, for more information about RFPs.

RFP by Fax, Snail Mail, E-Mail, or Online?

A big question these days is how to submit an RFP. The most common way is to submit RFPs by fax or e-mail. Less common is using the old-fashioned U.S. mail. However, many facilities allow the submission of online RFPs (discussed in Chapter 5). Planners are still getting used to this process. Be aware that it does take some time to enter the information into online forms, and some online forms may not allow you to describe all of your requirements, but try it to see how it works for you.

Another thing you need to make a decision about is who to send your RFP to. Use Chapter 4 as a guide to make this decision. You can use the following routes:

- Hotel(s) and conference centers directly
- Convention and visitors bureau (CVB)
- National or global sales office (NSO/GSO)
- Online RFP services (see Chapter 5)
- Meeting- or event-management company

Now, before you go off and start sending out your RFP, it is best to have a contact name at each facility. If you send it without one, it will be more difficult to follow up. Once you have a name or e-mail address, it will be much easier to track someone down if no one returns your calls. Contacting a professional affiliation is a good place to get a specific facility contact name.

Ask and You May Receive

Booking a meeting or event is a two-way street. Each party brings something to the table, and it needs to be a win-win situation to have a really successful outcome. In the past, items such as complimentary rooms and complimentary meeting space were industry standards. Now, what you bring to the table also determines your meeting/event facility costs.

The following is a list of potential *concessions* to ask for if they apply to your situation:

◆ One complimentary guestroom for every X number paid for on a cumulative basis (ask for 1 per 50, 40, or even 30), often referred to as the "comp policy"

◆ Upgrades to suites or to concierge or club floors at the group rate

◆ Complimentary meeting/event space

◆ VIP *amenities*

◆ Complimentary daily newspaper for all in-house guests

◆ Complimentary airport transportation if available

> **Meeting Speak**
>
> A **concession** is something you get over and above the standard offering. An **amenity** is an item placed in a guestroom such as food and beverages or some other gift. In-room amenities also include shampoos, bathrobes, and other extra stuff!

◆ Complimentary parking

◆ Complimentary refreshment break(s) (be specific)

◆ Complimentary transportation to offsite events

◆ Refreshments and cookies for your registration area

◆ Three-week cutoff date (industry standard is 30 days)

◆ Use of radios ("walkie-talkies") onsite (state the number needed and dates for use)

◆ One complimentary microphone in each meeting room

◆ Complimentary welcome reception

◆ Staff or speaker/faculty rooms at a reduced rate

◆ Late checkout for VIPs and staff

◆ Free local calls or toll-free access numbers from guestrooms

◆ Free or reduced-cost Internet access in guestrooms or meeting rooms

◆ Free parking for VIPs and staff

◆ Waive package receiving/shipping fees

- Food and beverage discount
- Audio-visual equipment discount
- Complimentary use of sign easels
- Complimentary health club passes

Be prepared to support your requests with solid business that warrants the concessions. But if you don't ask, you can't get.

Also talk to the local CVB or sponsors about assisting with some of your meeting or event costs. Sometimes they are able to provide transportation to offsite events or provide other services at no cost. You may also be able to negotiate with the hotel a dollar amount per room night as a credit (also known as a rebate) toward some of your expenses. It always pays to ask.

Special Accommodations

Special accommodations are items or services that you or the facility provide to attendees. These can include dietary, medical, and other personal requests. If you know of any special needs in advance, make sure they are included in your RFP.

Food for Thought

Prepare in advance by making a list of what you need to learn on your site inspection. If you don't prepare, you will have a tour based only on what the sales manager wants you to see and learn about the property—not necessarily all that you need to know.

The Americans with Disabilities Act (ADA)

The Americans with Disabilities Act (ADA) calls for "reasonable accommodation" for people with disabilities. As a meeting/event planner, you need to be aware of the law and provide for such accommodations. Your meeting/event site also has to be in compliance with these laws. The definition of a reasonable accommodation is the subject of debate. Depending on the situation, you may be required to provide sign-language interpreters, assisted-listening devices, or closed-caption systems. For more information about ADA, go to www.ada.gov.

See It Up Close and Personal

We can't emphasize it enough: If you can visit the site in advance, do so. Brochures, videos, and virtual site inspections are good tools to help you narrow down the potential sites, but they don't take the place of experiencing the facility in person. You cannot experience what the service is like or see what the property's condition is unless you go and see it for yourself. Also consider taking a video or digital camera along. This way, you can record the details for the staff or committee back at the office.

Guided Tours

Any hotel, conference center, convention and visitors bureau (CVB), or national sales office (NSO) can arrange a site inspection for you. These are scheduled in advance and are usually private, individual tours. You may tour just one or two hotels on a trip arranged by you, or you can go on a CVB-scheduled site visit to multiple hotels, a convention center, area attractions, and potential reception facilities.

Most CVBs periodically have *familiarization (FAM) trips* for meeting and event planners. Typically, a CVB hosts a group of planners and provides a one- to three-day area tour. Virtually every minute is packed with need-to-see sites in the city. These trips are complimentary to planners and usually include airfare, a hotel room, and all meals. The CVB wants to make a positive and lasting impression. Expect to be "wowed," however, realize that your attendees, who will be staying in standard rooms during your meeting/event, may not have the same experience at the same location where you were entertained as a VIP. Make sure you get a "real" feel for each property you visit.

> **Meeting Speak**
>
> A familiarization (FAM) **trip** is hosted by a destination, a CVB and its members, or an individual hotel for the sole purpose of showcasing the city or a specific hotel as a meeting location. Warning: Only partake if you are sure you have potential business. Going on a FAM trip for the heck of it is unethical, and your reputation will suffer.

Another bonus when scheduling a site visit through a CVB is that all of the scheduling is done for you. You just show up and take the tour. They usually drive you from site to site and can add last-minute additions to the itinerary if needed.

Front of the House

Front of the house refers to all the space accessible to the public: lobby areas, meeting space, food and beverage outlets, and the like. Carefully look at the entire facility. How well do they keep it clean? Are the employees you come in contact with friendly and knowledgeable?

Back of the House

Back of the house refers to the areas accessible only to the staff and includes hallways behind the meeting space, kitchens, laundry areas, security, and the like.

On your site visit, ask to have a tour of these areas, too. How properties take care of them is a good indication of their pride in the facility and their attention to detail. Are they clean or dirty? Neat or messy? Safe or hazardous? It is also good to know where the convention services, banquet offices, and AV storage are located. (They are frequently located in the back of the house.) Eat in the employee cafeteria to learn how the facility treats their line and management staff.

Site Checklist

You need to be prepared for your site inspection. All site visits are unique because each meeting or event has its own goals and objectives. Be sure to evaluate the properties based on their ability to help you achieve them.

The Inside Scoop
Take notes during your site visits. Create a checklist (or use the one in Appendix A and fine-tune it to your needs) with items that are important to your organization and meeting or use tools provided by APEX. Some lists have planners checking for dust bunnies under the beds. Use your time wisely.

Virtual Inspections and Colleague Recommendations

If you absolutely cannot conduct a site visit, find out if the facilities have a website with a virtual-tour capability. At the very least, ask for a video. Obviously, these will only show the good stuff, but it is better than nothing. A virtual tour in advance of your site visit is also helpful to prepare for your tour. Brochure pictures can be very deceiving. Ask other planners about their experiences with a property—whether you can see it before booking or not.

Decisions, Decisions, Decisions

The site decision is not that difficult if you have carefully laid the groundwork for the meeting or event. Look at it from this perspective:

◆ Is the facility conducive to achieving your goals and objectives?

◆ Which site do you feel most comfortable with?

◆ Has the preferred site presented an acceptable proposal?

◆ Can the attendees easily travel (by air and ground) to the site?

◆ Can you work with them? Do they listen to you? Do they understand your needs and concerns?

◆ If you conducted a site visit, was the service good? Was the facility in good condition?

◆ Whom can you call that recently met there? Ask for the names of recent planners who held a meeting or similar special event there and call at least two references.

Sometimes the decision to pick a site will fall to someone who did not participate in the site tours—a boss or committee, perhaps. It's easier for them to look at hard numbers (rates, concessions, and so on) than it is to understand other important factors (service, quality of rooms, and so on). In these cases, you must prepare a very thorough report and list the pros and cons. If you really like a specific site, be prepared to defend your position. Otherwise, the best site (in your professional opinion) may lose out to a site that looks better on paper.

Inform the Suppliers

Once you make a site decision, don't forget to inform all the properties that sent a proposal. Tell them in writing the reason your group is not selecting their facility, send them a thank you note, and move on. This is good business etiquette (we're sure you were taught good manners!) and they will remember your follow-through next time you send them an RFP.

Announce Your Decision

Finally, tell all your stakeholders of the site selection. These are the first people who should know because they can start talking it up!

Also tell your staff as soon as you know. Once the site is determined, they (or you) can begin working on other important aspects of your meeting or event that hinge on the dates and location.

The Least You Need to Know

- ◆ Carefully match your goals and objectives with your location and facility to make your meeting or event more successful.

- ◆ Ask for what you want in the RFP because the facility will base its proposal on your expressed needs.

- ◆ Site visits are a valuable (and often critical) tool for making a location decision.

- ◆ Always let the bidding facilities and all stakeholders know your decision and reasons in a timely manner.

Negotiating the Best Deal

In This Chapter

- ◆ Identify the vendors you need to consider when planning a meeting or event

- ◆ Learn what is and is not negotiable

- ◆ See how to protect your organization during the negotiating process

- ◆ Learn the most common items that are often overlooked when negotiating contracts

- ◆ Understand insurance issues and how to get proper coverage for your meeting or event

Everyone is looking for the best deal and the meeting and event industry is no different than any other. With such a variety of vendors that can be used for meetings and events, we can't possibly cover all the best negotiating strategies in one book. We can, however, discuss how to negotiate with the most widely used vendors. We will also focus on the big one—hotel negotiations.

In Chapter 10 we discussed the request for proposal (RFP) process for hotels and other meeting and event venues. You can and should consider submitting RFPs to your other vendors as well. Now that you know how to submit an RFP, this chapter will focus on the negotiation stages after you have received proposals or quotes from your vendors.

Vendors You Need

Make a list of the vendors you need for your meeting or event. To help you identify them, let's look at a list of those most commonly considered:

- ◆ Airlines and ground transportation providers
- ◆ Awards and promotional-gift companies
- ◆ Copying services
- ◆ Decorating companies
- ◆ Desktop-publishing companies
- ◆ Destination-management companies (DMC)
- ◆ Entertainers
- ◆ Exhibition-services companies
- ◆ Ground-transportation companies
- ◆ Insurance brokers
- ◆ Meeting facilities
- ◆ Meeting-supply companies
- ◆ Online registration providers
- ◆ Production companies
- ◆ Speakers
- ◆ Temporary help providers
- ◆ Website providers

Finding these vendors is easy. You may have already located all or at least some of them when you prepared your budget and sent out RFPs. If not, ask your meeting or event venue or the local convention and visitors bureau (CVB) for recommendations. Also check out meeting trade magazines, browse the web, and consult with members of your planning committee and other knowledgeable colleagues.

Needs, Wants, and Everything in Between

The key to negotiating is to do some homework before making any inquiries. Here are some things to think about:

♦ Know the value that your business brings to each vendor.

♦ Think long-term vendor relationships.

♦ Understand the business/economic climate.

♦ Buy for multiple meetings or events, not just one (if possible).

♦ Network and ask for vendor recommendations.

The best rule of thumb is to first understand your goals and objectives, then prioritize your needs, and then determine your "wish list" of products and services. This list should contain items that would be great to have but are not deal breakers.

When inquiring about vendors and their services, ask them what they need to give you a proposal. You can gain valuable insight by asking a few questions. Whether you ask for quick quotes or full-blown proposals, get everything in writing.

> **Don't Drop the Ball**
>
> If you plan meetings in more than one city, look for vendors that have branch offices in those locations. Then you can give them more business and save time and money in the process. Network! Network! Network!

Everything's Negotiable (Almost)

Once you have proposals/quotes in hand, review them carefully. Do they address all your needs? Don't be afraid to go back to a vendor and readdress your most important issues. If a proposal does not address an item from your RFP, find out why. Then select the finalists. When responding, be honest and up front. It is fair to tell your first-choice vendor how they can get the business, but only if you are prepared to give it to them!

Occasionally, a vendor will approach you with the question, "If I give you what you want, will you definitely give me business?" That is being refreshingly direct. Your answer should be up front and honest. Describe your decision-making process for them and when they will have an answer. *Then follow through!*

Attrition

It is imperative you understand *attrition* when negotiating contracts. If you experience guestroom or food and beverage attrition, you must pay the facility a sum (also called *damages*) to recoup the facility's lost profit. See Chapter 12 for more detailed information on contract attrition as it relates to both rooms and food and beverage.

Meeting Speak

Attrition (also called *slippage* or *drop off*) is a reduction in numbers from what you originally promised the meeting or event facility. The "numbers" typically refer to the total number of guestrooms blocked for your program, and the guaranteed amount of food and beverage expected to be served (also called *meal covers*) from which the facility forecasts its potential revenue and profit.

According to attorney and former hotel director of sales, John S. Foster, Esq., CHME (you will meet him in Chapter 12), "The sole purpose of an attrition clause is to shift the risk of low pick up or underperformance from the facility to the meeting sponsor." This can apply to guest rooms, food and beverage covers, or both.

Attrition calculations are usually proposed by the facility and can be calculated many different ways. It is your responsibility to understand and negotiate attrition calculations that are agreeable to you and the hotel. Make sure the calculation uses "lost profit" instead of "lost revenue" and stipulates that your damages will be reduced by any guestrooms or food and beverage that the hotel resells. You can also make sure you have the opportunity to reduce your room block up to an agreed upon percentage of the total room block at specific intervals prior to arrival. The reduced block now becomes the number of rooms you are liable for.

Say, for example, your room block is 1,000 rooms and you are allowed to reduce it up to 15 percent at some time specified in the contract. If necessary, this would allow you to reduce your total block by 150 rooms, down to an 850-room block. So, if you picked up 800 rooms, you pay the hotel for 50 rooms times their lost profit (if that is what you negotiated for your contract).

If the group rate was $100 and their profit margin is 75 percent, you would pay $75 times 50 rooms or $3,750 in attrition. Make sure the profit percentage is clearly stated in the contract. In addition, be sure to determine from the state office of tax and revenue if any attrition damages will be taxed and at what percentage.

Meeting Room Rental

Sometimes a facility may charge meeting room rental based on room pick up or lack thereof. For a meeting with a total of 1,000 room nights and a maximum of $15,000 in meeting room rental, a meeting room rental calculation might look like this:

Meeting Room Rental Requirements

Percentage of Room Block Picked Up	Total Meeting Room Rental
85 percent or higher	Complimentary
75 to 84 percent	$5,000
65 to 74 percent	$10,000
64 percent and lower	$15,000

The Inside Scoop

According to former hotel director of sales and industry attorney, John S. Foster, Esq., CHME, the contract should provide for either attrition fees or meeting room rental based on a sliding scale but not both. They are both intended to accomplish the same objective: compensating the hotel for a group's low pickup. There are two exceptions to this: If the group needs more meeting space than it is entitled to receive on a complimentary basis from the hotel or if the group insists on a specific meeting space that the hotel would not normally give to the group based on the group's attendance. In today's climate, more hotels are negotiating both conditions in a contract.

Understand that setting up your meeting or event in a facility is not free. Staff members have to be paid to set up the chairs and tables and prepare the meals. They also clean the public spaces, answer the phones, direct attendees, park cars, and serve food. You will be asked to pay meeting room rental at some point. Your job is to negotiate the best contract for your group. You should work to reduce or eliminate meeting room rental, but depending upon your specific circumstance, it may be necessary to agree to pay meeting room rental.

Keep in mind, hotels need to put "heads in beds" and make a profit for their owners and management company, often different entities. If you book an adequate number of sleeping rooms they usually (but not always) are willing to waive meeting room charges. The number of sleeping rooms required to tip the scales in your favor will depend on the facility's total number of guest rooms and the amount of meeting space you are requesting. There has to be a balance. If you are negotiating with a facility such as a convention center, whereby sleeping rooms are not an issue, you don't have that type of leverage.

Unexpected Charges

During negotiations, it is easy to overlook many items that could potentially have an impact on your bottom line and the success of your meeting. Read the contract with a fine-tooth comb so you are not surprised when your bill arrives. Any items that you are required to pay for should be incorporated into your RFP and contract.

If there are any "automatic fees" (such as gratuities, porterage or luggage handling, resort fees, shipping charges, and service charges) associated with a vendor, they should appear in the contract; otherwise, you should never pay them if you state in the contract that all fees have been disclosed in the contract. Ask to review the facility's standard contract in the beginning so you will understand all the issues in advance.

During the RFP and proposal process, ask for a copy of the vendor's standard contract and a list of their policies. The contract is where many miscellaneous charges are itemized. Then you can clarify any issues in advance of finalizing the contract.

Items Often Overlooked When Negotiating Contracts

Vendor	Items Often Overlooked
Hotels	Attrition fees (including taxes on such)
	Automatic housekeeper gratuities or other service charges
	AV equipment setup fees
	Banquet surcharges for serving less than x people (usually for less than 25 or 50)
	Box storage fees
	Cleaning fees
	Computer-usage charges
	Copying charges
	Cutoff dates

Vendor	Items Often Overlooked
	Deposits
	Early departure fees
	Easel rental fees
	Electrical and mechanical services
	Fax sending and receiving charges
	Guestroom phone call access fees
	Health club fees
	Internet access fees
	Labor to hang banners and signs and for meeting room setup
	Late checkout fees
	Meeting room key charges
	Meeting room rental
	Meeting room set changes the day of the meeting
	Outdoor venue surcharges
	Package-delivery fees
	Package shipping, receiving, and handling charges
	Parking
	Per-person service fees
	Resort fees
	Security
	Taxes on meeting room rental
Convention centers	Most of the items listed for hotels plus ...
	Doormen/electricians/engineers/maintenance
	Stagehands
	Labor to change a room set
	Loading dock access
	Staging, risers for meeting rooms
	Tablecloths, table skirting
Other vendors	Deposits
	Gratuities

continues

Items Often Overlooked When Negotiating Contracts (continued)

Vendor	Items Often Overlooked
	Excessive shipping or rush charges
	Labor or setup fees
	Special service fees
	Transportation and other expenses

Written Documents

Once you have the proposal or quote and the contract in hand, carefully compare the two and note any differences. Make sure you include a statement in your contract that says any miscellaneous charges not stated in the contract will not be paid for unless agreed to in writing by both parties.

Non-Negotiables

There are a few items you will not be able to negotiate (but you can always try!). This industry has taxes, license fees, insurance, *service charges*, and *gratuities* to contend with. These are a necessary part of planning any meeting or event. These costs need to be included in the budgeting and execution of your meeting or event.

> **Meeting Speak**
>
> A **service charge** is a mandatory charge added to a service. For example, hotels often charge a flat service charge for food and beverage and audio-visual services. A **gratuity** (also known as a **tip**) is a voluntary amount of money given in exchange for a service performed. Service charges are taxed; gratuities usually are not.

Music licensing, insurance, and other fees may be a surprise for your committee, boss, and other people outside the industry, but they are very important to safeguarding the outcome of the program itself.

Music Licensing

Music is protected under U.S. copyright law as intellectual property just like books, movies, photos, and articles. Any time music is played to third parties via CD, cassette, video, and so on, a music license is required. Copyrighted music cannot be played or performed in public without permission from the copyright owner. If you are playing music at your event, you probably owe music license fees.

There are currently three organizations that charge and collect the fees associated with playing music in public:

- ◆ Broadcast Music, Inc. (BMI) (www.bmi.com)

- ◆ American Society of Composers, Authors, and Publishers (ASCAP) (www.ascap.com)

- ◆ Society of European Stage Authors and Composers (SESAC) (www.sesac.com)

Depending on the music you play, you may need a license from one or all three organizations. Don't assume that these fees for your meeting are covered by those (band, DJ) who will play the music. Contact these licensing agencies for more information.

Service Charges, Gratuities, and Uncle Sam

We all have to pay service charges, gratuities, and taxes, so always take them into consideration when planning budgets and looking at potential meeting and event sites.

Service charges are taxable to the meeting sponsor, but gratuities should not be. Most hotels keep a portion of the service charge and disburse the rest to the service staff. You may be able to negotiate to have the portion that goes to the staff billed separately and not taxed. This gets a bit complicated, so consult an attorney for the appropriate contractual language if you take this route! For larger meetings and events, it may be worth the effort.

Food for Thought

Service fees, gratuities, and taxes can total upward of 20 to 30 percent of your bill. Make sure you understand the formulas used to calculate each and incorporate them into your budget and registration fees.

If your organization is tax exempt, tell your vendors early on, and provide a copy of your exemption certificate. Not all states allow organizations that are exempt from taxes in their home location or on the federal level to be exempt from state and local sales tax in the meeting venue. To determine whether your group qualifies, contact the sales tax division of the state government where your meeting or event is held. If your group qualifies, the state sales tax office will issue a certificate stating that the state exempts your organization from paying sales tax. Be aware that cities and counties are separate taxing authorities from the state. They must be contacted as well if you want to avoid tax assessments on this level.

Remember that it is your responsibility to obtain and furnish your exemption certificate(s) to the hotel or other vendor. Without the certificate(s), they have no authority not to collect taxes from your group. You can always check with your vendor for more information, but don't expect them to be fully knowledgeable about tax exemptions. It is the planner's responsibility to do the footwork.

Insurance

Insurance—you have to have it; your vendors need to have it; you need to understand it. Find an insurance broker or attorney who understands the meetings business and make sure you are covered in case of an incident. There are so many potential situations that could result in a claim against you or your organization that it can make you dizzy. These include liquor or host liquor liability, personal injury, convention/meeting cancellation, fire, property damage, and theft.

Insurance policies include, but are not limited to, the following types:

◆ **Commercial general liability (CGL).** This covers bodily injury and property damage. Host liquor liability is included, which protects you if you have alcohol served at your event by another party such as the hotel or caterer.

◆ **Convention cancellation and interruption.** This protects your organization from any disruption that results in a financial loss for your event or meeting. This could include fire, earthquake, strike, destruction of a meeting facility, and other causes. Be sure to review policies for caveats and exclusions before purchasing.

Don't Drop the Ball

Many professional associations offer insurance programs that address the many issues meeting and event planners are likely to encounter. You need someone well-versed in the meetings/events industry to help you determine your exposure and risk, and to determine the amount of coverage required. Call today.

Regarding terrorism and war or hurricanes, earthquakes, and major storms: coverage can generally be purchased as an add-on to meeting and event cancellation insurance, but since 9/11 it has become very expensive. It is a good idea to get several competitive quotes as prices can vary greatly. Fear of travel (by attendees) is not covered, but terrorism insurance would typically pay off if airports, roads, or facilities closed, and the attack was certified by the U.S. government. However, one school of thought contends if there is a major terrorist attack, canceling your meeting or event will probably be among the least of your concerns. If the area where you are holding your meeting/event is prone to seasonal storms, the additional cost (which could easily more than double the price of the policy) may be warranted.

Although communicable diseases (like SARS) are no longer covered in cancellation insurance policies, you can include communicable disease termination clauses in hotel contracts so that the contract could be terminated without liability if outbreak would occur.

Purchasing limited or full insurance protection is an individual decision. Each group must weigh the risks and benefits, based on the odds and the budget.

◆ **Directors and officers (D&O).** This covers volunteers, trustees, employees, officers, and committee members conducting business on behalf of the association, in case of a lawsuit.

◆ **Professional liability/error and omissions.** This is a policy for independent or third-party planners who need coverage while they provide their services to other organizations.

◆ **Liquor liability.** This protects against claims if your organization serves alcoholic beverages and is sued for some reason.

Have all vendors and exhibitors provide you with complete certificates of insurance prior to the meeting or event. These certificates should include general liability and worker's compensation. You can also ask to be named as an additional insured on their policy for liability, property, and medical payments. Make sure you understand your own policy so you know when and if you need to obtain additional coverage.

Once you find the right insurance agent or attorney, review your meetings and events with him or her and ask for an analysis of your potential exposure to lawsuits or claims against you and your organization. Every year or two, review your policy with your insurance agent. Things change and your policy should be kept current.

The Least You Need to Know

◆ Demonstrating the value of your business to each vendor is crucial to successful negotiations.

◆ Make sure attrition calculations are based on lost profit and not lost revenue.

◆ Hidden charges that a facility imposes while onsite are important to address in the negotiation stage.

◆ Music licensing fees, service fees, gratuities, taxes, and insurance are often unexpected and unavoidable costs; budget appropriately.

Hotel Contracts: Signing on the Dotted Line

In This Chapter

- ◆ Define the items that should be in a hotel contract
- ◆ Learn the difference between canceling and terminating a meeting-facility contract
- ◆ See what indemnification means to you as a planner
- ◆ Understand the difference between damages and penalties and which are enforceable
- ◆ Learn the difference between actual damages and liquidated damages
- ◆ Know how to sign contracts on behalf of an organization

Because we are not legal eagles, we have asked John S. Foster, Esq., CHME, a meetings-industry attorney and former hotel director of sales, to help us out with the important topic of hotel contracts. John is an attorney and counsel whose Atlanta-based firm—Foster, Jensen & Gulley, LLC—specializes in the legal aspects of meetings and conventions, trade shows and events, and association management. He has been named one of the 25 most influential people in the meetings industry by *MeetingNews*. Many thanks to John for assisting in authoring this chapter.

Recent disputes and lawsuits between meeting sponsors and hotels continue to emphasize the principle that it's better (and cheaper) to *stay* out of trouble than to have to *get* out of trouble. If you are involved in a lawsuit, as a plaintiff or defendant, there is no guarantee that your side will prevail.

The best way for meeting and event sponsors and suppliers to avoid controversies and lawsuits is to write a successful contract that clearly specifies the intent of the parties. This chapter provides guidelines and suggestions to assist both planners and suppliers in avoiding expensive and time-consuming lawsuits.

Disclaimer: The advice given in this chapter is intended to be for educational purposes and is not intended to be legal advice. All meeting professionals should seek specific legal advice suitable to their particular group and their meeting from an attorney experienced in the legal aspects of the meetings, conventions, and trade shows.

It's More Than Dates, Rates, and Space

It used to be done with a handshake. Not anymore. Just when you think selecting a meeting or event site is the challenging part, you get to jump one more hurdle.

You know the dates and have agreed to the rates, but the success of your meeting or event hinges on the performance by you, the meeting sponsor, and the hotel. A well-written, fair contract is essential to create the rules by which both parties must abide. A meeting or event represents significant financial gains, but it also carries significant risks. To sufficiently cover both parties, a contract must address numerous issues. Many nonlawyers on both sides believe that a short contract is better than a longer contract. This is not necessarily the case. If your shorter contract fails to address an issue that later becomes the subject of a messy and expensive dispute, your shorter contract has failed one of its essential objectives—to be a road map for the meeting/event and to steer the parties around pitfalls that lead to future disputes.

In order to thoroughly describe the components of a hotel contract, the remainder of this chapter is a bunch of lists. Remember that we're talking about the big "L"—legal stuff. So go get your favorite beverage and read on. *This* is what you really need to know.

General Provisions and Guestroom Issues

The following 17 items address general meeting information including guestrooms, reservations, *comp* rooms, and other room-related stipulations that should be addressed in your contracts.

1. **Identity of parties.** Use legal names, if known, which include the names of the owners of the property.

2. **Intent to contract statement.** Include language stating that the parties intend the document to be a contract and intend to be bound by the terms.

Meeting Speak

The meetings-industry term **comp** is short for "complimentary," or no charge.

3. **Purpose of meeting.** Explain the purpose of the meeting and state that all performance assumptions in the contract are based on the meeting sponsor's ability to fully accomplish this purpose. [Example: The purpose of this meeting is to bring together attendees from throughout the United States whose business involves widget manufacturing. All performance assumptions in this contract are based on meeting sponsor's ability to fully accomplish this purpose.]

4. **Meeting/event/conference name and dates.** State the official conference name and conference dates of the meeting or event.

5. **Authorized contacts.** Specify the name, title, address, and phone number of the contact(s) for each party who has the authority to negotiate and amend the contract.

6. **Guestroom block.** State arrival/departure patterns, the type of rooms/suites, and the number of each per night. Specify number of rooms per suite.

7. **Room block review dates and allowable attrition.** Guest room attrition damages can be based on either: a) a minimum amount of revenue guaranteed, or b) a minimum number of room nights guaranteed. Hotels prefer the minimum revenue method. Meeting sponsors prefer the minimum room night method. The following is based on the room night method:

   ♦ Adjustment date(s) for reviewing the group's history.

   ♦ If the meeting is more than a year away, state a formula for determining the revised block. (Example: averaging actual pickup on peak night of the same or similar meeting for the past three years.)

◆ Final review date(s) when the block will be reviewed and adjusted for the last time without liability to the meeting or event sponsor.

◆ The percentage of slippage or block reduction the group is allowed from the final adjustment date(s) through the meeting.

◆ Formula based on lost profit for determining damages or a sliding scale for meeting-room rental owed to the hotel, if any.

◆ Requirement that the hotel will take affirmative steps to resell the unused rooms and apply the number to reduce any attrition damages.

◆ Establish when money owed to the hotel, if any, will be paid.

8. **Check-in/out times.** The time a guest can check in to the hotel and the time by which a guest has to check out. Stipulate early departure fees, if any, and that each guest may revise their departure date without liability up to and including the day of check-in. State that early departure fees charged by the hotel will be applied to reduce the group's attrition damages, if any.

9. **Room rates.**

◆ Specify rates by room type such as single, double, standard, or deluxe. If the meeting or event is more than one year out, set the date when the hotel will quote definite rates.

◆ Specify the formula to be used in setting definite rates for meetings/events one or more years out: percentage cap on current rates, guaranteed percentage off definite future rack rates, or change in consumer price index (urban) for the hotel's city or region.

◆ Specify that if the hotel offers lower "promotional" rates over the meeting/event dates and some of your attendees receive them, then those rooms get counted in your room pickup. You can try to get the hotel to agree that a lower rate will not be offered over your dates to the general public, or at least not to other groups.

◆ Include an audit provision that stipulates the hotel will provide the meeting sponsor access to the in-house guest list so that the meeting sponsor can independently ascertain the accuracy of the hotel's pick-up and occupancy reports. The audit provision should also state that the meeting sponsor's representative will sign a confidentiality contract stating that the information will not be disclosed to additional parties or used for any other purpose. Your registration list will be compared to the hotel's reservation list. Any meeting attendee found outside your room block should be credited to your total room pickup regardless of the rate paid from the final adjustment date(s) through the meeting.

   ◆ Specify all suite types, arrival/departure dates for each, and rates. Specify the number of bedrooms with each suite included in the rate and the rate for additional bedrooms.

   ◆ Specify current sales tax and hotel bed tax, and how the group will be notified if and when taxes increase.

   ◆ Specify if there are any applicable resort fees, and if so, if they are taxed and at what percentage.

10. **Meeting/event planner/agent of record.** If the group is represented by an independent meeting or event planner or a travel agent, spell out what authority the planner/agent has and whether the planner/agent has the authority to contractually represent the group. If a commission arrangement is involved, spell out the commission rate and when it will be paid. If you are being paid a commission it is best to state that the commission is not transferable to other parties and cannot be used to offset meeting or event costs at the facility.

11. **Complimentary rooms and staff rates.** Set the formula for determining the number of comps. Specify that comps will be figured on a cumulative basis and that unused comp rooms can be applied to a master account in an equivalent dollar amount as a credit. (Comp rooms are not really complimentary. They are earned by the group's performance, therefore justifying receiving credit if they go unused.) Specify whether additional comp rooms will be extended to convention staff or guest speakers or whether a percentage discount will be given.

12. **Reservations.**

   ◆ Specify whether the meeting/event's sponsor, a third-party housing bureau, or the hotel is handling housing.

   ◆ Specify the method: reservation cards, call-in, rooming list, housing bureau, or other form.

   ◆ Dishonored reservations: Determine what compensation the hotel will make for guests that are *walked* (that is, given free sleeping room at comparable hotel, free transportation to and from the substitute hotel, long-distance phone calls to office and family, whether or not the hotel will bring the guest back and if a note of apology and amenity will be sent to the walked guest from the hotel general manager).

◆ Cutoff date: Specify the last date the hotel will hold the block of rooms before releasing the unsold rooms (if any) back into the hotel's general inventory.

◆ Specify what rate will be offered after the cut-off date. Meeting sponsors prefer that the hotel extend the negotiated group rate after the cut-off date. If the hotel wants the right to charge higher rates then the contract should state that no attrition damages would apply. (Raising the rates is a deterrent to the meeting sponsor's ability to fill its block.)

◆ Specify if name changes will be allowed after the cut-off date.

◆ Overbooked hotel prior to cut-off date: This is a reverse attrition clause for the hotel. If it is a breach of contract for the group not to pick up all of the rooms in its block, then the contract should state that the hotel is in breach if it does not make available all of the rooms in the block prior to the cut-off date. This clause should specify liquidated damages owed the meeting sponsor if the hotel sells into the group's block (for higher rated business) and turns potential attendees away before the cut-off date. This can be tracked through pre-meeting pick-up reports and test reservations made by the meeting sponsor to see if the block is being honored. The contract should also state that no attrition damages will apply if this situation occurs (because the hotel has interfered with the group's ability to meet performance requirements).

◆ Specify when the hotel will send out confirmations and whether the planner is to receive copies with pick-up reports.

◆ Specify whether or not room reservation deposits or cancellation fees collected from individuals will be applied to applicable attrition or cancellation fees.

13. **Deposits.** Specify the hotel deposit policy and spell out any conditions under which deposits will be refunded, within what timeframe, whether deposits will be placed in escrow, and the terms of the escrow. Also require that an invoice will be issued for each deposit due.

14. **Billing arrangements.** Specify what is paid individually and what goes on the master account (M/A). Identify who is authorized to sign the M/A. Specify credit information required by the hotel and whether an advance deposit is required (specify dates, amount, and escrow requirements). If certain functions are to be sponsored by third parties, specify procedures.

15. **Report of meeting/event.** Specify whether the hotel will furnish the meeting planner with actual group revenue, including rooms picked up, food and beverage, and other income, at the conclusion of the meeting or event.

16. **Suites.** Specify whether all requests for suites are to be approved by the planner.

17. **Parking.** What is the cost? How is VIP parking handled?

> **CAUTION**
>
> **Don't Drop the Ball**
>
> It's important to understand where you are in the negotiation process. This is John's Golden Rule of Contract Negotiations: If you ask for something from the other party before you have a contract, it's called "negotiating." If you ask for something after you have a contract, it's called "begging."

Meeting/Event Space Provisions

Make sure you understand how the hotel is charging you for any meeting-room rental fees. Calculations can be very complicated, and you must understand them. Here's a list of what you need to know:

1. **Meeting and function space requirements.** Be detailed about initial space requirements. Agree on and specify the date that the final program will be submitted. If group needs a *hold all space*, determine the hotel's policy. Is a 24-hour-space hold needed? Specify the date when the hotel will provide definite meeting-room names. Does the hotel reserve the right to move the group to another space? Can this be negotiated? Will the hotel agree to pay for reprinting programs if the group is moved to an alternate space? Note: If the hotel wants the right to reassign meeting space, specify that the new meeting space must meet requirements for minimum square footage per person in specific set-ups.

> **Meeting Speak**
>
> **Hold all space** means that all meeting space in the hotel is being held by a group. If you have a hold all space, it should be stated in the contract along with a date when your agenda is due.

State in the contract that no meeting space will be released to affiliate groups without the meeting sponsor's written consent.

2. **Function space rental.** Specify the hotel's criteria for waiving rental. (Note: In most instances, a room rental clause is not applicable if the hotel also includes an attrition clause. Hotels generally give complimentary meeting space based on the group's rooms-to-space-ratio. Example: If a group is using 30 percent of the hotel's group rooms it is entitled to 30 percent of the meeting space without charge. If the amount of space needed is higher, then rental usually applies.) Agree on sliding-scale formula, if applicable. *Important*: Specify that rooms paid for under the attrition clause count toward the group's pick-up when determining meeting room rental. Set a firm price for function space, if applicable. This avoids "double-dipping" by the hotel where it charges twice to cure the same problem; that is, low pick-up.

3. **Services and equipment.** Specify whether the hotel charges for setup and teardown of meeting rooms. Specify what equipment the hotel provides on a complimentary basis and a cutoff date for ordering equipment. (The contract should require the hotel to provide all chairs and tables to set each meeting room to its maximum capacity without the group paying to rent more.)

4. **Signage.** Determine whether the hotel will provide signage for the group and at what cost. What are the hotel's rules for displaying signs?

> **Food for Thought**
>
> A lawsuit is a process in which you go in as a pig and come out as a sausage. In other words, the process is never neat, clean, or simple, and both parties come out a different shape than when they went in.

Food and Beverage

We are halfway there! These are the points you need to consider about food and beverage:

1. **Food and beverage functions.** Give the hotel preliminary figures for anticipated attendance. Determine a date for the final guarantee and for what percentage over the guarantee the hotel will prepare. Determine how far in advance firm food and beverage (F&B) prices will be confirmed. Will the hotel guarantee a certain F&B percentage maximum rate increase per year?

This increase can be stated as a cap or on the change in the consumer price index from the date the contract is signed to the meeting date.

2. **Taxes/gratuities.** What is the hotel policy and formula for each? Does state law require the hotel to tax the service charge? Can the group agree to pay a gratuity and therefore avoid paying tax on the gratuity?

3. **Bartender and waiter charges and training.** Determine hotel policy on these. Does the hotel have a minimum charge for F&B functions? What are their procedures in place to minimize liquor liability?

4. **Attrition.** If the hotel insists on including an attrition clause for F&B functions, include an original estimate of catered F&B revenue that the meeting sponsor will spend. Also include a review date or dates when the parties will establish a final figure for catering food and beverage revenue that the group will spend at the hotel. It should include a percentage of attrition allowed to the group from the figure previously projected. The industry average is currently 20 to 25 percent. Get the hotel to agree to reduce any damages by any food and beverage functions it resells or any business the hotel is able to book after the notice of reduced attendance at food and beverage functions is received by the hotel. (The same criteria should be used if a food function is cancelled.)

Sometimes a group cancellation is beneficial to a hotel because it allows the hotel to accept a more profitable piece of business that wants the rooms and space. If this occurs, the hotel has not been damaged by the first group's reduction or cancellation. In your contract, make sure you have clearly stated the resell provisions and have a mechanism to calculate the reduced damages.

Understanding Contract Damages

Actual damages is the amount owed to the injured party for losses caused or gains prevented as a direct result of the breach. Actual damages can be ascertained only after the time for performance of the contract has passed. As a matter of social policy and law, the injured party may not sit idly by and let damages accumulate. The law does not permit the aggrieved party to recover from the other party those damages that were reasonably foreseeable and could have been avoided with reasonable effort. This is generally referred to as the "rule of avoidable damages" or the "duty to mitigate."

Liquidated damages is an amount (or formula) agreed to by the parties at the time of the contract, and before any breach occurs, as reasonable compensation if the contract is breached. A liquidated damage clause is enforceable only if it meets strict criteria for reasonableness. While courts usually will enforce whatever terms the parties agree to as evidenced by the contract (see the following section), the enforcement of the liquidated damage clause is the exception to this rule. Liquidated damage clauses are frequently struck down in court if the amount stipulated is out of proportion to the actual damages. Generally, reasonableness must be judged as of the time of contracting rather than as of the time of the breach and ensuing damage. Additionally, liquidated damages must be tied to a specific breach, not just any breach.

General Contract Damage Rules

Here's a rundown on penalties versus damages:

◆ Breach by one party entitles the other party to damages (but not penalties).

◆ Generally, damages are defined as lost profits, not 100 percent of lost revenue (i.e., benefit of the bargain).

◆ "Lost profit" is defined as gross revenue minus variable expenses. Hotels track this by department (rooms, food and beverage, and so on).

◆ Damages are collectible to the extent they are foreseeable, certain, and contemplated by both parties.

◆ "Liquidated damages": Contract law allows parties to agree to specific damages in advance rather than requiring the injured party to prove actual damages. This may be expressed as a flat fee, sliding scale, or formula. To be enforceable, actual damages must be difficult or impossible to calculate, and the liquidated damage amount must be a close approximation of the actual damages and not a penalty. To be a close approximation of actual damages, the liquidated damage provision should be a formula based on industry average profit margin, as follows: guest rooms, 70 to 80 percent; catered food functions, 25 to 35 percent; alcoholic beverage functions, 80 to 85 percent. (Because these are averages, some hotels may fall outside these percentages.)

◆ Penalties are not allowed in contract law. Penalties exist if one side would tend to benefit more by enforcing the liquidated damage clause than if the contract were performed (called "unjust enrichment").

◆ Injured party has a duty to mitigate its damages (doctrine of avoidable damages), unless the parties agree to reasonable liquidated damages.

The food and beverage attrition formula should state the final amount of catering food and beverage revenue guaranteed by the group, minus the actual catering food and beverage revenue spent by the group, minus revenue from resold functions or space. The resulting figure should then be multiplied by an agreed upon percentage to represent estimated lost profit. Industry average is 25 to 35 percent. The resulting amount represents the damages for catering food and beverage attrition, subject to an audit by both parties.

Don't Drop the Ball

Pay attention to the special limitations of the exhibit area such as floor load limits, dock space, storage space, and union jurisdictions, if applicable. Determine when union contracts expire so you aren't caught in the middle of union negotiations.

Exhibit Space Provisions

Contracting for exhibit space is a different process than booking meeting space. Read on for exhibit-specific info:

1. **Exhibit space.** Includes move-in/out dates, rental price, and what is and is not included: signage, carpet, pipe and drape, general daily maintenance, HVAC to the group's satisfaction, and so on. If floor sales are allowed, do exhibitors have to obtain a sales license and pay sales tax?

2. **Discuss special requirements.** Includes items such as insurance certificates, hold-harmless clauses, licenses or permits needed, security personnel, the hotel's policy on concession sales, fire safety, rules of the house such as prohibited activities and health code requirements, and medical personnel onsite.

3. **Have exhibit floor plan approved by fire marshal.** Have the facility sign a statement that, during the dates of the meeting, the facility and exhibit space will meet or exceed all local fire safety and health code regulations.

4. **Payment terms for rental charges.** What are the criteria for charging rental fees (flat fee basis versus per booth basis)?

Cancellation or Termination?

Although you never plan to cancel a meeting or an event, you need to agree with the property on how to part ways. Every contract should contain reciprocal provisions for

Don't Drop the Ball

Understand the difference between termination and cancellation. If a contract is "terminated" for acts of God or other similar circumstances, neither party has any obligation to the other. If a contract is "cancelled," it means one party has breached or defaulted on its performance and owes the other party damages unless otherwise stipulated in the contract.

cancellation by either side. If you get this right in the contract, if you ever need to cancel, your job will be a little easier. Here is what you need to address in the contract:

1. **Termination and excuse of performance.** Under what terms can the contract be terminated without either side incurring damages to the other? This might include acts of God, acts of third parties not under the control of either party to the contract, change in management or chain affiliation, terrorism, foreclosure or bankruptcy, or the inability of a specific percentage (usually 30 percent or higher) of attendees unable to get to the meeting or event, and so on.

2. **Cancellation by the group:**

   ◆ Define the term "cancellation" to differentiate it from "attrition" and "termination."

   ◆ Establish the right of the parties to cancel or modify the terms by mutual agreement at any time.

   ◆ Establish that, if cancellation by the group occurs for reasons other than those outlined in the termination clause, a cancellation fee or liquidated damages are due to the hotel.

   ◆ Establish the sliding scale or fixed amount applicable for determining the cancellation fee owed to the hotel based on when the cancellation occurs. The cancellation fee should be based on a percentage of the anticipated revenue, not to exceed the estimated departmental profit margin of the hotel for the anticipated revenue sources specified in the contract. If the formula or flat fee is a reasonable approximation of actual damages and not a penalty, it is called a liquidated damage clause.

   ◆ Establish how anticipated lost revenue is calculated. The formula should explain exactly what revenue sources are included in "lost revenue," and it should exclude sales tax unless required by state or local law.

- Be aware that many hotels expect meeting sponsors to pay for lost "ancillary revenue" for unused guest rooms. Ancillary revenue is the discretionary, uncontracted revenue from ancillary activities such as: room service, in-room movies, purchases in the gift shop, drinks in the bar, and so on. This is highly negotiable and most hotels will drop the requirement to pay if asked.

- Unless the damages are a reasonable and valid liquidated damage provision, establish the duty of the hotel to reduce its damages and credit those room nights and revenues against the cancellation fee.

   If a sliding scale is used for liquidated damages, the formula can factor in resold rooms so that additional credit for resold rooms is not required as matter of law. Meeting sponsors can still negotiate to receive credit for resold rooms over and above the sliding scale. To keep the formula balanced for the hotel, credit for resold rooms should be given by the hotel in the same percentage as applicable in the sliding scale for the meeting sponsor based on when cancellation occurs. (Example: If the sliding scale states that the meeting sponsor will pay 50 percent of the guest room revenue if cancellation occurs one year out, credit for resold rooms should be given at 50 percent.)

- Establish when the cancellation fee is due and payable. Payment can be set to be at the time of cancellation or after the anticipated meeting dates to determine whether the hotel has recouped any business.

3. **Cancellation by the hotel:**

   - Define the term "cancellation" by the hotel to differentiate it from "termination." It should include: a) failure to provide facilities, or b) failure to give reasonable assurances of its ability and intent to provide facilities after notice of foreclosure or bankruptcy.

   - Establish the right of the parties to cancel or modify the terms by mutual agreement at any time.

   - Establish the group's right to damages if cancellation by the hotel occurs for reasons other than those outlined in the termination clause.

   - Establish how damages will be calculated to compensate the group either as: a) a sliding scale based on percentage of revenue and when the cancellation occurs, b) a specific sum, or c) actual out-of-pocket expenses and lost profits. Expenses you would incur if the hotel cancelled your contract include expenses to research alternate facilities (airfare, long-distance phone calls, and so on) and the difference in the increased cost of the alternate facility (room rate, F&B prices, meeting-room rental, additional mailings, and so on).

◆ Specify when damages will be paid by the hotel to the meeting sponsor, either at the time of cancellation or after actual amounts are incurred.

◆ Establish the hotel's duty to return deposits within a specific timeframe.

Beyond Your Control

The following clauses protect you from things beyond your control. The last thing you need is a jackhammer on the other side of the wall during your meeting or event:

1. **Other meetings/events at the hotel.** Determine if it's appropriate for the group to restrict the hotel from booking competitors' groups over the same dates. Specify the terms of this restriction and the procedures for releasing function space. You can also state direct competitors' names in the contract to prevent them from meeting next door to your meeting or event.

2. **Construction, remodeling, and noise control.** The hotel should advise the group of any construction or remodeling to be performed in the hotel or in the vicinity over the meeting dates. Determine and specify whether group wants the right to terminate the contract if the construction will be detrimental to the meeting/event.

   Specify that, if noise becomes an issue to the extent that the meeting/event is impaired, the meeting sponsor will be due compensation in the form of a credit on the master account. The parties will have to negotiate what a reasonable amount is based on the circumstances.

3. **Deterioration in quality.** For all bookings, the facility should warrant that the quality of its service and the condition of its physical facilities will be the same or better at the time of the meeting/event as they were when the contract was signed.

People Provisions

Here are some other things to think about:

1. **Use of outside contractors.** Specify whether the meeting sponsor wants, or will be allowed, the right to use outside contractors for services not specifically reserved to the hotel, and if there are any additional fees to be paid or provisions to be made. (This also applies to convention centers, and may apply to any other facility you use, including museums, restaurants, clubs, and so on.)

2. **Staff and staffing.** Specify specific performance standards, and the hotel's duty to assign an adequate number of personnel to handle the meeting/event you use, including museums, restaurants, clubs, and so on.

3. **Ownership and management changes.** Require the hotel to notify the group if this happens. Specify the effect of ownership or management changes on the contract.

More Legal Terminology

You really need a lawyer to sift through everything in a contract. However, to get you started, the following are often standard clauses in most vendor contracts:

1. **Mutual indemnification and hold harmless.** Each party should agree to indemnify each other for its own negligent acts or omissions. Specify that the hotel will specifically indemnify the sponsoring organization for alcohol-related claims, defects in the facilities, and defects in equipment provided by the hotel. Don't agree to indemnify other people or entities for their negligence. If someone asks you to sign an *indemnification* clause, make sure you understand what risks and responsibilities you are being asked to assume or seek legal counsel.

2. **Insurance.** The hotel and group should both agree to carry adequate liability

Meeting Speak

Indemnification is an agreement in which one party agrees to protect the other party from liability, damages, or out-of-pocket expenses that may occur in connection with a particular transaction. **Mutual indemnification** means that each party will be responsible for its own negligent acts or omissions if it causes a loss to the other party or causes the other party to defend itself against an asserted claim in connection with a particular transaction.

insurance that protects both parties against claims arising from activities in the hotel. Stipulate the amount of insurance and specify that the group and the hotel are responsible to each other for property damage only up to the amount of insurance.

3. **Warranties, duties, and responsibilities of parties.** The hotel should warrant compliance with all federal, state, and local fire-safety and health codes, including compliance with the Americans with Disabilities Act (ADA) and the Hotel and Motel Fire Safety Act. The meeting/event sponsor also should warrant its compliance with the ADA in the areas it controls. Include provisions for hotel security and deterioration in quality.

4. **Costs to enforce agreement.** The contract should provide that, in the event the parties must resort to a dispute-resolution method, as previously outlined, the party prevailing in the action shall be entitled to attorney's fees and costs in bringing the action.

5. **Procedure for notices.** Stipulate where legal notices or notices about termination or cancellation should be sent. This usually corresponds with the names listed as contacts at the beginning of the contract.

6. **Restrictions on assignment by either side.** Stipulate that neither party may assign this contract to a third party without written permission from the other party to this contract.

7. **Counterparts.** Stipulate that the final contract may be executed in one or more counterparts, that each counterpart shall be considered an original, and that all counterparts taken together shall be considered one and the same instrument. Stipulate that facsimiles and photocopies are as valid as originals.

8. **Waiver and severability clause.** If any provision is found to be unenforceable, the remainder of the contract is still valid. No right or remedy specified in the contract shall be waived by either party except in writing.

9. **Dispute resolution/choice of law/venue and jurisdiction.** The parties should determine how disputes will be handled: arbitration, alternative dispute resolution, mediation, or litigation. If arbitration is chosen, parties should reserve the right to use the courts for equitable remedies. Specify the jurisdiction, venue, and choice of law.

10. **Effect of agreement.** Stipulate that the contract does not create a joint venture or agency relationship.

11. **Paragraph headings.** Stipulate that paragraph headings, numbers, letters, and emphasis marks have been inserted for the convenience of reference only, and if there is any conflict between any such headings, numbers, letters, or emphasis marks and the text of this contract, the text shall control.

12. **Merger of terms and modification.** Stipulate that the contract contains all the terms and conditions agreed to between the parties and that no changes may be made to the contract except in written form signed by the parties.

13. **Co-authorship of contract.** If the contract is negotiated and prepared jointly by both parties, stipulate that, in any dispute in connection with this contract, ambiguous terms shall not be construed against either party.

14. **Authorized signatures.** Who is authorized to sign? Make sure titles are used and make sure the parties warrant and represent that they are signing individually or on behalf of their organizations.

In our legal system, you can sign contracts in only one of two capacities, as the principal or as the agent. If you sign as the principal, you are personally liable for performance. If you sign as the agent, your acts are imputed to the principal as long as the principal authorized your acts. If you signed as an agent but weren't authorized or if you don't indicate your agent status, you become the principal. If a contract is valid when signed, it remains valid even if the parties that signed it, including agents, are no longer employed by the principal.

Hotel, facility, and other meeting/event vendor contracts are getting more complicated and are covering more ground. In meetings-industry circles, legal issues and contracts are always hot topics. If you educate yourself about the items described in this chapter and incorporate them into your hotel contracts, you increase your chances of a successful meeting. For more information, buy one of John Foster's books on meeting and facility contracts. Contact John via his website: www.FJGLaw. net, at 404-873-5200, or John.Foster@FJGLaw.net. To find out more about hospitality industry attorneys, contact the Academy of Hospitality Industry Attorneys at www.ahiattorneys.org or 303-892-6966.

Always add a term that states that neither the meeting sponsor nor its attendees will be responsible for additional charges, gratuities, or service fees not included in the contract unless later agreed to in writing by the meeting sponsor or the attendee, respectively.

The Least You Need to Know

♦ Make sure everything your organization needs from the facility or vendor and vice versa is included in the contract.

♦ Attrition can be applied to both guestrooms and food and beverage. Make sure all sliding scales use a formula for calculating attrition damages based on estimated lost profit.

♦ Always sign contracts as an agent on behalf of your organization. Otherwise, you are personally liable.

♦ Penalties are not enforceable in contract law. The correct term is damages, which means lost profit or out-of-pocket expenses incurred.

Chapter 13

Marketing—Early and Often

In This Chapter

- ◆ Understand that meeting or event goals and objectives contribute to your marketing campaign
- ◆ Find out what to put in a marketing brochure or online
- ◆ See how technology can enhance marketing efforts
- ◆ Understand that the timing of your marketing pieces makes a big difference

Marketing your meeting or event is serious business. Marketing and promotion are necessary if you want strong attendance. Good marketing allows potential attendees to understand why they need to attend and what's in it for them.

Once again, your goals and objectives play an important role. If they are clear and provide the right message, your promotional campaign should be easy. In this chapter, we will explore what goes into your marketing pieces and your marketing strategy, and we'll take a look at how to deliver your message.

The Marketing Message

Whoever is responsible for marketing and promotion needs to understand the reason for the meeting or the event. You need to demonstrate to the decision-makers, sponsors, exhibitors, and especially the attendees that you have a meeting/event people want to attend.

It's marketing's role to take your goals and objectives and repackage them into a positive campaign that gets attention, sparks the interest of your intended audience, and makes it easy for them to attend.

To help you define your marketing message, start by answering the following questions:

◆ What are the goals of the meeting/event?

◆ What are the meeting/event objectives?

◆ What is the financial objective?

◆ Who should attend? Who should not attend?

◆ What are the benefits of attendance to the attendee?

> ### The Inside Scoop
>
> Many companies waste thousands of dollars on meetings that accomplish nothing. You need to let the potential audience know the agenda in advance and why the meeting is important to them. You also need to show how some fun was built into the agenda. Unhappy attendees bring down the morale of the entire crew, and an entire meeting can be sabotaged.

There may be other issues that factor into your marketing direction. Even if you are having a mandatory company meeting, your marketing message should still focus on the goals and objectives to promote buy-in and build excitement. After all, everyone is so busy that they really need to understand the benefits of being away from work or family. They want to know what's in it for them. Nothing is worse than having to go to a boring sales meeting and knowing it is going to be boring ahead of time!

Marketing Philosophy

Your marketing message depends on your target audience. Let's take a look at two different scenarios. You will see that each scenario has a very different audience, but both want the same end result—a successful meeting. There are many ways to deliver your message, but first you need to determine what the message is and how to package it.

Scenario #1: You Have to Attend the Sales Meeting

Pretend you work for a corporation that is planning a sales meeting. There is no need to spend money on a meeting brochure because a memo or company e-mail will do the trick. You have a captive audience and you just need to tell the sales team the dates and give them airplane tickets. How motivated will they be when they hear a directive telling them they have to attend? They already know that.

How about a little motivation? Create a theme, and put some fun into it. Add excitement by getting them involved in the theme. Let them in on the agenda ahead of time, promote your fabulous keynote speaker, and pique their interest with some activities geared specifically to their enjoyment. Don't just send out the mandatory meeting memo and leave it at that. Generate some "buzz" and create posters, games, or whatever gets your crew interested. By promoting the meeting again and again, attendees will start to look forward to coming together, instead of dreading it.

Scenario #2: Please Come to This Meeting

Now you work for a large trade association and are planning an annual conference. Attendance is usually around 1,000 people, but competition for attendees is tough. You really need to appeal to the attendees' needs. Promotional material must grab their attention and provide detailed information. An agenda is very important. Include information on the speakers; they bring credibility to the meeting and are one of the key motivators to attract an audience. You need to answer the question "What's in it for me?" (meaning, of course, what's in it for *them*) and get people to take action by registering. Highlight three to five reasons to attend—it will help your potential audience sell the meeting to those who may pay for their participation.

> **Food for Thought**
>
> Give potential meeting attendees a several reasons why they should attend by using action words such as "how to," "learn," "increase," "identify," "improve," "discover," "understand," and "find out" to describe what's in it for them.

Also consider that meeting costs play a significant role in the decision to attend meetings. Your attendees may have to get approval from supervisors or others to pay for these costs, or they may have to pay for it themselves. Either way, your audience must justify the value of being away from work, families, or community obligations as well as the financial cost. Other barriers that prevent people from attending meetings are too many meetings, too little time to attend meetings, and too much time out of the office.

When considering your marketing philosophy, you must take many issues into consideration. For example, you want to hold your meeting in an interesting location, but depending on your audience, promoting all of the fun things to do (say, in Las Vegas or Orlando) may backfire if the meeting venue makes it sound like a vacation. If your program is too much like the last one or is too similar to a competing program, you need to figure out a way to make your meeting be and sound different and better.

Getting the Word Out

Once you know your audience, you can use the following methods to reach out and "touch" them:

- Advertisement
- E-mail broadcast
- Fax distribution list
- Mailing list
- Networking
- Partnerships with other organizations
- Past attendee
- Press release/media
- Referral
- Website
- Word of mouth

Food for Thought

Offer discounted registration fees to attendees who bring in new people to your next meeting or event. The more new people they bring in, the greater the discount. Also consider giving discounts to multiple participants from one organization.

Create a marketing plan using a combination of the preceding distribution methods. Understand your potential audience and make sure you have determined the best way to reach these people. Add a question to your registration form and meeting-evaluation form that asks how they heard about the meeting. This can tell you where to advertise more.

Review your marketing plan every year and for every meeting or event. What is effective today may be obsolete tomorrow. Pay careful attention to what marketing vehicle reached the most people and produced the greatest results. It is your responsibility to get the word out in the right places.

Hard Copy

Brochures are expensive, but they set the image for the event. Plus, many people just like something they can touch. Brochures need to have visual impact. Professional, well-written brochures or flyers are a must. Use color if possible and a good-quality paper. Be smart about the type size and design. Some may want to copy the brochure to provide to others; make it easy to do so with color and design.

Before you set your sights on a specific brochure design, paper, color, size, and so on, determine the costs. You may even want to hire a graphic designer or desktop publisher to produce the marketing pieces. It will most likely cost more money than doing it yourself, but the expertise will be well worth the money. A professional will know how to pull together a brochure that fits your budget and will also understand design techniques that will capture your audience's attention and consistently promote your company's image or your event's theme through use of a brand, color-scheme, or logo.

Be aware that U.S. mail has certain size and weight restrictions. Before you spend a lot of time and money printing beautiful invitations or announcements, take a mockup to the post office to understand what it will cost to mail.

Brochures also need strong content. Be sure your promotional materials include the following:

- Meeting or event title or theme if applicable
- Meeting/event days of the week and date(s)
- Meeting/event agenda including times
- Speakers/entertainers with brief bios
- Location, address, phone, fax, e-mail, website
- Who should attend
- Benefits of attending
- Goals and objectives (from the attendees' perspective)
- Testimonials from previous attendees, if applicable

- Registration fees and deadlines (received by versus postmarked by)
- Special incentive offers for early or multiple registrations sent together
- Sponsors

- Exhibitors if applicable
- *CEUs*, if applicable
- Housing information (name of facilities, address, rates, and a URL), cutoff dates, and methods by which to make reservations
- Spouse/guest activities
- Airline and ground transportation information
- Complete registration form or RSVP procedures
- Online registration information

Meeting Speak

CEUs are continuing education units. Many professional associations require that individuals earn a specific number of CEUs to maintain their original certification status. Check with your industry trade association on how your attendees may qualify/earn them at your meeting.

Promotions in Cyberspace

Technology is making it easier to promote your meetings and events. Today you can advertise, register, customize, and keep track of attendees online. There are some really cool ways you can reach your audience.

If your organization has a website, you should put your meeting or event information on it. This information is dynamic and should be updated frequently. When attendees know they can get current, accurate information about the meeting or event on the web—they will. It's cost effective and efficient. Create listservs or blogs for pre-meeting buzz and discussions of issues. These generate interest by the occasional user.

Food for Thought

Don't just announce your meeting or event once or twice, do it several times. With web and e-mail technology, it's easier than ever to get the word out and send strategic reminders. Consider slightly different messages targeted specifically to subgroups.

Another efficient communication tool these days is the e-mail distribution list. Depending on your audience, most people use e-mail. You can easily create distribution lists of your targeted audience and e-mail people short and sweet informational notes. Use this method to tell them to "save the date," to point them to your meeting/event website, and to send them important program updates. E-mail communication is also an excellent way to send registration confirmations and reminders.

Up and coming in online meeting and event marketing are some new websites that help you get the word out. They are companies that help you create customized e-mail, announcements, and invitations online. Check out Cvent (www.cvent.com), Senada (www.senada.com), or View Central (www.viewcentral.com) to see what we mean. You can go to one of these websites and complete templates about an upcoming meeting or event. They even allow you to use your logo and theme. You provide an e-mail address list of potential attendees, and the software creates a personalized e-mail from "your organization." One of the great features is that the software allows you to require, track, and manage RSVPs. If you need to send reminders, you can do that, too.

It may be prudent to send a reminder notice to those who have already registered when the program approaches. Sometimes people forget where they are to be when—or someone else registered them and they were unaware. Sometimes people lose their original email and just want another reminder, too.

Those who have not yet registered for your program may need several polite reminders at key intervals (for example, before the early registration deadline or the hotel cut-off date) to do so.

Web-based programs offer a lot of features and flexibility—more than we can describe here. Price-wise they can vary considerably, so do your homework. Consider that the increased cost of purchasing an online program will replace much in terms of the current time-consuming, inefficient manual process you may be using now. We expect this type of technology will continue to get better over time, as more and more users take advantage of it.

Ads

Advertise in your trade publications and other regional or local publications and the trade publications of competitors. Newsletters are also a good place to reach potential attendees. For example, if your audience is CPAs, then the local, regional, and even national CPA associations would be a great place to find attendees. Print ads can be expensive, so be sure you are reaching the right audience or barter for exchange of services for ad space.

Media

Keep an up-to-date list of appropriate media in your area. Send press releases to announce your meetings and events. Also use the CVB for media contacts in the city where you are holding the meeting or event. In some cases, the CVB will even send the press releases for you.

Be creative. Is there an innovative way to announce your program? The media is more apt to give you ink if it is unique and newsworthy. In other words, make it exciting!

Partnering: If You Can't Beat 'Em, Join 'Em

Is there a way to partner with other industry organizations and hold joint meetings or events? If there are two similar meetings taking place, does it make sense to join forces and have one meeting together? In the long run, both organizations just might benefit. Your attendees will love it because they can attend two meetings for the price of a single airfare and will spend less time away from home and the office. Pooling the resources of two meetings allows you to create a stronger program, reach a larger audience, and have a stronger base for negotiations with potential meeting properties because you are bringing in a bigger group, possibly for a longer period.

Timing Is Key

Start early. Some organizations announce their annual meeting dates 5 to 10 years in advance. Do what makes sense in your situation, but the earlier you get on people's calendars the better. You also need to avoid scheduling over other meetings or holidays that impact your audience, so it helps to know when the key meetings in your industry are held.

For employee meetings, there may be a particular month in which it makes sense to hold the meeting. For example, an annual sales meeting may be held in the first or last month of the fiscal year for planning purposes. It also helps the sales staff plan personal trips because they know the first or second week of a certain month will be the sales meeting.

Meetings that are scheduled during the same days/dates every year make it easy for people to plan ahead.

Events are often held to commemorate anniversaries or celebrate special occasions. Invitations and announcements still need to be sent out well in advance if you want good, strong attendance. Never assume your program is more important than what may already be set in stone on your potential attendee's calendar.

The Least You Need to Know

- You must demonstrate the benefits of attending your meeting or event to your audience.

- Clearly written, easy-to-understand marketing materials are best.

- Web software allows you to reach a much broader market at a fraction of the cost.

- The earlier you can announce your meeting or event, the greater the chance you will attract your desired audience.

Chapter 14

Exhibits and Expositions: Should You Do It?

In This Chapter

◆ Learn how to determine whether exhibits make sense for your meeting

◆ Understand what it takes to run a successful exhibit program

◆ See where to turn for help in finding potential exhibitors

◆ Discover what an exhibitor prospectus is

◆ Learn how to get attendees to the show

A successful exhibit opportunity means getting the right buyers and the right sellers together in the same room. How do you do this? You have to create the show, demonstrate to both attendees and exhibitors that it is worth their time and money, market it, sell exhibit booths, get attendees, and produce it. Did you know that an exhibit tradeshow can be a revenue generator for associations and other organizations? It also can be very time consuming and expensive, and if not done right, a flop.

In this chapter, we will walk you through these issues. You will understand what it takes to be successful in the exhibit tradeshow arena. You will also learn how to keep exhibitors and attendees happy so that they achieve a return on their investment of time, money, and effort.

Exposition or Tradeshow?

Every year, in many cities across the country, local builders and remodelers have home-remodeling shows. These expositions are open to the public, and you pay a fee at the door. This is different from a tradeshow, which is only open to registered attendees. This chapter is about tradeshows and does not deal with the issues of public expositions, which usually are larger and more complex to plan and manage, although there are similarities.

Weighing the Options

So someone suggests you need exhibits at your meeting. Before jumping on the bandwagon, ask yourself the following questions:

- Why is it beneficial to have exhibits?

- Do we need 8×10 or 10×10 exhibit booths, or will tabletop exhibits suffice?

- When will the attendees have time to visit the exhibits?

- Will exhibits be on display throughout the meeting, limited to several hours, or for specific times over the course of one or more days?

- Will they be scheduled in parallel with other sessions?

- Will they provide value to both attendees and exhibitors?

- Is there sufficient space for them?

- What is a reasonable fee to exhibit?

- What impact will exhibits have on the meeting's budget (both income and expense)?

- Who would be interested in exhibiting? Are there enough exhibitors?

- Will the exhibitors receive a return on their investment?

Exhibiting in a tradeshow can cost thousands of dollars. Costs include the booth and materials (and shipping them), travel expenses, promotional brochures and giveaways, time out of the office for one or more people, and booth registration fees. To keep exhibitors coming back year after year, they need to show a return on their investment to their organization.

> **Food for Thought**
>
> Your tradeshow floor can be open all day, but at least a portion of the day should be dedicated only to exhibits. Consider having some of the meals and breaks in the exhibit hall.

Full-scale tradeshows should be considered only if both your attendees and exhibitors will really benefit from them. If you want to have exhibits on a smaller, less costly scale, try tabletop exhibits or displays. You provide each exhibitor with a draped and skirted table. Each exhibitor is allowed to bring in brochures and small displays. You generally do not need an exhibitor services company, because electrical power and telephone/Internet capabilities pretty much are all an exhibitor would require (if that). Your convention services manager will help with the details. Refer to your meeting's goals and objectives. (This is a perfect example of why you need them.) How does a tradeshow or a simple tabletop exhibit setting fit into the scheme of things? Does either make sense?

If you decide to go the tradeshow route, here are some ideas for incorporating exhibits into your agenda:

- ◆ Have the opening reception in the exhibit hall.

- ◆ Schedule continental breakfasts, breaks, and lunches in the exhibit hall.

- ◆ Have a demonstration stage in the exhibit hall. Invite exhibitors to demonstrate their latest product or to give short presentations on how their services can help attendees.

- ◆ Have a grand-prize drawing in the exhibit hall at the end of the conference.

- ◆ Schedule a window of time during the morning or afternoon for exhibits only when there is not a conflict with sessions or other official program activity.

Location, Location, Location (Again)

Convention centers are specifically designed to hold expositions and tradeshows, but in some cases you can use a ballroom in a hotel. (Conference centers are typically not used for tradeshows or large exhibitions. Their size and purpose differ from convention centers.) It's really an issue of space availability and the complexity of your program that determines your location decision. Here are some things to consider when deciding which to use:

- Building regulations
- Facility rental fees
- Insurance
- Loading dock access
- Security
- Shipping procedures
- Space needs
- Union jurisdictions

> **Don't Drop the Ball**
>
> Locate the nearest freight elevator or loading dock to your exhibits. Inform your exhibitors of the location and let them know where, when, and how they can bring their materials into the facility.

Here are some other considerations: Can you charge enough to cover your costs? Will the attendees have easy access to the show? Can the exhibitors move in easily? What additional fees will the exhibitors be charged by the facility? Can you plug in your own electrical cords, or are there union restrictions? Is there an open-dock policy, or do the exhibitors have to hire someone to carry their exhibit material in for them? Can your exhibitors exhibit what they want to? For example, if your exhibitors are car manufacturers, can they display a car? What are the building policies on it? What is the floor load capacity? Will some of the exhibits be too heavy?

> **Meeting Speak**
>
> **Net square foot (NSF)** is the method some facilities charge for exhibit space. Net square footage is the space the exhibitors actually use and does not include aisles, pillars, food stations, and seating. The **gross square footage** of an exhibit hall is the total square footage of the room (length × width of the room).

How Facilities Sell Exhibit Space

Facilities charge for exhibit space in a variety of ways. Take a look:

- Flat fee per day
- Flat fee for length of show
- Per booth
- Per *net square foot* (for length of show)

Usually it is the convention centers that charge on a net square foot (NSF) basis. Typically, hotels will rent you the space for a flat fee, although this is not always the case. Be aware that facilities charging you on an NSF basis will have different calculation methods.

Exhibit booth sizes typically rented to exhibitors are 8×10 feet (80 square feet) or 10×10 feet (100 square feet).

If you have 100 exhibitors all using 10×10 exhibit booths, then the net square footage being used is 100 exhibits $\times$ 100 square feet each, or 10,000 NSF. If the facility charged 80¢ per net square foot, then your charge would be $10,000 \times 80$¢ = $8,000.

How to Sell Space to Exhibitors

You sell booth space to exhibitors as a booth package. Typically, a booth includes an eight-foot pipe and drape back wall and three-foot-high side rails. Sometimes a table and two chairs are also part of the package. Anything else (carpeting and other furnishings, power, lights, and so on) is extra and is paid for by the exhibitor. You can create a package according to your tradeshow needs.

In addition to selling a booth to exhibitors, you can sell them ad space in the program and sponsorship opportunities. Also think about charging a premium for the best booth locations: corners, near food stations, in front of the main door, island booths, and other unique configurations.

Exposition Services Contractor (ESC)

Who provides the booth package? The *exposition services contractor* (sometimes called the decorator). Exposition services contractors are vendors that specialize in a variety of services including booth design and setup, furniture rental, floor plan diagramming, and signage. They also handle the delivery and setup of the exhibitors' show materials, the teardown and shipping back to the exhibitors' offices, as well as acting as a subcontractor for other services.

There is a unique relationship between you (the meeting host), the exhibitor, and the exposition services contractor. You hire the exposition services contractor and design the show (with his or her assistance). Once you have decided

Meeting Speak

The **exposition services contractor** (or decorator) is the company that provides the booth, signs, setup, and other services needed for a tradeshow or exposition.

what your standard booth includes, the exposition services contractor quotes you a per-booth fee that you collect directly from the exhibitors. The exposition services contractor prepares an exhibit services kit that outlines all of the services provided. If an exhibitor needs additional services such as electricians, furniture rental, florists, audio-visual technicians, security staff, plumbers, sign makers, and photographers, the exhibitor contracts with the exposition services contractor directly. The exhibitor pays for additional services not offered in the booth package.

The following table looks at the responsibilities of the meeting host and the exposition services contractor:

Responsibility	Host	ESC
Select show location	X	
Determine standard booth options	X	
Create/mail exhibitor prospectus	X	
Design floor plan and flow	X	X
Determine exhibition fee	X	
Collect exhibition fee	X	
Create exhibitor kit	X	X
Mail exhibitor kits	X	X
Make booth assignments	X	
Provide additional exhibit services		X
Collect fees for additional services		X

Don't Drop the Ball

Before you sign a contract with an exposition services contractor, read all of the company's materials, ask lots of questions, and check references for shows similar to yours. Understand your responsibilities as well as theirs. Get all costs in writing and make sure you budget for them.

A budget for an exhibit tradeshow is much different from a typical meeting budget without exhibits. When it gets right down to it, the rules, regulations, contractors, and other issues can be very confusing even to the most experienced planner. Some costs are absorbed by the exhibitor, others by the meeting sponsor.

If you are considering a tradeshow, call an exposition services contractor and discuss the services and fees. Two nationwide contractors are Freeman Decorating (www.freemanco.com) and GES Exposition Services (www.gesexpo.com).

Other items you may need from the exhibitor services contractor are registration booths, furniture, and additional pipe and drape. Registration booths are floor-standing booths you can use for your registration area. Furniture can be used to create a more relaxing lounge area in the exhibit hall or other areas. Make sure to negotiate on these items. Depending on your show's size, registration booths are often provided at no charge. The pipe and drape can be used to hide office areas and to drape off sections of the exhibit hall.

Determining Potential Exhibitors

Before you can invite potential exhibitors to show their wares, you have to know what the attendees want and need to see. What products and services do your attendees use? Make a list of vendors they use on a regular basis and add those they use on a less frequent basis. Also think about which companies would like to access your audience. This is a good starting point.

Do a little research before jumping in with both feet. Ask potential exhibitors if they would exhibit in your show. Ask previous attendees if it would benefit them to have a tradeshow. You will learn a lot just by talking to a few people about the idea. If you already have a show, reexamine it. Do some research. What would make it more beneficial to both sides?

When looking for potential exhibitors, look in your own back yard. Who are your attendees currently doing business with? Don't overlook the obvious!

The Exhibit Prospectus

An exhibitor prospectus and application form contain all the information a potential exhibitor needs to know to make an informed decision about exhibiting. These can be two different documents or can be incorporated into one. Here are some things to include in the prospectus:

- Information about the show's location
- The dates of the show including move in/move out and exhibit hours
- Why they should exhibit
- An attendee profile
- Rules and regulations

- A floor plan (draft)
- Statistics on last year's show if available (number of attendees, testimonials, and success stories)
- How booth assignments are made (first-come, first-served; random; or lottery)
- The booth fee and when deposit/payment is due
- The cancellation policy
- Exhibitor services contractor information
- Music licensing information

Here are some things to include on the application:

- The organization's name
- A contact name/title/address/phone/fax/e-mail for correspondence and the program
- Exhibitor names for name badges (state how many are included) and if they are a full conference or exhibit only registration
- A statement to sign saying that they understand the show rules and regulations and will abide by them
- Booth number and location preference (ask for top three, if applicable)
- How the booth sign should read—be sure to specify how many characters and spaces are allowed
- What products and services are being exhibited
- When and where to return the application
- Twenty-five words or less about the product or service (if you need this information for the attendee program)
- Liability waiver
- Insurance statement (they need to have proof of insurance)

> **The Inside Scoop**
>
> Most booth packages include two or three complimentary registrations. Sometimes exhibitors are invited to educational sessions and all meal functions, and in other cases they are not. Establish guidelines and communicate them to the exhibitors. Try to include them in as many events as you can. They want to network, too.

Determine early on how you are going to market and communicate information about the show to potential exhibitors. Make sure complete information is available on your website.

To give you ideas, save other tradeshow brochures when they come to you in the mail and search the web for ideas on how you can create your brochures and prospectus. Ask your exposition services contractor for samples from other successful shows.

Rules and Regs

Every show must have rules and regulations. You need to communicate with the exhibitors regarding move-in procedures, move-out procedures, security information, liability waiver, insurance requirements, shipping and storage, booth construction and obstructions, the booth assignment procedure, and the procedure for enforcement of rules and regulations. Each tradeshow will have rules that pertain to its specific industry. For example, a food show may require that visqueen (plastic sheeting) be laid on top of carpet if cooking is done in the booth. You get the idea.

The booth-assignment procedure can be first-come, first-served, or at your discretion. Always reserve the right to reassign booth space if necessary and pay attention to competitors. In certain industries, you will need to ask them if there is any organization they do not want to be near on the floor.

Issues Onsite

If you use an exposition services contractor, your exhibitors will check in directly with this company. Exhibitors will also need to check in with you to receive their conference packet and other information. Sometimes the meeting host places a registration table next to the exhibitor services company on the show floor so that the exhibitors can check in with both at the same time.

Set Up and Move In

Moving in can be a lengthy affair depending on the facility and the number of exhibitors. Publish specific move-in hours that must be adhered to. Depending on the facility, only so many exhibitors can use the loading dock at the same time. Sometimes exhibitors are allowed to "carry in" their stuff through the front doors as long as they do not need carts and other assistance. Other times, they are required to use the loading dock. Ask the facility about these rules.

When a loading dock is very busy, some facilities require a *marshalling yard*. This is an area away from the facility where exhibitors wait to be called to the dock in an orderly fashion. Unless your show is really big, you won't need one. But now at least you know what one is.

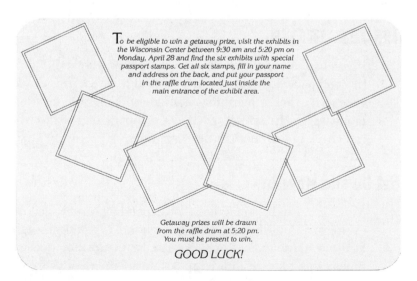

Meeting Speak _____

A **marshalling yard** is an area away from the facility where exhibitors wait to be called to the dock for unloading. It is "take a number" and wait.

After all the exhibitors are set up, you may be required to do a walk-through with the facility manager and/or fire marshal. They will determine if all the facility's rules and regulations are being followed and that there are no municipal code violations. For smaller shows, you probably won't see the fire marshal, but he or she could drop by at any time!

The Hook

Your show is open. Congratulations! But no one is visiting the booths! This is a show sponsor's worst nightmare. Here are some things you can do to lure them in.

Have a fun theme in the exhibition hall. Encourage all exhibitors to join the theme and decorate their booths accordingly. Have the attendees vote on their favorite booth. Make it a contest. They have to go into the hall to see which booth they like best!

An example of a game to encourage booth traffic.

To be eligible to win a getaway prize, visit the exhibits in the Wisconsin Center between 9:30 am and 5:20 pm on Monday, April 28 and find the six exhibits with special passport stamps. Get all six stamps, fill in your name and address on the back, and put your passport in the raffle drum located just inside the main entrance of the exhibit area.

Getaway prizes will be drawn from the raffle drum at 5:20 pm. You must be present to win.

GOOD LUCK!

Some organizations create games that offer prizes for attending booths in the exhibit area. For one show, an Exhibit Passport Getaway was created. Attendees had to find the six different booths with special stamps and get their passports stamped. Once they did that, they placed their passports in a raffle drum, and they were eligible for drawings at the end of the day. The prizes were hotel and restaurant certificates. The following figure is an example of this type of passport.

Outside cover of passport game.

(Courtesy of the Workplace Learning Conference and Pete Manesis)

There are a number of neat ideas like this to provide incentive to your attendees. Ask your exhibitors in advance to provide prizes and to solicit local companies as well as organizations involved in the conference to provide prizes.

Tear Down and Move Out

What goes in must come out. Make sure you state in the rules when teardown can begin. If just one exhibitor packs up early, then others will follow, and you run the risk of having your entire show shut down early.

The rules that applied for bringing stuff in still apply when taking it out. Before the show is over, the exposition services contractor will

The Inside Scoop

Most shows do not allow direct sales on the floor during show hours. If you want to allow this, check into the local sales tax regulations. Your exposition services contractor or the local convention and visitors bureau (CVB) can tell you where to call.

have instructed the exhibitors how to get their boxes shipped out. Exhibitors can even hire the exposition services contractor to tear down, pack, and ship the items for them.

If you have a tabletop show, be prepared to assist exhibitors with shipping options, or at the very least provide them with a list of phone numbers for the major shipping companies. The exhibitors can then arrange for the company to pick up the booth and/or boxes at the meeting facility.

Got the Itch? Want to Learn More?

Interested in learning more about exhibit management? There are opportunities all over the web to help you become more knowledgeable about exposition management.

Check out the International Association for Exhibition Management (IAEM) at www.iaem.org. They have a link on their website to Tradeshow Store.com (www.tradeshowstore.com) where you can purchase books and publications to help you as you learn the ropes about organizing and executing exhibit events.

Another good site is the Trade Show Exhibitors Association (www.tsea.org). An annual education conference with networking opportunities and industry discounts are some of the benefits of membership. The Certified Manager of Exhibits (CME) is offered through TSEA; it's the only certification program in exhibit management and marketing.

The Least You Need to Know

- Have valid reasons and plenty of market research to support having a tradeshow.

- An exposition services contractor provides booth packages and is the subcontractor for other services such as additional labor, florists, electricians, plumbers, and shipping.

- The exhibitor prospectus contains all the details of the tradeshow including who the audience is, why exhibitors should participate, the dates and times of the show, rules and regulations, and other details.

- Tabletop exhibit shows are smaller and are managed by you and your convention services manager. They are great if you do not have the space or enough exhibitors to have a full-fledged tradeshow.

Part 3

Care and Feeding

You need to learn about the essentials of taking care of your attendees. How should you set up the meeting rooms? What kinds of giveaways and amenities should you order? What about name badges? Are there really any decisions about putting a name on a piece of paper? You bet there are!

Here you'll get the scoop on how to find and hire speakers, make travel arrangements, and order food, beverages, and audio-visual equipment. You'll also learn about the registration process and software programs you need to investigate.

Chapter 15

The Meeting Setup

In This Chapter

- Learn how the meeting room set plays a big role in delivery, education, and attendee satisfaction

- Understand why the audience, program, format/schedule, and venue must be in sync

- See how room sets, speakers, audiences, and floor plans fit together for successful meetings

- Define meeting ground rules and understand their importance

How your meeting rooms are set up can make the difference between a successful meeting and one memorable for the wrong reasons. The placement of tables and chairs is just as important as the other details. A smart planner will work with those planning the content to determine how the meeting room should best be set and not leave it up to the venue. In this chapter, you will learn how room diagramming tools can help you, and which room sets are conducive to more effective learning.

It's also important to set a few ground rules for your meeting. The world is full of electronic intrusions and impolite people, and you don't want either to disrupt the meetings. Take a seat and get ready to set the stage for great performances!

Seating Is Important: Understanding Room Configurations

Adults learn more when they can interact with other people. A session that allows for peer-to-peer learning is often more valuable than just one speaker talking to an audience.

Whenever possible, you should face your audience to the long wall in any room. That way, you expose more people to the front/stage area. This is especially important if you have a long and narrow room. Also consider the direction from which people will enter the room. Try to have them enter from the back. You do not want people entering from the front or sides when the speaker is talking.

> **CAUTION**
>
> **Don't Drop the Ball**
>
> Schedule breaks that allow enough time for the attendees to interact with each other, use restroom facilities, make calls, and eat. Fifteen to 30 minutes is the norm.

Let's explore how room sets can have an effect on your entire meeting. Here we will explain exactly how each room set works in a meeting situation. (Thanks to MeetingMatrix [www.meetingmatrix.com] for providing the diagrams.)

◆ **Classroom or schoolroom.** This set consists of rows of tables with chairs. It is a true "school" setting and allows the participants to take notes and spread out handouts, use laptops and other materials. Classroom tables are 18 or 30 inches wide and 6 or 8 feet long. The 18-inch tables are often referred to as "skinnies." Optimally, you will want to seat two people per 6-foot table or three people per 8-foot table. You need to specify your room sets in your RFP—so facilities can match your space needs to their meeting rooms. Facilities will often set for three people per 6-foot and four people per 8-foot table to be space efficient. Those ratios can be uncomfortable and confining.

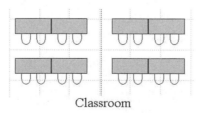

Classroom

◆ **Theater.** This is similar to a classroom, but without the tables. It is a good set when you have to maximize the amount of people in the room and when notes are not likely to be taken and sessions are not overly long.

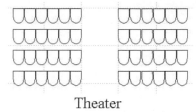

Theater

◆ **Chevron or herringbone.** These are used with classroom and theater sets. All the rows are angled inward toward the center, giving attendees a better view of other participants and the front of the room. You can also curve the rows. These also allow for more aisles, ensuring easy access for participants.

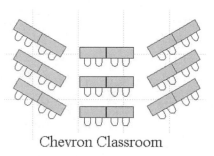

Chevron Classroom

◆ **Conference, T-shape, U-shape, or hollow square.** These are used for smaller (typically up to 30-person) meetings such as board, committee, and staff meetings. Tables are generally 8 feet long and 30 inches wide and can be placed together to make any configuration. As a rule of thumb (just like classroom seating), allow 2 to 3 feet of table space per person.

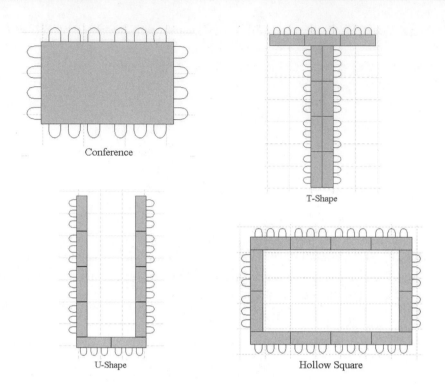

Conference

T-Shape

U-Shape

Hollow Square

◆ **Crescent.** This is sometimes called one-half or three-quarter round. Round banquet tables are set with chairs around half to three quarters of the table, facing the front or center of the room. A standard 60-inch round seats 8 to 10 people, but in a half-round configuration, it would typically be set for 5 to 7. This is used for meetings at which small group activity and note taking are used. It allows speakers to design interactive activities and encourages good interaction among participants.

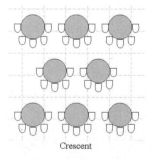

Crescent

◆ **Banquet rounds.** This configuration is mostly used for food functions. The tables generally come in 60-inch or 72-inch diameters and seat between 8 and 12 people each. When setting for formal dining, opt for 72-inch rounds whenever possible, to allow more space for extra wine and water glasses, silverware, menu cards, place cards, comfort, and so on.

Round Tables

◆ **Reception.** This setup generally makes use of smaller "cocktail" rounds, and perhaps cabaret (42" height for standing only) tables, sometimes called "hiboys." Determine the amount of space needed for bars (1:100 people for a general reception; 1:50 people for a VIP reception) and food stations.

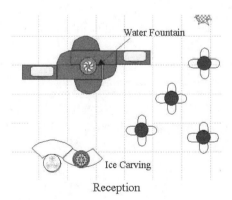

Reception

It is recommended that you visit the facility before designing the room set. If you don't see the room, you are relying on pictures and a floor plan given to you by the facility. Their idea and your idea of a good meeting set for your group could very well be two different things. Keep in mind, however, that they use the room every day in a multitude of configurations and they have probably witnessed great sets as well as

The Inside Scoop

Where do people usually sit when they enter a room? In the back. Some savvy planners place rope and stanchions across the back rows in a room to force people to the front. You can also put reserved signs on rounds. It also helps to have staff stationed throughout the room to help fill in the seats up front.

disasters, so they are in a position to offer good practical suggestions. That said, ask for their suggestions, but trust your own instincts. The final call is yours. Try not to get into the rut of using classroom or theater-style seating. One of the best ways to set a meeting room is often crescent style. The attendees can network, take notes, and have plenty of space to spread their stuff out. The crescent set takes up more space than theater or classroom, but it can provide a better learning atmosphere. Negotiate the space with the facility and explain the session objectives and desired outcomes that will be supported with this set.

Math for Meetings: Setup Specs

All meeting facilities have meeting-space charts (sometimes called specs) that show the maximum number of people that will fit into each meeting room for each setup style or configuration. The only way to make sure the space is adequate is to create a diagram to scale. Many times, the facility can provide you with a computer-generated diagram. Ask them. In addition, companies such as MeetingMatrix and Room Viewer can make a planner's job easier by creating room diagrams, which use industry-standard calculations and fire codes. Many of the room-diagramming software companies have already produced standard floor plans for thousands of hotels across the United States. Check out their websites in Chapter 5.

As a rule of thumb, take the total square footage of the room divided by the approximate square footage needed per person to arrive at the number of people that will fit in a given room. Here are the approximate calculations according to industry-accepted standards:

Room Set	Space Calculation
Classroom—18-inch tables	14 to 15 square feet per person
Classroom—30-inch tables	17 to 18 square feet per person
Theater	9 to 11 square feet per person
Banquet—60-inch rounds	12 square feet per person
Banquet—72-inch rounds	13 square feet per person
Reception	10 to 12 square feet per person

There is a handy web-based tool for calculating how large your room needs to be based on the number of people you need to accommodate in a variety of room sets. Go to www.meetingscoach.com/calculator.cfm or www.mpoint.com—click on search engines, then cool tools/space calculator.

So, if you have a 1,200-square-foot room and want to set it theater style, divide 1,200 by 9 to 11 square feet (let's say 10). The answer is 120 people, give or take.

Next you have to allow for head tables, audio-visual, staging, pillars, and other space hogs. See why we encourage the use of room-diagramming software? It eliminates the guess-work and provides a floor plan that will work. Then you simply give the diagram to the facility so that there is no miscommunication about your set—very professional!

If you really want to know how a setup will work in any given meeting space, talk to the convention services manager or audio-visual personnel. They work with many meetings on a daily basis and have probably seen it all.

> **The Inside Scoop**
>
> Facility meeting-space charts are not all created equal. They usually tell you the maximum number of people for each set. The maximum number typically does not take into account staging, aisles, columns or pillars, low ceilings, or hanging chandeliers that can have an impact on audio-visual, refreshments in the back of the room, and so on.

Know and Understand Your Audience

Today's audiences expect sophisticated educational methods and more interaction. It helps to understand a bit about the various generations sitting in your audience before planning your program. Many thanks to Joe Guertin, a professional speaker from Oak Creek, Wisconsin, for this information. Here's the short list:

Generation Type	Who They Are
Veterans (pre-Boomers)	As attendees, they will pay attention but need to relate. Refrain from using new terms and catch phrases. Give them respect. Also make sure your handouts and visuals make use of a larger font for easier reading.
Baby Boomers (born 1948–1964)	They like programs that mix education and fun, such as golf. They will ask for clarification on issues they don't understand. Q&A time is important.

continues

continued

Generation Type	Who They Are
Generation X (born 1965–1980)	Grew up on MTV and technology. They like interaction and movement. Static presentations are boring to them. Sessions with personal relevance pique their interest.
Generation Y (also called Nexters or Millennials)	Short attention spans and time constraints will play a role in the meetings they attend. They are impatient. Family is important. Sessions need to be shorter with a hands-on approach and possibly include family programs, too.

People have different styles of learning and participation. Most learn best by seeing (visual learning), but others learn by hearing (auditory learning), and some like the hands-on approach and need to experience it (experiential learning). Provide the appropriate combination of all three learning styles to reach your audience. In other words, use handouts, appropriate visuals, and hands-on experiences throughout each session and the entire meeting.

Food for Thought

Place standing floor microphones throughout the room or pass handheld wireless mics so the audience can ask questions and everyone can clearly hear the questions.

In addition, you need to consider the makeup of your audience when designing your meeting. Your audience may be ethnically or religiously diverse. For example, placing the Annual Oldtimers Convention in a high-altitude location might not be smart. Neither is holding a meeting on a major Canadian holiday when a significant portion of your attendees is Canadian. Make sure you take into consideration holidays, food necessities, physical requirements, and other concerns when making decisions.

Interactive Sessions

Speakers and session design impact the amount of interaction that goes on in meetings. Ask speakers how they get the audience involved and what you can do to help them create a great program.

Because your speakers will have a big impact on you reaching your goals and objectives, make sure you review these items with each speaker and provide them with an audience profile.

Also ask your speakers to integrate questions and responses throughout the session. It is important for the audience to be able to clarify the information presented and to be able to speak directly with the presenter.

You can also build in time for small discussion groups and interactive learning. Consider assigning topics or areas for discussion and have each group report back to the large group on the outcome of the discussion. Getting everyone involved is one of the keys to successful learning.

Breakout Seating: The Fine Art of Educated Guessing

Have you ever been to a meeting and found that some of the breakout sessions were not well attended and others were overcrowded? What can you, as the planner, do to avoid this? To begin with, make sure you figure out in advance the number of seats you will need in each breakout. It can be helpful to ask attendees to pre-register for concurrent sessions, or use meeting history and discussions with organizers to determine what topics (or speakers) are "hot."

If you have 200 attendees with four breakout sessions, theoretically each session should seat 50 people. If one breakout topic is perceived to be more popular than the others, you should try to adjust accordingly. Speakers may only want 25 people for their sessions because of the topic or need for greater discussion. You can post a monitor at each breakout session door to close the session when it is full. Have a sign ready to put on the door indicating the session is full.

Ask the CSM and banquet staff to "stand by" to make necessary adjustments should one room have an overflow problem. They will be much happier to be forewarned than to be unprepared for the unexpected and have to make a mad dash with chairs at the last minute.

Set for what you need, but do not overset the rooms or they will give the appearance that your audience is not as large as expected. In the previous example, if your breakout rooms seat 75 but you only need 50, make sure the hotel sets to your needs and not the maximum set. You can always have more chairs stacked up in the back of the room, or brought in quickly, if needed. Don't assume that everyone registered for the meeting will attend every session. The experienced planner knows, it just ain't true!

Session Monitors

A meeting with various breakouts should have a monitor in each session. This person helps keep the sessions running smoothly, because you can't be everywhere all the time. He or she introduces the speaker, keeps the meeting on track, gets help with audio-visual equipment if needed, and distributes and collects the evaluations (if applicable). The monitor is often a volunteer. Be sure you have a backup plan when using volunteers. If there are any no-shows, having an alternate who can step in at the last minute is a plus.

Provide monitors with instructions to tell them what they are required to do. Also prepare a form for each to complete. This form includes the number of attendees at the session, comments about the session, and a few feedback questions about being a monitor. Always try to improve the process for the next time!

Floor Plans

When finalizing the agenda and assigning sessions to specific meeting rooms, carefully look at where the meeting rooms are located. Are they near one another? How long will it take participants to walk from session to session? Where will the refreshment breaks be placed? Are the meeting rooms easy to find? Are the signs sufficient, or do you need to make additional ones? Is an elevator or escalator needed to access some session rooms? Note the locations of restrooms and areas where wireless devices can be used. Do a walk-through to experience how a participant will exit a room and move to the next activity.

Also take into consideration the room sets for each session. Assign sessions with similar sets and A/V to the same rooms throughout the day. You will want to avoid changing or "flipping" room sets midday because it takes time and often incurs an additional labor fee.

Plan to have any general session room setup changes occur in the evening after the programs are over. Think about this ahead of time, particularly if your lunch or dinner is in the general session room. In this case, it is generally best to use rounds or half-rounds all day.

Setting the Ground Rules or "Norms" for the Meeting

There are usually a few important items all attendees need to know. This information can and should be stated in the registration materials, the onsite brochure, a welcome packet, or some other appropriate place. It's usually a good idea to mention these items in your announcements as well.

Create a policy for smoking and alcohol consumption. Be sure to consult with the meeting facility for their regulations as well as find out what state laws are. For company meetings, policies may already be in place. If this is the case, a gentle reminder is usually all that is needed. State that company policies apply at your meetings, just like in the office. For other meetings, adopting these policies can reduce and eliminate problems onsite. We encourage you to establish your own policies based on your situation. These are just a few guidelines to get you started.

Don't Drop the Ball

Ask the meeting facility, at the time of the RFP, for its policy on smoking and alcohol service, and tell them your organization's policies and attendee preferences. Find out about the training provided to employees and the policy-enforcement procedures.

- ◆ **Smoking.** "Inferno Explosives Company meetings are designated as nonsmoking. Outside the meeting rooms, we adhere to the facility smoking policy." (Make sure the facility has designated smoking areas, and know where they are. When booking your meeting, know if your participants are smokers or not; more and more states and municipalities are designating facilities—hotels, bars, restaurants—non-smoking.)

- ◆ **Alcohol.** "Please drink responsibly and don't drink and drive."

- ◆ **Electronic intrusions.** "To make sure all attendees have an interruption-free meeting experience, please turn off your phone or pager (or use the vibrate mode)." (Most people are now used to using PDAs or other devices to take notes during meetings. Establish and state the norms of use.)

The Least You Need to Know

- ◆ Seating that allows interaction with other attendees promotes a better learning environment.

- ◆ Understand your audience and your speakers so you can create the right learning environment.

- ◆ Session monitors help keep your breakout sessions on track and let you know if something needs attention.

- ◆ Establish policies on drinking, smoking, and using electronic devices for your meetings.

The Stuff That Meetings and Events Are Made Of

In This Chapter

- ◆ Enhance meetings and events with an array of gifts and giveaways
- ◆ Learn how to make your name badges stand out
- ◆ Make your attendees feel special with amenities
- ◆ Identify vendors who provide the "stuff"

We all go to meetings and events, and most of the time, we leave with more "stuff" than we had when we arrived. We're not referring to just the notes, handouts, and programs. What about the other items we acquire throughout the meeting or event—the gifts, goodies, treats, and giveaways?

As a planner, you'll want to stay abreast on the latest in name badges, badge ribbons, registration supplies, plaques and awards, certificates, and other materials. This chapter looks at the world of supplies, gifts, giveaways, and "other stuff" that makes your meetings and special events memorable. Beware, however: There is a lot to choose from!

Vendors Everywhere

Before we launch into what is out there, we want to identify the players. The meetings industry has a vast number of vendors who supply planners with promotional products and supplies. Some call themselves promotional products companies, advertising specialty companies, or meeting-supply companies, while others focus on incentives and awards and others on corporate or business gifts. When doing searches on the web, you can search the following topics or keywords and pull up a lot of info:

- Advertising specialties
- Business gifts
- Corporate gifts
- Promotional products
- Incentive gifts
- Meeting supplies
- Tradeshow promotional items

The possibilities are endless with respect to promotional gifts and giveaways. You can find items that range from inexpensive refrigerator magnets to top-of-the-line crystal vases. You just need to know the purpose of the gift, your budget, and the message you want to send.

Name Badges and Ribbons

One of the most important and most noticeable items for meetings is the name badge. For attendees who do not know each other and for those who see each other once a year, a name badge provides the initial introduction. When designing your name badge, limit the amount of information that goes on the badge. The attendee's name, company or organization, city, state, and country (if the event is international) are the most common and most useful. Don't try to list too much or the text size will get too small to read from a distance. The key is to make your badges easy to read!

> **CAUTION**
>
> **Don't Drop the Ball**
>
> For safety and security reasons, be sure to advise all attendees not to wear their name badges or carry their conference tote bags outside the facility.

Consider the following for your name badges:

◆ **Font size.** Make them big and bold—readable from a short distance ("Impact" is a good font choice).

◆ **Meeting info.** Add the meeting name and/or dates (this text can be very small).

◆ **Logo.** Use it to represent the meeting or organization.

◆ **Colors.** Use them to highlight the meeting info, logo, and even attendee info.

◆ **Holder style.** Will they be pinned, clipped, or hung around the neck?

Believe it or not, there are considerable options for name badge style, size, and accompaniments. You can purchase preprinted matching stock that includes the name badge, name tents, signage, tickets, and jumbo registration envelopes. Or the stock can be blank so you can print your own logo or design to give your meeting a professional, coordinated look. There are even companies that will customize these items with your logo or meeting theme, eliminating the need to print them yourself or outsource to a printer.

Professionally printed name badge with lanyard and ribbons.

The Inside Scoop

Make sure you schedule ample time to print your name badges. Factor in time to have them preprinted with your meeting information prior to customizing with participant information. With attendees registering at the last minute, or onsite, some label makers (such as DYMO Labelwriter—www.dymo.com) can print names on clear or white tape, which can be affixed to preprinted name badges at the last minute. This also makes it a snap when you only need to print one or a few badges.

When determining the attendee information to print on your name badge, the following printing order works well:

Line One: First name with a minimum 40–42-point font.

Line Two: First and last names with a minimum 18–22-point font. (Consider adding suffixes such as "MD," "DDS," or "CMP" as part of the formal full name, if appropriate for your group.)

Line Three: Organization name with a minimum 16–18-point font.

Line Four: City and state the attendee is from with a minimum 18–22-point font.

Line Five: (Optional) Country or region with a minimum 18–22-point font.

Name badges should have two to four lines. Five gets to be too much but can be used if really necessary. You can skip line one above, but having an individual's first name only on the first line makes it easier to read his or her name from a distance.

In addition to the name badges, you will have to select appropriate name badge holders. Many attendees prefer holders with both a pin and clip backing. There also is a growing trend to supply lanyards (a necklace or neck-cord that attaches to the name badge, often adjustable and printed with the meeting or event sponsor's name or logo) or use badge holders with small pouches that allow the name badge to hang around the neck Women especially like these because they don't like pins sticking in business clothing (think silk blouses) and frequently don't have anywhere to attach a clip.

Consider categorization of your attendees. Do you want to identify specific groups such as exhibitors, sponsors, committee members, or guests? If you do, then pre-printed or color-coded badge holders or ribbons that attach to your name badges are the way to go. Consider purchasing stackable ribbons. These ribbons (approximately 4 inches wide by 1½ inches tall) are attached below the badge holder, layered on top of each other, so you can wear many at once (if you are special, that is). They come in a large variety of colors and preprinted titles. And yes, you can have your logo imprinted and have your own titles custom made. Who knew?

Totes and Carryalls

Another popular item to give your attendees is something in which to carry all their stuff. Totes, carryalls, attaches, bags, and briefcases are great because they can be used again and again. Most will sport the meeting or event name, theme, or logo on it for all the world to see.

If cost is an issue, evaluate your quantity. You can get volume discounts (the more you buy, the less it costs per bag), but also consider getting your bags paid for by a sponsor. You can imprint or embroider your meeting info or theme on one side and sponsor logos on the other. Another thing you can do is ask for "specials." Frequently, promotional product vendors will have sales or specials—ask them.

> **Food for Thought**
>
> Attach a blank luggage tag (with your logo, of course) to each bag and ask attendees to put their name on it or insert a business card (or preprint attendee names on luggage tags for that special touch). All the bags look alike, and some are invariably lost because they cannot be identified. What a useful gift!

Awards and Special Recognition

There are several occasions when special gifts are needed. Recipients of awards, speakers, sponsors, VIPs, and committee and conference chairs all fall into this category. Again, there is a large selection of special, elegant, and classy gifts. Base your selection on your audience:

- ◆ Awards (plaques, trophies, statues, etc.)
- ◆ Books (about the venue, topic, etc.)
- ◆ Bookmarks
- ◆ Business card holders

- ◆ Clocks

- ◆ Crystal (boxes, bowls, vases, etc.)

- ◆ Desk sets (pens, notepads, calculators, etc.)

- ◆ Donation to a speaker's charity or local organization

- ◆ Frames

- ◆ Key chains

- ◆ Lapel pins

- ◆ Laser pointers

- ◆ Letter openers

- ◆ Paperweights

- ◆ Pen and pencil sets

- ◆ Watches

The list is endless, and it's a lot of fun browsing catalogs and websites to imagine the possibilities. Because some of these items are more expensive and are for special recipients, the challenge is to select items that people will like, use, and enjoy. After all, as a recognition piece, you will want the gifts to elicit good memories.

Also consider handing out gift certificates so the recipients can select their own gifts. You can choose a bookstore or a national department store. Another nice gift is a certificate for dinner at a nice restaurant where the recipient lives. This takes more time to arrange, but it makes the gift more special. Doesn't everyone love to eat?

> **The Inside Scoop**
>
> Did you know that many well-known companies have a corporate sales or business gifts department? If you're looking for something extra special, check out Tiffany (www.tiffany.com), Nambe (www.nambe.com), and Lands' End (www.landsend.com) for starters.

In this world of over-consumption, more of those who are to receive awards or other recognition prefer that a donation be made in their name to a cause affiliated with the group or the individual. Consider doing so and announcing it with a tasteful handwritten card to the recipient.

Be sure to take into consideration how the recipient will get the gift home. Make it small enough to carry in the person's luggage or make arrangements to have it shipped to a home or office. The recipient will appreciate it.

Giveaways and Amenities

Giveaways and amenities are any "gift-like" items given to attendees at a meeting, usually for promotional purposes. Everyone likes free stuff, and it's a nice touch to be able to provide your attendees with well-selected mementos. In some circumstances, you or the meeting sponsor will want to provide your attendees with special treats every day.

So what do you give and when do you give it? Here are some suggestions.

At the Meeting

The most obvious place to give stuff away is in the registration packets or bags, but you may want to spread it out and give your attendees little surprises throughout the meeting. Meals, especially sit-down lunches and dinners, are an opportunity to place gifts at a table. Remember to keep it small. You also can place your gifts on chairs at the general session, such as a book written by the speaker. This works especially well if the gift ties in with the theme of presentation.

If you have little giveaways that don't have to be given specifically to each attendee, placing them at registration, computer banks, lounges, or breaks works well. Items in this category include pens, pencils, key chains, bottled water with the meeting logo, candies, notepads, rulers, and so on.

Food for Thought

Amenities that fit the theme of the meeting location make an impact: coffee in Seattle, macadamia nuts in Hawaii, Wisconsin cheese in Milwaukee. You get the idea.

Amenities in the Guest Room

What a nice surprise. You come back to your hotel room from a long day; you're tired, your mind is mush, and what do you see? A gift, maybe even personally addressed to you, from a meeting sponsor or perhaps the hotel (negotiate VIP amenities and delivery charges into your contract). These types of amenities are placed in your attendees' rooms by the hotel at your request and usually for a fee. These amenities can be larger (a bottle of wine, a gift basket) because the attendees won't need to carry it all day in their nifty tote bags. Room amenities are usually reserved for keynote speakers, committee members, and other VIPs, but if you have the funds or generous sponsors, room amenities for all of your attendees are a nice touch.

Because amenities are delivered to the rooms, you can work with the hotel to provide creative deserts, milk and cookies, fruit and cheese, or whatever flips their switch. Whatever you come up with, your attendee will feel special.

The Selection Is Endless

It's not possible to list all the choices for gifts and amenities. Start with all the items listed earlier in the "Awards and Special Recognition" section and add the following:

- Apparel (caps, shirts, jackets)
- Attachés and briefcases
- Backpacks, bags, fanny packs, totes
- Binders and portfolios
- Bottled water with meeting or sponsor logo
- Calendars and clipboards
- Candy and chocolates
- Clips and pins
- Computer accessories (cases, CD/disk holders, mouse pads)
- Cups, glasses, mugs, and sports bottles
- Donations, noted with an announcement card
- Electronics (calculators, cameras, radios)
- First-aid and travel kits
- Food and beverage (the list is endless)
- Golf, golf, and more golf stuff
- Luggage and travel items
- Music (CDs and tapes)
- Pocket/purse accessories (key chains, business card holders)
- Sports products
- Tools and knives

◆ Toys, puzzles, and games

◆ Writing utensils

Yes, there are companies that sell all of this and much, much more—just for your meeting or event. You can get some great ideas for your own meeting or event by attending a few tradeshows. Exhibitors are experts at putting logos, whether engraved, imprinted, or embroidered, on just about anything.

Trinkets at the Tradeshow

Tradeshows are notorious for giving away lots of stuff. They're mostly small, trinket-type items, but you can find some really neat things. In Miami, one resourceful fellow walked out of a tradeshow with a pair of giveaway flip-flops and a pair of swimming trunks—he went right to the beach. You can bet he thought those items were quite useful.

At tradeshows, the exhibitors want to get and keep your attention, so naturally they entice you with cookies, candy, and a variety of interesting freebies—all with their name on it. Here is where you can pick up notepads, refrigerator magnets, letter openers, lip gloss, luggage tags, yo-yos, flashing buttons, bottled water with a logo, and scads of pens (and pins).

"Logo It"

Everything we've talked about can have a logo or other important info imprinted, engraved, or embroidered on it. After all, the freebies really aren't free. Someone—a sponsor, the host, or the attendee—pays for it one way or another.

When deciding on what to put on your giveaways, keep it simple. Your logo, phone number, website, or a pertinent catch phrase is really all you need. If you have a meeting theme, try to select an item that ties into your theme.

Logos are powerful, especially to sponsors. Pay special attention to their instructions for logo reproduction—color, proportion, size, and placement can be critical. Otherwise, you may end up with an upset sponsor or have to redo the job.

Everything Under the Sun

There are many items that you need to plan, manage, and produce for your meetings. Here is yet another list of meeting-related stuff:

◆ Badge carrying cases

◆ Ballot, evaluation, and comment boxes

◆ Bells

◆ Buttons

◆ Carts

◆ Certificates

◆ Directional arrows

◆ Display stands

◆ Easels

◆ Gavels

◆ ID bracelets

◆ Laser pointers

◆ Literature holders

◆ Raffle drums

◆ Registration envelopes

◆ Shipping boxes

◆ Shipping cases (hard)

◆ Signage holders and carrying cases

◆ Signage pedestals

◆ Stock roll tickets

◆ Ticket-tag bracelets

◆ Timers

◆ Walkie-talkies or radios

Where do you go to find this "stuff"? Check out the following companies—you'll be amazed at what they offer:

- 4imprint (www.4imprint.com)

- Awards.com (www.awards.com)

- Branders (www.branders.com)

- Marco (www.marcomeetings.com)

- *pc/nametag* (www.pcnametag.com)

A word of caution: It's fun to look at all the stuff, but before you know it, your bill can get out of control. It is best to have a list and a realistic idea of your budget before you shop.

The Least You Need to Know

- Make name badges stand out. Use large, easy-to-read fonts, such as Impact, and themed designs to give them a professional, coordinated look.

- Don't give out all your giveaways at registration. Surprise and treat your attendees throughout the meeting.

- An enormous selection of items can be printed with a logo and given as give-aways.

- Look beyond the office-supply companies. There are companies that specialize in providing meeting and event-related supplies.

Yakety-Yak: Working with Speakers

In This Chapter

◆ Find the right speakers for your program

◆ Learn about options for finding the right speakers

◆ Find out what to include in speaker contracts

◆ Know how to prepare your speakers for your audience

Selecting the right speaker or speakers for your meeting or event is a crucial step in the planning process. Do you hire a professional keynote speaker or entice an expert from within your industry? We've all heard horror stories about keynote speakers who have missed the mark in front of hundreds or thousands of people. There are also "subject matter experts" (SMEs) who know their stuff, but can't quite deliver it well. Can this happen to you? Sure it can. It happens for various reasons, but here are some of the common ones: 1) The speaker and audience were not properly matched; 2) the planner did not prepare the speaker about the organization, meeting goals and objectives, and/or audience profile; 3) the planner assumed that "expensive" means high quality; and 4) the SME wasn't trained to deliver the goods.

This chapter explains the ins and outs of selecting a speaker. Don't assume that just because you have a signed contract with a pro, come 8:00 Monday morning your speaker will be in the ballroom ready to go. What happens if his or her flight is cancelled or delayed? What happens if he or she oversleeps? What happens if his or her laptop is not compatible with the projector? Not to worry. We are here to clue you in on how to reduce the potential for a speaker disaster.

Setting the Stage for Excellence

First, review your meeting agenda and your goals and objectives (we warned you—goals and objectives play an important role all the way through this process). Where do you begin? There are five important steps:

1. Determine potential topics based on agenda, goals, objectives, and audience profile.

2. Determine how many speakers you need (including keynotes) and whether they will be professional speakers, industry experts (SMEs), or others.

3. Determine the nature of the presentations and whether they will be motivational, technical, educational, or entertaining.

4. Know your budget and audience.

5. Keep a list of recommended speakers.

By now you should have decided on the number of general sessions, breakouts, and general topics. If any changes are necessary to your agenda, the time to do it is now, before you hire and contract with speakers.

You also need to track speaker information in your database or by using meeting-management software. Contact information (including an assistant's name or the contact at a speakers bureau), audio-visual requirements, special requests and quirks, session title, and general description should be available in a report format.

For large conferences, breakout session tracks are generally offered. Tracks can be geared to the level of the audience (beginner, intermediate, or advanced) or to job position such as CEO, middle management, and administrative support roles. In your onsite program, consider color coding or assigning

Food for Thought

The right opening keynote speaker sets the tone for your entire meeting. Make sure the presentation is tied to your goals and objectives to get the audience on track from the start.

a symbol to each to clearly designate the different tracks. Let your speakers know your expectations for the level of their presentation, so they can properly prepare.

Where Do You Find Speakers?

Speakers are everywhere, including at the meetings you attend and advertised in trade magazines and newspapers. They are even found among the business professionals you meet and work with. No matter what type of speaker you are looking for, here are some of the best places to look for recommendations:

- ◆ Convention and visitors bureaus

- ◆ National Speakers Association (NSA)

- ◆ Your state or local speakers association

- ◆ Referrals

- ◆ Business or other publications

- ◆ Book publishers

- ◆ Speakers bureaus

- ◆ Meetings Industry websites

- ◆ Within your (the planner's) own industry

If you know what you want with regard to the meeting's topic and audience's experience level, finding a speaker is not difficult. Frequently, we see planners looking for someone who can produce a certain result, but they have no clue where to find one who can provide it. If you are looking for a professional speaker, we suggest the National Speakers Association (NSA). This group can put you in touch with your local or state speakers association, to help you find speakers in your own backyard or in the location of the meeting (which may eliminate or reduce speaker travel costs). NSA has a home page dedicated specifically to meeting planners; contact them at www.nsaspeaker.org.

Another easy way to find a professional speaker is through a speakers bureau. Speakers bureaus represent hundreds and even thousands of

Don't Drop the Ball

Raise your right hand and repeat after us: "I will always preview a potential keynote speaker in person, on videotape, or via a web demo, and check references before signing any contracts."

202 quality at fronts

professional speakers and act as an agent for them. Usually a bureau will charge the speaker so their fee is built into the overall fee structure, but sometimes the fee is passed on to the client.

Another organization (discussed in Chapter 1) is the International Association of Speakers Bureaus at www.iasbweb.org. This group can point you to many speakers bureaus.

Hired Guns

"Hired guns" are professional speakers who make speaking their full-time career. These days, professional speakers are generalists, specialists, or both and oftentimes (but not always) are represented by a speakers bureau.

Hired guns may be celebrities. You often hear about famous athletes who hit the speaking circuit during or after their sports careers. Just by name recognition alone, they can command some pretty high fees for their appearances. Celebrity speakers come in many flavors: CEOs, commentators, politicians, journalists, authors, writers, sports figures, and of course, entertainers and radio/TV/movie stars.

You also have the "expert" speakers. They usually have influence, are respected in their field, and have developed a niche. They may or may not be represented by a speakers bureau. The price range varies from speaker to speaker. You can cut a good deal on someone just starting out or shell out big bucks for someone in high demand.

Hiring the Hired Guns

Contracting with celebrities and experts is different than securing other types of speakers. Professional speakers will most likely require you to sign their contract. They also often have a list of extra needs. They may ask for the following:

> **The Inside Scoop**
>
> On a tight budget? Ask speakers if there is anything you can do to reduce their fees. Sometimes being flexible on travel schedules or dates allows them to piggy-back the trip with another speaking engagement or a personal vacation.

- First-class airfare
- First-class airfare for an assistant
- Limos
- Suites
- Special amenities in their room (gourmet food, bottled water, flowers, etc.)

Effective Speaker Contracts

Here are the most important items to address in speaker contracts:

◆ Day, date, and start/stop times of the presentation; location of presentation; special requests to arrive early or stay after the presentation to interact participants.

◆ The topic and any customization required.

◆ Q&A throughout the presentation (if any) and book signings if appropriate.

◆ Breakout sessions and additional costs (if any).

◆ Approval for video- or audiotaping of the program. If yes, have the speaker sign a release.

◆ A short bio and photo for introduction purposes and the program.

◆ A presentation outline and learner outcomes or session objectives.

◆ Handouts (if yes, who copies them and who owns the copyright?) and deadlines for receipt of originals with permission to reproduce them.

◆ A statement that ascertains the material (verbal or written) is the speaker's own work.

◆ Reimbursable expenses and caps on expenses, if any.

◆ Travel arrangements.

◆ Travel requirements (first-class airplane ticket?).

◆ Audio-visual requirements and room set requests.

◆ Date the deposit (if applicable) is due.

◆ No-show, cancellation, and termination clauses.

◆ The date final payment is due.

◆ The date expense reimbursement forms and receipts are due.

Food for Thought

If possible, let speakers have input as to when their sessions are scheduled. Also, when repeating a session, don't put a speaker on the schedule as both the first and last to present.

Speaker fees are based on many things including the date, the length of presentation, the topic, demand for the speaker, and their expertise. Some speakers will donate their time because your organization is near and dear to their heart, or they simply want the exposure. Some may only present at one or two conferences during their entire career. (For more information about speakers who donate their fees, contact www.heartofamerica.org—speaking from the heart.)

Breakout Speakers and Other One-Shot Deals

There are community, business, industry, and educational leaders who make presentations to groups and work well as breakout session speakers. These people can cover a variety of topics and enhance your program.

Not only are these individuals good for breakout sessions, also consider them for facilitating sessions or roundtable discussions on their area of expertise. Attendees particularly enjoy roundtable sessions because there is more intimate interaction with the expert.

You may choose to use a professional facilitator for a breakout session that will be highly interactive and in which you want someone who can ensure all participants have input.

Call for Presentations (CFP)

Identifying and selecting your non-keynote speakers is a different ballgame. To make a monumental task do-able, it is recommended that you create a *call for presentations (CFP)*, an application to speak at a meeting or conference.

Large conferences or those with multi-tracks often distribute a CFP. This document is an opportunity for many individuals to apply to speak at your conference. It provides you, the planner, with information in a consistent format from each potential speaker, which helps you make an informed decision.

The Inside Scoop

If a speaker agrees to be audio- or videotaped, ask him or her to sign a taping release form. Have your attorney prepare this document, which should be signed in advance of the conference. Basically, a release ascertains that the material is the speaker's own work, not previously copyrighted by anyone else, and that he or she agrees to be recorded. The speaker may also waive the right to any proceeds from sales of the tapes.

A standard CFP includes the following:

- Presenter contact information (name/organization/address/phone/fax/e-mail)

- The title of the proposed session

- The session description and at least three but not more than five learner outcomes/session objectives

- Track information or perceived level of knowledge of their audience (so they can prepare accordingly)

- The presenter bio, including credentials

- Audio-visual and room setup requirements

- A question regarding audio- or videotaping of the session

- Compensation the speaker requests for presenting and expenses (travel costs, complimentary registration or registration discount, name and bio in the program, etc.)

- Due date for the proposal and to whom it should be sent

Once you have received responses to the CFP, you need to make final selection(s). Acknowledge all proposals. Send those selected letters of confirmation. Send the people who are not selected a thank-you letter for submitting their application, explain why their session was not selected, and invite them to the conference.

Once you have selected your speakers, don't discard those who were not selected. You never know when one of your speakers will cancel and you might need to go back to your "honorable mentions" for a replacement.

Most speakers who do not charge a fee for their services are people who do not speak professionally for a living or who, because of their affiliation with an organization or profession, donate their time and expertise. They very likely will not have their own speaker contract, so you will have to prepare one. We recommend you review the preceding criteria for professional speaker contracts and simplify it to fit your situation.

Instead of offering an honorarium or speaking fee for breakout speakers, offer a registration discount or complimentary registration to the conference. Many speakers who are found among your industry experts and colleagues would normally attend the meeting anyway, so this saves them money and you have the advantage of their expertise. See Appendix A for a sample breakout speaker agreement letter.

Meeting/Event Scoop Sheet

Create a meeting or event information sheet for all speakers. This document is different from a contract and should provide all the essential information about the meeting or event. This should be created a few weeks in advance of the meeting or event, when you have compiled statistical registration data about their audience. The scoop sheet should contain the following:

- ◆ Confirmation of the day/date/time of the presentation, and expected time to be at the venue.

- ◆ Audience/attendee statistics; for example, the number of males/females, a sampling of job titles, age ranges, where attendees are from, and the number of expected attendees for the session.

- ◆ A review of meeting/event goals and objectives.

- ◆ The visual and handout expectations and procedures. (Should they send to you in advance; who makes the copies and brings them to the meeting?)

- ◆ The guestroom reservation confirmation number, if applicable.

- ◆ Transportation details, if applicable.

- ◆ A meeting program if it is available, or at least a final agenda with meeting room assignments. Also include a facility floor plan and driving directions.

- ◆ Information on the speaker ready room (performers call this the "green room"), or rehearsal room.

- ◆ Instructions regarding payment of speaker fees and expense reimbursement, if applicable.

Books, Tapes, and Other Sale Items

Address issues regarding audiotaping, publication of articles, and book and tape sales in advance of the meeting. Don't wait until the speaker shows up onsite with 50 boxes of books and tapes to sell.

Recording speakers on audio- or videotape is a common practice in today's meeting world. This allows attendees to take the sessions home with them, and it also lets people who were unable to attend the meeting see or hear the sessions. You need to get prior permission to tape a speaker. Do it before the meeting. Most professional speakers do not allow taping of their sessions.

Taping and Publication Release

There are companies that provide taping services. They tape, reproduce, and sell the tapes and CDs onsite during your meeting! These items are also for sale for a few months after the meeting.

In addition, make sure you ask the facility what charges you will incur as a result of this process. Most will charge a "patch" fee, which allows the taping company to access the facility's sound system. You will also need to provide a microphone for all speakers being taped.

The breakout speaker agreement letter in Appendix A has a basic speaker taping release form. You should consult with an attorney to ensure that your form is properly customized for your organization. This is a sample only and needs approval from your attorney.

In addition, if any of the speaker's material is published in your newsletter, magazine, or other printed format, your speaker should sign an appropriate copyright release form.

Book and Tape Sales

Frequently professional speakers will want to sell their books, tapes, CDs, T-shirts … you name it. Many meeting participants appreciate buying a signed item from a speaker they've enjoyed. Any reasonable request should be considered, but think about how you and your organization can benefit from this opportunity, too. For example, agree to sell their tapes or books after the session and, to increase sales, have the speaker donate a percentage back to the organization or to a charity.

You can also buy the books or tapes in advance (negotiate a discount) and give them to every attendee. This reinforces the meeting's message because attendees get to take it home, and the item is perceived as a valuable gift.

Getting Them There and Other VIP Issues

If they are flying in, meet your keynote and VIP speakers at the airport. Whether or not a limo or car service is picking them up, consider whether a company executive, committee member, or other appropriate person should go to meet them personally.

Many times, your breakout speakers are on their own for transportation and other travel arrangements. You should offer them assistance and detailed information regarding travel to the destination and meeting site.

CAUTION

Don't Drop the Ball

Always have water (professionals often request "no ice") on stage near where the speaker will present. Usually a bottle of water and a glass are sufficient. A glass is a must because it looks unprofessional to have your speaker guzzling from a bottle! Ask your speaker what he or she prefers.

When your speakers arrive at the meeting, give them a map of the meeting facility, an onsite brochure, and the same packet you give to all attendees. Introduce them to the monitor, if any, assigned to their session, and what to do if they need assistance with the audio-visual equipment.

Always let speakers know the sequence of events as it pertains to them. Introduce them to the person who will introduce them to the audience, and let them know whether they should be seated in the front of the room or enter from backstage.

Speaker Ready Room or Green Room

Reserve a room just for your speakers to practice and review their presentations. Stock the speaker ready room with basic audio-visual equipment (you should know what they are using based on their audio-visual requests) and, if the budget allows, food and beverage. Have bottled water, soda, coffee, tea, decaf coffee, and snacks available. Performers and entertainers refer to this type of room as a "green room" and will use it not only as a dressing room and to rehearse, but to relax in during breaks. Make sure it is stocked according to their contract requirements.

Cancellations, No-Shows, and Your Backup Plan

Okay, it is inevitable at some point in your career that a speaker will be a no-show! Just what do you do if a speaker or entertainer doesn't show up? The show (or meeting) must go on! Make sure the speaker contract stipulates what arrangements will be made if they are late or don't show up as agreed upon. Always have a backup plan. If you went through a speakers bureau, they will be your first point of contact and will provide you with a backup speaker or another solution to the problem.

It's always best to consider your options *in advance*. If you were stuck onsite at the eleventh hour in a sticky situation, who could serve as a stand-in? The CEO? The association's executive director? An articulate participant? A local radio or TV personality? If the speaker runs late, would there be a way to switch the program around to have them appear later? Could you spend the time wisely with the audience in some other way? Go to your backup plan.

Another idea (if you have a few hours) is to contact the local Convention and Visitors Bureau (CVB). They might know of a local speaker you could call to ask if he or she could fill in. You won't have time to preview this person, but it may be your best and only option. Be honest with the audience, and hopefully they will understand.

You can also turn the time into a facilitated discussion among meeting participants. They will relish this additional time to compare notes and solve problems.

Monitors

Even the most seasoned meeting and event planners acknowledge they cannot be everywhere at one time. Monitors are very helpful when assigned to each breakout. These individuals will make sure that all is progressing as scheduled, and if not, should be instructed how to troubleshoot (or notify you) on the spot.

CAUTION

Don't Drop the Ball

Clarify in advance who is responsible for making copies of speaker handout materials. Always obtain a hardcopy or backup flash drive or CD of the original, just in case you need to make copies at the last minute.

Speaker Support: Handle with Care

Some speakers will inevitably arrive late or unprepared, and need last-minute copies, have a laptop that isn't working or a missing presentation, or other miscellaneous items. Most larger hotels have a business center that can handle these requests, but it will cost you some bucks. There are a few things you can do to avoid this scenario.

First, work directly with speakers in advance to assist them in preparing for the meeting. If you are responsible for supplying the handouts, request their originals well ahead of time (best via e-mail for the cleanest copy) and make photocopies at the office and a copy on a flash drive.

You will also find speakers who need to make changes to their presentation at the last minute, when the business office is closed or line is too long, and they will look to you for help. If possible, have a spare, secret laptop at registration and let them have access to it. Remember, they may be anxious or nervous, and your help will mean a lot to them.

Rehearse, Rehearse, Rehearse

Always have your general session speakers arrive early for a rehearsal. (Be sure you have blocked the space and have the AV set for rehearsals.) Start from the beginning and run through the entire program, with an audio-visual technician present, if possible. Never skimp on audio-visual requirements (more on this in Chapter 20). Leave nothing to chance, and never "wing" it. One time during a rehearsal, we realized that the second set of stairs to the stage was not there! The speaker had no easy way to access the stage. Luckily, we were in rehearsal and it was no big deal. Conduct a rehearsal as if it were the actual presentation. Leave enough time to make changes if necessary. Show time will be a breeze!

The Least You Need to Know

- ◆ Prepare your speakers in advance as to the meeting's goals and objectives and the audience profile.

- ◆ Carefully review your speakers' contracts, so there are no misunderstandings.

- ◆ Industry hot topics and networking provide valuable leads to find speakers.

- ◆ Take good care of your speakers. Focus on their needs so they can focus on imparting valuable information to your audience.

Chapter 18

Planes, Trains, and Automobiles: Working with Transportation Providers

In This Chapter

- ◆ Get your attendees to the meeting site
- ◆ Learn about the Transportation Security Administration (TSA)
- ◆ Discover the benefits of "meet and greet"
- ◆ Learn what to ask ground transportation providers
- ◆ Know what attendees who drive need to know
- ◆ Learn about "city-wide" meetings

How efficiently attendees get to your meeting and how easily they move around once they get there takes a lot of coordination. In this area, you definitely need to rely on trusted, competent, and efficient transportation providers. In some cases, as with commercial airlines, their performance is out of your hands—but you can still try to get your attendees airfare deals.

When considering the broad category of available transportation options, components can include domestic and international air, private or chartered jets, helicopters, private or public train cars, sea-going vessels and cruise ships, and private automobiles, taxi, or limousine service. However, the reality is that, for the majority of your meetings, commercial airlines will get your attendees to the city and then ground transportation providers will move your attendees locally. That's the focus of this chapter.

Getting There

In many cases (unless you are dealing with VIPs or high-visibility corporate meetings), the meeting host is not responsible for getting the attendees to the meeting site. There are, however, some important things you can do to make it easier for them. Because air travel is the primary mode of transportation, you should research the major airlines servicing the airport nearest your meeting, as well as those in neighboring cities. Sometimes smaller outlying airports provide more efficient and less expensive airfares. Convention and Visitors Bureaus (CVBs) can help with this research.

Some airlines have meetings programs in which they provide the following:

♦ Special group fares or airfare discounts

♦ Promotional support

♦ Free tickets based on volume

♦ Passenger lists (also referred as a manifest) with arrival/departure times

Each airline's meetings program has a different level of support. Negotiated discounts will vary depending on the type of fare, when the passenger books a ticket, and how many passengers are expected, in addition to other criteria. In some cases there are no group discounts available.

Airlines will ask you where your attendees are coming from, the meeting dates and location, and your passenger estimate. Usually 10 or more tickets will qualify as a group booking. However, this varies by airline.

Many airlines have a group department that handles meeting contracts. Once a contract is signed, you will be assigned a group code for publication in your meeting materials. Your attendees must reference this code to identify them as part of your group and qualify for the special fare. Make sure you let all attendees know the convention identifier code for each airline discount you have negotiated. The only way to take advantage of any discount is to use the code when booking the flight.

Most meeting attendees choose to take care of their own flights using their own resources. Besides having airline preferences, there are many websites offering discounted fares so in some cases, the group fares are not the lowest fares available.

Before They Head Out

The Transportation Security Administration (TSA) was created in 2001 in response to the terrorist attacks of September 11. At the time of this writing, TSA is part of the Department of Homeland Security and its mission is to protect the U.S. transportation system. Because getting your attendees to your meetings and events is integral to your success, it is necessary for you to be aware of important TSA requirements and updates as they occur. The TSA website (www.tsa.gov) is easy to use and is frequently updated. They have an excellent "must-read" section and many links about all avenues of transportation. Don't assume that all of your attendees know the ins and outs of the new security measures. When in doubt put relevant information in their conference materials.

Meet and Greet

Say what? *Meet and greet?* Sometimes you will want to have staff or volunteers stationed at various locations throughout the airport to "meet" your attendees upon arrival and "greet" them. This is usually done in the baggage claim areas, due to security regulations. New security regulations may not allow the number of greeters previously stationed. Check with the airport authority and TSA for more information. Greeters with banners or signs and clipboards should be equipped with cell phones, walkie-talkies, and a manifest (list of names with arrival times and flight numbers) to direct your attendees to designated ground transportation. Smiling, of course.

Meeting Speak

Meet and greet is commonly used at airports to meet special passengers and either direct them to ground transportation or take them to their final destination.

When using meet and greet for groups, the attendees may either pay for transportation to their hotel, or be directed to complimentary shuttle buses. The meet and greet is there simply to help them locate the ground transportation. You, the meeting host, pay for the meet and greet service.

Meet and greet is also frequently used for VIPs, executives, and speakers. Some companies have services where you can request a representative to greet your attendees or VIPs at the airport baggage claim, carry their baggage, escort them to their waiting car service or a taxi, and assist them at hotel check-in. In these cases, you pay the company directly and cover the transportation cost and gratuities. Providers of these services are ground transportation, limousine, and destination-management companies. The cost of these services will depend on the city or location, type of vehicle, length of time, and services required. Meet and greet makes a strong, professional impression.

Flights get delayed and things happen. Whenever possible, get a cell phone number for your VIP, executive, or speaker and give it to the meet and greet company so it can contact the passenger if he or she doesn't connect with the greeter.

Ground Transportation

In most cases, the attendees are responsible for getting and paying for their travel to the hotel or venue. At the very least, you should research local transportation options and provide this information in your meeting materials.

> ### The Inside Scoop
>
> Nothing changes more than travel schedules—either by choice or by fate. If you are responsible for coordinating travel for your attendees, be prepared for a lot of changes and wrong information. Really good transportation companies know this, too. Find one that is flexible and that works with you when things don't go as planned.

Start with the headquarters hotel and ask how they transport their guests to and from the property. They may have a dedicated shuttle service. If so, you could negotiate this in your hotel contract to have service provided free or at a reduced cost. If there is a charge, ask if they can add the cost directly to the individual's hotel bill or direct bill your organization, as appropriate. Whatever arrangements you work out with the hotel, make sure you inform the attendees in advance so they know what to expect, including whether tipping is expected or prepaid. Conference centers often provide their own transportation, at no cost or minimal cost.

If the property does not have its own airport transportation, it should have recommendations regarding local shuttle or limo services. Call these vendors and a few others, if possible, to compare costs and services.

Here are some of the questions you need to ask transportation companies:

- How long have you been in business?

- How many vehicles do you own?

- What kind of vehicles are they?

- What is their condition? Their age? When did they last pass inspection?

- What is the cost? Are there discounts for groups?

- Do children ride free or at a discount? Are child-safety seats required in vans or cars? What is the cost?

- What are your hours of operation?

- Can the drivers be contacted at all times? Are they full or part time? Do they wear uniforms? Are they employees of your company or contract workers?

- What is the company's safety record?

- What are your emergency procedures, and how are drivers trained?

- Are the drivers trained in CPR? Are they required to take drug and alcohol tests?

- Is there a contact available to you 24 hours a day? At what number?

- How many of your vehicles are nonsmoking? How many allow smokers?

- How far is it to the airport? How long does it take during peak and nonpeak traffic times?

- Do you make other stops or is this door-to-door service?

- Are reservations required? Is the service paid for in advance?

- When do return reservations need to be made?

- What is your insurance coverage?

- Are backup vehicles available for overflow or breakdowns?

- How does an individual locate the transportation?

Make sure you provide your attendees with the hours of operation of all selected ground transportation companies. You don't want attendees arriving at midnight thinking they can just hop on the shuttle. Also, it's a good idea to provide alternate transportation, including taxicab information (phone numbers and estimated costs), for people who will arrive late or get delayed. During your site inspection, find out how late transportation is available at the airport and check the condition of the cabs. And remember to give attendees information on parking costs. It can be expensive, especially in big cities. They may decide to take alternative transportation or share a ride instead.

If your meeting is one in which the meeting host pays for all of the attendees' travel costs, such as for a corporate or incentive meeting, you still need to do the same research and ask the same questions. The difference is that you are contracting directly with transportation providers, so you can expect dedicated, even customized service to meet your needs.

Also influencing your transportation decisions are circumstances beyond your control, such as labor strikes, weather, traffic jams, road construction, and traffic accidents. Therefore when making decisions about transportation, prepare for these occurrences. They impact your choices of transportation and the vendors, or even your choice of cities.

Food for Thought

Provide distance information in both English and metric units for the benefit of your foreign attendees. Go to www. onlineconversion.com for online calculators!

Remember that you are researching ground transportation companies on behalf of your attendees, and it's important to check out the company's reputation. You don't want your attendees riding in dirty, run-down vehicles or being driven by rude drivers—what a horrible first impression of your meeting. Ask around or use the companies yourself, so you know.

Driving Directions

Some attendees will decide to rent a car at the airport or drive from their home. You will need to obtain and provide complete, accurate driving directions to the property and parking information.

You need to consider from which direction people will be coming and also provide directions from (and returning to) the airport. You can easily get this information from the hotel or meeting venue. They will most likely have prewritten directions and maps available. Many properties will have this information on their website. Simply provide a link from your website to theirs!

If possible, make sure the directions have road numbers/names and ramp exit numbers. Add how many miles from point A to point B and estimate driving times. This is very helpful, especially to people who are unfamiliar with the area. A great place to get point-to-point directions is www.mapquest.com.

As your meeting/event date approaches, research potential driving obstacles such as road closures, construction, or weather-related problems like snow or ice. The concierge, bell captain, or local Convention and Visitors Bureau (CVB) will know about these obstacles. You can inform attendees via your website or do an e-mail blast. It can save them considerable time and, most importantly, prevent frustration.

Moving the Masses

Okay, everyone has arrived. They are happily attending sessions, eating great food, and networking away, but now you want to take them to an offsite location. You need to hire motor coaches. Where do you start?

Know the answers to the following questions, because any motor coach or ground transportation company will ask:

- How far away (and where) is the offsite location?
- When do they need to arrive/depart that venue?
- How many people are being transported?
- Is it a single trip or a continuous loop?
- Is there nearby parking for the vehicle? Where can buses be staged at the pickup and drop-off locations?
- When should the vehicles arrive for pickup?
- Where (specific location) will the vehicles pick up and drop off passengers at both ends?
- Do they all need to arrive/depart at the same time?
- Are they all nonsmoking?
- Do the vehicles have restrooms? Public address (PA) systems?

Don't Drop the Ball

Chartering motor coaches for tours or offsite events can be expensive. Don't guess. Be sure to factor their costs into your budget.

You will also need to ask the same questions about operations procedures and drivers that you asked the ground transportation companies earlier in this chapter.

Motor coaches and buses come in a variety of sizes (maximum number of passenger seats or "pax"). Most have luggage storage and restrooms, public address systems, and air-conditioning; many have TVs and VCRs. Because demand is high and gas and maintenance costs continue to increase, don't be surprised to find a four- or five-hour minimum rental or fuel surcharge. They will ask you to sign a contract and make a deposit. Read it carefully and make sure you understand it, especially the liability issues.

You can also rent school buses for some events. These are cheaper but are limited in availability during school hours. Sometimes a school bus is the perfect way to transport your attendees! Make sure you request newer vehicles only; school buses can experience a lot of wear and tear. If you do rent school buses, know your audience and ensure these will be appropriate for their transportation.

Here are some other things to consider:

◆ Can attendees leave belongings securely on the motor coach?

◆ Will the motor coaches be accessible but secured during the event?

◆ Will you feed the drivers or are they on their own?

◆ Will you or the company provide signage for the vehicle?

◆ Will you or the company provide detailed driving directions?

◆ Will you need a guide? Will you or the company provide the guide?

◆ What is expected in terms of tipping the driver?

You may have a situation in which you need to transport attendees to different locations simultaneously, such as for site tours. Pay special attention to directing people to the right motor coach (consider using tickets or tour hosts), and once people are on the bus, reconfirm the destination. Also give the drivers accurate directions and depart promptly. Keep in touch with drivers via radios and cell phones. Unless you are renting one motor coach, you will have several drivers. Get the cell phone number for each driver (not only the transportation company) in advance.

It is a good idea to verify that the driver knows the right directions. Be prepared to provide another copy of the map and directions, and review any detours or route changes.

Try to provide your own signage for each motor coach. You then have control over size, color, spelling, and readability. Prepare easily recognizable signs (consider adding your logo or a strong color theme) for inside the motor coach, as well as at the pick-up and drop-off locations.

City-Wides

A *city-wide* refers to a meeting that is so large it cannot be contained in one or even two hotels. City-wides usually use convention centers for the meeting venue, and attendees stay at multiple hotels throughout the city, sometimes extending into neighboring communities. The challenge is to provide transportation for your attendees throughout the meeting so that they can get from their hotels to the convention center or other venues and back, quickly and easily.

Meeting Speak

City-wide meetings are large meetings that cannot be hosted at a single hotel venue. Attendees stay in hotels throughout the city and surrounding communities and usually meet at a convention center or other large venue.

For city-wides, motor coaches will need to run on a continuous loop schedule. Usage will usually be heaviest in the morning before your meeting begins and when your meeting is over each day. You may even decide not to run them in the middle of the meeting when you expect passenger counts to be low.

Another way to provide continuous service is to provide it on-demand. That is, instead of running buses on a fixed schedule, always have a bus at each hotel and at the convention center or other venues. As it gets reasonably full, it can depart and another bus will take its place. This may not save you any money, but it will decrease the number of almost-empty buses traveling the city streets. Ask the company providing the motor coaches to help you with a schedule and to assist in determining how many coaches you need. They know their business best!

The Least You Need to Know

◆ Although the meeting host is not responsible for getting attendees to the meeting site, there are some important things you can do to make it easier for them.

◆ Stay aware of important TSA requirements and updates by checking their website frequently.

◆ Meet and greet makes a nice first impression and makes it easier for attendees and VIPs to get to their hotels.

◆ Prior to the meeting, provide attendees with accurate information for all ground transportation options.

◆ In your ground transportation plans, factor in alternative solutions in case of bad weather, traffic jams, road construction, or traffic accidents.

19

Food and Beverage Management

In This Chapter

- ◆ Test your knowledge of food and beverage (F&B) planning
- ◆ Learn some basic rules to apply to any meeting or event meal-planning process
- ◆ Discover food and beverage tricks of the trade
- ◆ Understand banquet event orders (BEOs)

There are a lot of things to know about food and beverage (F&B) planning. Of course, the catering or food and beverage manager at the meeting facility will assist you in this process. However, it helps to have a basic understanding so you know what questions to ask and how to get the biggest bang for your buck.

In this chapter, we will provide you with helpful hints for planning breakfasts, lunches, dinners, breaks, and receptions. You will learn some neat tricks of the trade and a bit about negotiating. Then, it's down to the paperwork, finalizing your meal plans and determining how many to guarantee. Get ready, get set, go!

Pop Quiz

Do you like to entertain? Do you think it is easy to plan meals for hundreds of people? What exactly do you need to know? Before we get started, let's take a short quiz on the subject of food and beverage planning.

1. How many (industry standard) cups of coffee are in a gallon?

    a. 20

    b. 8

    c. 13

    d. 25

2. Who pays for the beverages at a cash bar?

    a. Attendees

    b. Meeting host

    c. Meeting facility

    d. Bartender

3. Who pays for the beverages at a hosted bar?

    a. Meeting facility

    b. Meeting host

    c. Attendees

    d. Bartender

4. A guarantee is …

    a. The number of people the meeting sponsor tells the meeting facility to prepare for.

    b. The service promise from a meeting facility.

    c. The total number of people registered for your meeting.

    d. A promise from the chef that the food will be good.

5. At most facilities, how many additional people will the facility prepare to serve over your guarantee?

    a. 10 to 15 percent more than the guarantee

    b. 0 to 5 percent more than the guarantee

    c. 8 percent more than the guarantee

    d. 15 to 20 percent more than the guarantee

6. How are you billed for a meal function?

    a. The number you guaranteed

    b. Your guarantee or actual served—whatever is greater

    c. Your guarantee or actual served—whatever is less

    d. The total registered for your meeting

7. A buffet is usually more expensive on a per-person basis than a plated meal.

    a. True

    b. False

8. On average, how many bartenders should be scheduled for a reception?

    a. 1 bartender for every 75 to 100 people

    b. 1 bartender for every 25 to 50 people

    c. 1 bartender for every 150 to 175 people

    d. 1 bartender for every 125 to 150 people

9. "On consumption" for bottled beverages or packaged foods means …

    a. You pay for only what you open.

    b. You pay for what you order.

    c. You pay for what was opened plus 10 percent.

    d. You must consume all the food and beverage you order.

10. On average, how many servers should be scheduled for a plated meal function?

    a. 1 server for every 20 to 25 people

    b. 1 server for every 15 to 20 people

    c. 1 server for every 25 to 30 people

    d. 1 server for every 10 to 15 people

Answers:

1. a, 2. a, 3. b, 4. a, 5. b, 6. b, 7. a, 8. a, 9. a, 10. a

If you answered …

8 to 10 correct: Congratulations! You are ahead of the game!

5 to 7 correct: Read this chapter twice.

4 or fewer correct: Read this chapter three times.

0 correct: Hire a professional meeting planner.

A Few Rules to Get You Started

See what we mean? Planning, serving, and managing meals for the multitudes can be a real eye-opening experience. It is very different from personal gatherings, large or small. Let's start with some guidelines about this process:

◆ **You don't have to order off the menu.** Ask the catering manager to ask the chef for other ideas (in particular, what is in season, and what would be his/her preference) and make special requests when needed.

Don't Drop the Ball

Evaluate whether to order by quantity or per person. Quantity means specifying exact quantities of food versus per-person packages. Often it is less expensive to order your morning coffee and continental breakfast foods by the gallon and dozen.

◆ **Plan for the taste of the majority, not yourself.** Consider your audience. Age, nationality, religion, and special meal circumstances are considerations in your F&B selections. Just because *you* don't like mushroom-stuffed chicken breasts and tiramisu doesn't mean you shouldn't serve it.

◆ **Always order "on consumption" when possible.** If you order 350 sodas for the morning break and only use (consume) 325, then you only pay for 325. If you don't do this, some facilities will charge you for 350. They may then resell the other 25 cans to another group or maybe back to you! This applies to bottled beverages and prepackaged food items such as granola bars and bags of chips. Ask that wait staff consult with you before replenishing quantities beyond what you guaranteed.

♦ **Commit to high-quality, healthy food.** Ask the facility what food items are in season and how to keep the menus healthy.

♦ **For large, important meal functions, do a tasting.** Most facilities will allow you to taste the potential meal selections in advance. If you can't decide between two or three dishes, ask for a tasting. Be aware though that a meal prepared for 4 or 5 for a tasting may not be the same as one prepared for 350.

♦ **Understand the food and beverage policies.** Most facilities will charge you a fee to bring in your own food and beverage or will flat out disallow it. Obviously, they are in business to sell you these items and have to guard against their liability and your participants getting sick. Ask if there is there anything you are allowed to bring in and what the corkage charges are to do so. Sometimes organizations will put their logo on prepackaged food and beverages (such as bottled water) and will want to distribute these items to attendees. Try to negotiate this if possible. It can amount to considerable savings.

♦ **Use leftover food not purchased on consumption for the next break.** Items like breakfast breads can be "retrayed" and put out at the mid-morning break. You also could have them delivered to the staff office or donated to a local shelter or food kitchen if you have pre-arranged this with the hotel and contracted a "good Samaritan" clause.

♦ **Ask how many servers and bartenders will be assigned to your functions.** Service levels vary at every facility and knowing how many dedicated servers and bartenders you have will give you an indication of what to expect from the facility. If you require more servers per table than allotted, ask the facility to add more. It may cost a bit but it may be what makes the event special.

♦ **Carefully consider the appropriate type of service for a meal.** Need a quick lunch? Maybe a box lunch is the answer. What people to mingle? Try a buffet. Use a variety of service methods. If you have a buffet, use double-sided buffets whenever possible and have at least one double-sided buffet line for every 75 to 100 people. Contrary to popular misconception, sit-down (plated) meals often provide faster, more economical service than buffets.

◆ **Use decorative props and themes for breaks and meals.** Ask the hotel what props, centerpieces, and decorations it has in inventory. Try to negotiate them into your facility contract at no charge. You can also rent props from companies specializing in themed events. Local DMCs, CVBs, and your facility contact can provide the resources.

Before we take a look at all the various meal functions, you need to know that all meeting facilities have banquet menus available to you for planning purposes. You will have the option of selecting plated meals, buffets, break packages, and *à la carte* items. These are either sold at a per-person price, by the dozen, gallon, or piece. If you order on a per-person basis, the facility is responsible for providing enough food to feed your guaranteed number. If you order in quantity (by the gallon, dozen, or piece), the facility is only responsible for the amount you order. The pressure is on you to order the right amount of food. All prices are then subject to applicable service charge/gratuity and taxes. Find out the tax and service charge/gratuity percentages and factor them into your budget. If service charges are added, they are most likely taxable, which can significantly add to your bottom line. On average, they are 20 to 30 percent of the total food and beverage bill.

Meeting Speak

The term **à la carte** means each item is priced and sold individually on the menu.

At conference centers, you pay a per-person price called a complete meeting package or CMP (not to be confused, of course, with the meetings industry certification of CMP or "certified meeting professional"). This price includes a person's guest room, three meals a day, continuous refreshment breaks (allowing you not to have to guess how much to order), basic A/V equipment, and other items associated with a meeting. Having a meeting at a conference center takes the guess work out of food and beverage planning and provides meetings with added advantages: sessions can break when it's a natural breaking point and participants can eat when they are hungry. Check out www.iacconline.org to learn about other benefits of using conference centers.

You should always obtain a copy of the menus when you begin the site selection process so you can take a look at the prices, creativity, and food options. Along with the menus, many facilities have catering policies and a general information sheet. These will explain the specific food and beverage policies at that facility. These might include when your menu selections and guarantees are due, table linen choices, floral arrangements, ice carvings, coat checks, extra labor charges, liquor liability issues, liability statements, and so on.

Finally, when you book a meeting at a facility, try to negotiate firm menu prices. Most facilities will guarantee food and beverage prices six to nine months in advance of the functions. You can ask them to guarantee current menu prices at the time of booking or at least get a firm date on when your prices are guaranteed. In some cases, you can negotiate for a 10 percent, 15 percent, or greater discount on menu prices.

Breakfast

Breakfast is important. Your attendees are hungry in the morning and, at the very least, will be looking for coffee, tea, juice, or soft drinks. It depends on the location and attendee profile, but as a general rule, order 65 percent hot and 35 percent cold beverages in the morning. The reverse is true in the afternoon. For coffee, the rule of thumb is 70 percent regular and 30 percent decaffeinated. Offer hot tea, too. And be sure to have regular, diet, and caffeine-free sodas.

For breakfast, you have several choices. From the catering menu, you can order a sit-down, plated meal; a full breakfast buffet; or a continental breakfast. Your agenda, your budget, and your audience determine which you select. An awards breakfast is the perfect candidate for a sit-down, plated breakfast (and will very likely cost less than an awards banquet). A full breakfast buffet presents more food options and covers a wide variety of tastes. A continental breakfast is good when you are not presenting a program, and the attendees will be arriving at various times.

> **Food for Thought**
>
> Offer fresh fruit for breakfast. A lot of less expensive continental breakfasts do not include it. Usually there is an additional per-person charge to add it, but most people will appreciate it. Whole fruit (on-consumption) is better than sliced as people can take it with them.

Another option is to create your own breakfast buffet. Take a look at the à la carte prices. Does it make sense to start with the less expensive continental breakfast and add yogurt, fruit, and French toast? Or would it be more economical to order in quantity: breakfast breads by the dozen, fruit by the platter or person, whole fruit by the piece, and beverages by the gallon? Then you could add an omelet bar (fresh omelets cooked to order). Determine what you want and play with the menus. Ask the catering manager for recommendations on how to package your desired result.

Breaks

Breaks can be a source of motivation and fun for your attendees. Some meeting facilities have created some really creative break ideas. Obviously, it depends on your budget (breaks can get pricey!), but no matter how much you can spend, try to be creative. Tie in your meeting theme or a theme that relates to the location, the season, or a regional sports team. Offer a combination of sweet, salty, and nutritious to please everyone. Or mix your offerings up over several days. Here are some ideas to ponder:

- Ice cream bars (if the facility has the capability to keep them frozen during the break)—they always bring out a smile!

- Popcorn served from a popcorn cart

- Fruit smoothies (yummy!)

- Small bags of trail mix/sunflower seeds

- Candy bars

- Whole fruit

- Granola bars

- Pizza

- A sports theme (for example, popcorn, peanuts, and caramel corn)

- Meats and cheeses for those on low-carb diets

You'll want to offer a variety of beverages in addition to food items. The standard coffee, tea, and soft drinks are fine, but also consider fresh lemonade, specialty coffees, fruit punch, or other specialty beverages. Offering items other than the standard fare adds variety and is a refreshing change for attendees. You may also request smaller items such as mini muffins, mini bagels, and other miniature items to reduce waste. Don't be afraid to ask the hotel to create special breaks just for your group, or to alter the location to liven things up. Can you have the break outside on a terrace or poolside?

Lunch

No matter what meals you are planning, take a look at all of them together to make sure you are using a variety of serving methods and the same food is not served twice. Lunch is a great opportunity to take a trip off the beaten path.

Offer a box lunch, serve pizza, give people an hour or more off on their own, or serve lunch in a section of the restaurant or another non-meeting room location. If you give them a lunchtime break on their own, offer suggestions for where to get lunch and make sure there are a variety of options nearby. See if the hotel will offer your attendees a discount if they eat in one of the onsite restaurants. (Do let the hotel know if there is likely to be a rush in their restaurants at lunchtime, so they can have additional staff on hand to keep service at its best.) Most hotels will comply and appreciate your effort to keep them in the facility.

> **The Inside Scoop**
>
> A conference we help plan for 1,000 people offers two options for lunch: a box lunch in the exhibit hall or a deli buffet in a roundtable discussion format. Attendees can purchase tickets for either, and both options are very popular!

Dinner

Dinner can be very extravagant or very simple. The goals, objectives, theme, time-frame, and purpose for the dinner will set the tone. It can be as simple as a backyard, poolside BBQ or as elaborate as a steak and lobster plated dinner with wine service. Before you decide, look at the menus. If there is something you want but don't see, talk to the chef.

For special dinners, consider decorating the room. Centerpieces, chair covers, special table linens, and props can make the difference between a plain setting and a memorable dining experience. Ensure centerpieces are low enough to allow all participants to converse with each other.

Consider ending your dinners with gourmet coffee stations. This is a great way to end the evening, and it fosters networking as people move about the room. Along with this, instead of serving dessert at the table after dinner, offer sweets tables near the coffee stations. Have a small assortment of desserts and chocolates available to satisfy everyone's sweet tooth. Attendees love this one! (Don't forget to accommodate your noncoffee drinkers with gourmet teas or hot chocolates!)

Receptions

Receptions are great because attendees can relax and get to know one another better, or receptions can *be* dinner. If you hold a reception in a famous museum, you may want the attendees to mingle about at various food stations, which will allow them to network the entire evening and experience the culture of the venue.

Ordering food and beverage in the right quantities for a reception depends on the time of day or evening that it starts, how long it goes on, and, of course, the number of guests invited. Work closely with the catering manager to make sure you have the right amount and an interesting variety of items on the menu.

Your reception menu is also determined by your budget, and whether it is followed by dinner. When the reception is the dinner, serve heavy hot hors d'oeuvres. Items to consider: pasta bars, mashed potato bars with all the toppings, and carving stations. A carving station features a chef slicing some sort of meat such as beef, ham, or turkey with rolls and condiments available. These types of items fill people up, and you look like you're going all out. Top it off with a variety of cold hors d'oeuvres including fruit and cheese.

Receptions held right before dinner should have a lighter menu. As a general rule of thumb, six to eight pieces of food (hors d'oeuvres) per person per hour are adequate. If you offer a heartier option such as a carving station or a pasta bar, you can get by with fewer pieces per person. Passed hors d'oeuvres (served on a tray carried by wait staff wearing white gloves) usually will stretch your budget a little further, as people tend to take less than they would at a buffet. It adds a classy touch as well.

If you order on a per-person basis, your guarantee will dictate the amount of food prepared. The facility is then responsible for making sure there is enough food. A per-person price will be for an agreed upon timeframe (for example, 1, 2, or 3 hours). If you order by quantity, the facility prepares only the specific amount of food you requested, so order carefully or you may run out.

You will have several options for the bar setup. The number one question is who pays for the drinks. The options are as follows:

- **Hosted bar.** The meeting sponsor pays for the drinks, either by the drink, per person per hour, or per bottle.

- **Cash bar.** Attendees pay for their own drinks.

- **Cash bar with tickets.** Attendees get a specified number of free drink tickets (paid for by the meeting host), and then pay cash for additional drinks. You determine how many free tickets.

Food for Thought

When you have a cash bar, you should also provide complimentary soft drinks, juices, and bottled water. It is a nice gesture for those who choose not to drink alcoholic beverages, and it can decrease your organization's liquor liability.

The most common way to pay for beverages at a hosted bar is per person per hour or by the drink.

You will designate either house, name, or premium brands and the attendees can order from that selection. Have soft drinks, water, and juices available, too. For bottle sales, make sure you obtain the beginning and ending inventory, which will tell you the precise brands and amount consumed.

Ask for a complete report on bar sales for your food and beverage pick-up report. This is great information to have when planning future functions.

Keep in mind each state has different laws regarding the sale and distribution of alcohol. Ask about local laws and facility policies and regulations that could affect your functions. Each state is different so be sure to discuss this with your catering manager during the planning phase.

Liquor Liability

At some point you will plan a reception or meal function where alcohol will be served. Your liability, should a guest or an attendee become intoxicated, is significant. Make no assumptions. Just because you are having a function in a hotel or with a caterer, don't assume that they are experienced, trained, or insured. Of course, they should be all of those things, but because liability is such an important and potentially costly issue, you can't leave anything to chance.

Here are some tips to help keep your social events fun and safe:

♦ Make sure that the vendors dispensing alcoholic beverages are licensed and insured and are compliant with state and local regulations.

♦ Consider purchasing or adding a liquor liability rider to your general liability coverage. Again, don't assume that your existing policy covers serving alcohol at your meetings and events.

♦ Do not purchase and serve alcohol yourself, even for a few people. Leave it up to the vendors who have the licenses.

♦ Don't offer a self-serve bar. Instead use trained bartenders.

♦ To reduce the amount people drink, consider using drink tickets. Each guest gets a predetermined number of tickets. Most people won't want to fork over cash for a drink, especially if the cost is high.

♦ Make sure you offer plenty of nonalcoholic beverages as well as ample food.

♦ Try to reduce the time that the bar is open. At the very least, close it well before the end of the function.

♦ Be responsible. If you suspect that someone is intoxicated, take charge and make sure that person gets settled in his or her room or back home safely.

For a cash bar, the attendee either pays the bartender directly or buys tickets from the cashier to give to the bartender. Ask about the additional cost of the bartenders and cashiers. It is standard to be quoted a flat or hourly fee for each bartender unless each bar achieves a predetermined amount of sales. This is negotiable, so ask about it. You need one bartender for every 75 to 100 people, so it is important to know what you are paying for. Cashiers are also charged on a flat or hourly fee basis. These charges often add up and can be a surprise on the master bill!

Ensure the music or entertainment at the reception or at dinner is subtle. People want to talk and hear what others are saying without shouting.

Tricks of the Trade

Planning food and beverage gets easier as you learn the ropes. Here are some tricks of the trade to give you a boost:

♦ **What's best—buffet or a plated meal?** A buffet is great for networking and for offering multiple entrée options. Attendees also do not get stuck at one table the entire night with the same people. Buffets are usually more expensive because more food needs to be put out and more options are offered.

Food for Thought _____

Have the facility preset salad and dessert on the table if you are on a tight schedule. Select items that hold well until they are eaten. Desserts (such as whole cakes, precut) can be used as centerpieces.

♦ **Carefully watch your food functions.** What do the attendees like? What don't they like? What special food needs—kosher or vegetarian for example—do you need to accommodate? Do you have enough food? What works well with other groups? Ask the wait staff, bartenders, and catering manager. Write this information down for your next meeting.

♦ **Is a minimum number of people required for a specific meal or event?** If you don't qualify, ask if you can combine with another in-house group to meet the requirement.

◆ **Ask the catering manager to have all the food on a buffet labeled.** If it fits into the theme, create unique names that describe the food.

◆ **Have a special dinner or reception offsite.** Select a museum or other unique venue, and work with either the facility catering office or another catering company.

◆ **Find out if the facility has standard centerpieces available to use.** Add votive candles on mirror tiles, or some flowers to embellish them. If you use floral centerpieces, ask the florist to create them to be reused for another function. Some florists will even come back the next day to make them look different. Don't forget to ask the facility to store them overnight in the cooler. And never have them so tall that you can't see across the table.

◆ **Always use double-sided buffets or multiple stations when possible.** Ask and double-check—do not assume the facility will do this.

◆ **Guarantees are generally due to the facility 48 to 72 hours prior to each meal function; for resorts and some off-site caterers, the guarantee is sometimes due one week prior to the event.** If you aren't sure how many to guarantee, err on the low end. You can sometimes raise them and often the overset will be increase enough.

◆ **Ask the facility to place reserved table signs if needed.** Specify which tables on your diagram. (See how handy a diagram is?)

◆ **If you are using a ticket system for meals, don't assume the hotel will collect them for you.** This detail, like all others, needs to be discussed in advance. Don't wait until the hungry herd is stampeding your event!

◆ **Ask for a fancy napkin fold.** This can jazz up your table setting.

◆ **If you do not have entertainment, ask if music can be piped into the room.** Sometimes you may have to pay for a CD player, but this is much cheaper than live entertainment! Even if the music is piped in, you will need to pay for music licensing—it's about who is listening not just who is playing the music.

Banquet Event Orders

Now it is time to create the *banquet event orders* (BEOs) or *banquet prospectuses* (BPs). A BEO or BP outlines the details of all the food and beverage functions. It includes start/stop times, the number of people, room setup, the menu, (usually, but not always) audio-visual equipment, bar setups, and other things pertinent to the meals and service. This is the document the catering department uses to prepare and serve the meals. The catering manager prepares this document based on specifications you, the planner, give the facility. The planner then is required to review and sign off on the BEOs, and return the signed copies to the catering manager.

Meeting Speak

A **food and beverage minimum** is an amount you must spend for food and beverage, generally not including taxes, gratuities, or service charges. If you spend below the amount, you pay the difference between the minimum and the actual amount spent.

You may also be asked to spend a *food and beverage minimum*. Based on your total meeting specifications, you may have to agree to pay for a minimum amount of food and beverage. This is negotiable and agreed to during the contract phase; pay attention to the fine print!

Banquet event orders are not just for meal functions. Many hotels use BEOs as documents to outline all of a group's meeting functions. These are also called function sheets. They list the times, the number of people expected, room set, audio-visual equipment, and any special information. The reason for doing this is that each facility must have a single format that all staff members understand. Usually, a BEO will be prepared for each unique event, even if nothing changes except the date. That means you could easily have dozens upon dozens of BEOs or function sheets for your meeting.

Review each BEO carefully because this is the document or work order from which the facility gets its instructions. With so many different eyes looking at them, you must be sure your instructions are clearly stated. Double-check each BEO, especially as it is updated.

Guarantees

This is where knowing your group, and paying attention to other factors such as outside activities and timing, really comes in handy. A *guarantee* is the number of people you tell the meeting facility to prepare for and for which you will be expected to pay. You either pay for the guaranteed number or the number of people served, whichever is greater. You will need to provide a guarantee for every meal function, as well as how many people to set for in each room or area.

Let's say you have 200 people registered for your meeting. It is highly unlikely that all 200 people will show up for each meal, even though you may wish to set the room for 200 to be on the safe side. As a general rule, you never guarantee the exact number of registrants; you should factor in if guests are also invited and may attend. This is one of the reasons you need to track your history and know the facility's overset percentage. Your meeting history sheet should include the number of registrants, guarantees, and the actual number served for each meal. Continental breakfasts are definitely a prime candidate for subtracting some people from your attendee count. Some people will come down at the posted time to eat, and others will skip it entirely, opting to sleep in a bit longer before the meeting begins.

Giving the facility an accurate count is necessary to make sure enough food is prepared. Many facilities will prepare some percentage over your guarantee. In other words, if you guarantee 100 people, and the overset is 5 percent, they will set for and be prepared to serve 105. Note that the overset does not always guarantee that those meals will be the same as the one you ordered and guaranteed for the 100. If 120 show up, most likely there will not be enough seats or food. What happens in this case? The facility scrambles to bring in tables and chairs, and the chef prepares more food. Everyone looks disorganized and unprepared—including you. And these people will have to eat late and the food served is subject to whatever the kitchen can pull together quickly.

If you order by quantity, then the guarantee is the quantity you ordered. How do you order in quantity? You need to consider three things when ordering this way: the attendees' appetites, the weather, and the food items. Make sure you have enough beverages and food items for all attendees and know what the facility can quickly replenish if you are running low. Make sure the BEO gives specific instructions about replenishing. Does the facility need to get your approval? Make sure to ask for the catering manager's input if you order by quantity.

Service and Presentation

One detail you shouldn't overlook is the timing of a meal. Always have the facility ready to go at least 15 minutes prior to the start of a food function. If there is a program (such as an awards banquet) with speakers giving talks during or in between courses, create a script with the start and stop times of every speaker.

> **CAUTION**
>
> **Don't Drop the Ball**
>
> Don't forget to make sure the BEOs state when the doors can open for seating. You do not want your attendees entering a room where a speaker is rehearsing and the waitstaff are still setting tables.

Include the time when the servers should leave the room, if required, if they can continue to refill coffee cups or not, and when it is okay for them to finally clear tables. Include the catering manager in this part of the scripting—he or she will know how much time is needed for serving and clearing.

Have the facility prepare floor diagrams of all your meal functions. This makes it easier for the meeting facility's staff to set the room to your specifications.

Also make sure your BEO states the number of bartenders and servers assigned to your function. As a general rule, you should have one server for every 20 to 25 people for a sit-down meal, one bartender for every 75 to 100 people, one cocktail server for every 50 people, and one double-sided buffet line for every 75 to 100 people. If your sit-down meal includes wine service, 16 to 20 people per server is the norm.

Special Needs

Make sure your registration forms include a place to state specific food requirements. Some people have dietary restrictions and some want vegetarian meals. Make sure to include these meals in your guarantee. Have food labeled, on buffets when you can, to alleviate any problems. Provide brightly colored cards to these attendees for sit-down meal functions that can say "kosher meal," "vegan meal," "vegetarian meal," and so on. They can discreetly place the card on the table and wait staff can discuss their needs with them before they are served.

Be flexible and accommodating, and everyone will walk away happy.

The Least You Need to Know

- ◆ Don't automatically select the per-person meal packages. Evaluate your food and beverage order based on à la carte prices for comparison.

- ◆ You don't always have to order off the menus. Talk to the catering manager and chef.

- ◆ Consider having heavy hors d'oeuvre receptions instead of sit-down dinners. This creates a better networking atmosphere.

- ◆ Check and double-check your BEOs for accuracy before signing off.

- ◆ Carefully track your meeting history so you can fine-tune your meal guarantees.

20

Strategies for Working with Audio-Visuals

In This Chapter

◆ See what audio-visual (A/V) is really about

◆ Learn what to ask the in-house audio-visual provider

◆ Discover often overlooked audio-visual costs

◆ Explore the latest media options

◆ Learn when to hire outside audio-visual and/or production companies

Just a few years ago, audio-visual (also known as A/V) requirements for meetings and events consisted mostly of a microphone or two, an overhead projector and screen, and maybe a 35mm slide projector. As with most everything, technology advances have changed what now constitutes standard A/V equipment, and as a result we are changing the way we communicate with our attendees. Today, computer-generated slide shows are the norm, and attendees are not even wowed anymore by giant screens, live video feeds, and high-tech laser light extravaganzas. Even a simple meeting or event can be quite a show, with quite a budget!

Because A/V is complex, this chapter is not an A/V technical primer. We do not discuss all the different types of equipment, formulas, or laws of physics; that's for trained A/V professionals. Instead, we provide a basic overview of A/V rental considerations and support issues. You will soon have enough knowledge to speak intelligently with A/V professionals to make your next meeting or event A/V rental order a breeze.

What Is A/V, Anyway?

A/V is more than just equipment; it's labor, power, and a plethora of items. When preparing your budget, factor in the following costs as they apply to your program:

- Audience response monitor (ARM) systems
- Audio, CD, and video duplication
- Bulletin boards
- Carts and projection stands
- Computers, monitors, and printers
- Extension cords and cables for connecting equipment
- Fax machines
- Labor (technical support, setup, riggers)
- Lasers and laser pointers
- Lecterns and podiums (and yes, there is a difference between the two: you stand *on* the podium *at* the lectern)
- Lighting
- Microphones (and associated equipment)
- Power
- Power strips
- Radios and walkie-talkies
- Recording equipment
- Screens
- Signs or flip charts, and the easels to hold them

- ◆ Staging (pipe and drape, risers, stages, etc.)

- ◆ Video equipment (TVs, VCRs, projectors, cameras, etc.)

Most meeting and event facilities either own their own equipment or have a separate A/V equipment rental company onsite. Before finalizing a facility contract, you should obtain an A/V price list (including labor) and find answers to the following questions:

- ◆ Who provides the A/V equipment, the meeting/event facility or an onsite company?

- ◆ If an onsite company, are you required to use that company? If you don't, are there any additional "usage" fees?

- ◆ Can the onsite company provide the level of service and skilled labor to manage your general sessions?

- ◆ Can you bring in your own equipment regardless of who provides the A/V?

- ◆ What is added to each rental item? Percentages for labor, service charges, gratuity, taxes? Ask how to calculate the total (for example, are service charges taxed?).

- ◆ For larger stage productions, what are the labor fees? Is union labor required?

> ### The Inside Scoop
>
> If you need A/V labor at odd hours, weekends, or holidays, prepare to pay higher hourly rates. If possible, plan to have your setup and teardown during regular hours.

For most small meetings and simple events, you will only need limited A/V equipment such as overhead, data, or video projectors; screens; microphones; and flip charts. A large show or general session might include, for example, computerized game shows, big-screen video teleconferences over satellite links, entertainers flying on the stage from above, fireworks, smoke and mirrors, you name it. If your budget allows for some big-time fun, you'll need to work with a full-service A/V production company. We'll discuss this in a bit.

A/V equipment is usually rented by the day for a flat rental fee for each piece of equipment. The rental fee includes setup and testing. As your program gets bigger and more involved, however, you should hire dedicated technical support to monitor your A/V in one or more rooms. The A/V provider charges an hourly rate for this

Food for Thought _____

If you have a general session and multiple breakouts, consider using your general session room as one of your breakout rooms. This will save you money on A/V costs for one breakout!

and will give you an estimate of the amount of time necessary. In addition to the hourly fee, there is usually a service charge and tax. For meetings and events with a lot of A/V, labor can be a significant expense. You may also need to hire labor to set up and tear down your staging. This labor includes carpenters, electricians, and riggers. Also check into union rules and regulations at the venue. Be sure to ask if union labor is included or is in addition to your A/V quotes.

Know What You Need

Every meeting and event has a message to communicate. Meetings are an excellent educational tool, but only if they are designed and produced with the organization's goals and objectives in mind. Special events also must address goals and objectives, but may require a little more pizzazz in terms of production and staging; let the experts guide you.

When you work with an A/V provider early in the planning stages, you will accomplish two things: You increase the scope of your A/V knowledge about current technologies available to you, and you identify and include all of the associated A/V costs in your budget. By now, you probably realize that A/V can be a considerable chunk of change; however, if there is one place you don't want to cut corners it's in your A/V planning. Why would you settle for anything less than an absolutely seamless audiovisual presentation for your speakers and attendees?

If possible, walk through your meeting or event venue with the A/V provider and a representative from the venue well in advance of finalizing your program. Look at ceiling height and the location of pillars, doors, chandeliers, windows, and mirrors. Look at the in-house lighting and listen to the sound system. Discuss the room set, both in terms of style and anticipated number of attendees. Make sure any room diagrams include your stage and any other equipment that uses space.

One thing you should do to determine your A/V needs is ask your speakers and entertainers what they need. As an example, the breakout speaker form in Appendix A includes a place to indicate A/V needs. For hired speakers and entertainers, A/V requirements (particularly if extensive) should be part of the contract agreed to by both parties in advance. (You'll find more about working with speakers in Chapter 17.)

When considering concurrent breakout room assignments, determine which speakers have similar A/V needs. Try to schedule them so they speak on the same day or in the same room. Your goal is to reduce the volume of A/V equipment by consolidating speakers with like needs in one location. Be sure to reconfirm all A/V with each speaker in writing a few weeks prior to his or her presentation.

You can also determine a "standard set" for your breakout rooms. For example, on your speaker contract or form, tell your speakers that each room will have a standard set including an overhead projector, screen, laser pointer, wired lavaliere microphone, and flip chart. Your form can then ask the speakers for additional equipment needs such as LCD projectors, VCRs, 35mm slide projectors, Internet connections, and so on, if your budget allows for add-ons.

Once you have decided on A/V requirements, make sure you get a written quote for every item. Don't assume that easels, carts, extension cords, and so on, are free. If you have a lot of A/V, you should get competitive bids from outside A/V companies. You might find better rates elsewhere, and the competition might motivate the in-house A/V provider to reduce its rates.

In most cases, your best bet is to use the onsite provider because it has the inventory onsite and knows the facility well.

> **CAUTION**
>
> **Don't Drop the Ball** _____
>
> If you own some A/V equipment and are proficient in using it, consider bringing it with you. Be sure to get prior approval from the meeting facility or you may get charged a surcharge for bringing in your own equipment. Keep in mind you will be responsible for keeping tabs on your own equipment, but you will save money. The disadvantage is you do not get technical support if something doesn't work. Make sure the facility can supply you with a backup if something goes wrong; otherwise, don't do it.

The Visual Basics

Most people are visual learners, so most speakers use visual tools. These may include flip charts, data projectors, overhead projectors, screens, or VCRs and monitors.

More and more speakers are moving from the 35mm projector to data projectors. The data projector is used to display computer presentations on a screen. The major consideration here is cost. They are very expensive. The higher the projector's

Meeting Speak

Merriam-Webster's Collegiate Dictionary defines **lumen** as "a unit of luminous flux equal to the light emitted in a unit of solid angle by a uniform point source of one candle intensity." Yeah, we knew that …. Actually, the more lumens a projector has, the brighter the projector output. But how many lumens you need depends on the screen size and the brightness of ambient light in your room.

resolution and *lumens*, the higher the cost. A good place to learn everything there is to know about data projectors is www.projectorpeople.com.

Naturally, most speakers will want the best projection system, but depending on the meeting room's size and the number of attendees, you may be able to use projectors with lower resolution and intensity and spend less. When deciding on the type of LCD projector to use, consult your A/V provider. Keep in mind there is a big difference between clearly projecting images of detailed data with a lot of small text (and unfortunately some speakers come with just that!) and images containing graphics and photos. Also consider if very precise color distinctions are required. Make sure to inquire about the various projectors and what is best for your specific needs.

Whatever you decide, test all your A/V equipment under the conditions in which it will be used. Then test it again.

Screen type and size are always considerations. You want to make sure that all attendees can see the screen(s), especially from the far sides and the very back. Do you need to "fly" additional screens overhead halfway back in the room? Also consider projection image quality. It may impact the type of screen(s) you use. In some cases, meeting rooms have screens that pull down from the ceiling. If possible, set the room so they can be used instead of renting another one.

For large general sessions, you need to decide whether you are using front- or rear-screen projection. Front-screen projection means the image is projected onto a screen from the front of the screen, usually within or behind the audience. The screens can be placed in front close to the wall. This is less expensive and takes less space.

Rear-scree projection means the image is projected from behind the screen. The advantage of rear over front projection is that, with rear projection, there are no visible projectors, cords, and wires. They are all behind the screens and stage. Rear projection also tolerates a wider range of light reduction in the room. The downside is that it takes up significant space behind the stage/screen. In most cases, the screens will be placed 25 to 30 feet from the wall, unless the A/V provider has (and you can afford to rent) special lenses that don't require moving that far back. You need to drape the stage/screen, and you may require other special equipment.

The bottom line is this: rear projection looks very professional, but is usually a costlier way to go and can be a "space-hog." The decision to use front- or rear-screen projection should be made when booking the meeting because space is an important consideration. With both front- and rear-screen projection, you will incur labor fees to run the projectors, keep the speakers on track, and in general manage the flow of the show.

Other visual devices typically used in meeting rooms are VCRs and, to a lesser extent, 35mm projectors. Considerations here are the size of the room and the number of attendees. Consult with your A/V provider to determine whether you need additional screens or monitors. For committee meetings with a high number of attendees using their personal computers simultaneously, additional power may need to be dropped into the room. Remember that every itty-bitty piece of equipment costs money.

Food for Thought

Have signs made with your conference or organization logo to attach to the lectern(s) (get size specifications from the facility). This covers the facility's logo and customizes your meeting. For large general sessions, have the same logo projected up on the screen(s) before and after the sessions.

The Audio Basics

Your venue will most likely have its own in-house sound or audio system. What you want to do is patch into that system. (Often times if outside A/V companies are brought in they will incur patch fees; check this out with the facility in advance.) Although this is relatively easy to do, be aware that there are a host of sound problems that can surface. Humming, feedback, squeaking, or just plain bad sound can happen. The A/V technical staff can solve these problems, and this is a good reason to have dedicated A/V personnel.

If you have a very important session or sessions, you should consider adding an additional sound system to either supplement or replace the in-house system. Naturally, this adds to the cost, but you have more control over the quality.

Every speaker needs a microphone (mic) unless it is a very small meeting. Here are your options:

- Handheld mic (wired or wireless)
- *Lavaliere* mic (wired or wireless)
- Lectern or podium mic
- Multidirectional mic
- Standing or floor mic
- Table mic

Your selection of microphones will depend on the type of presentation, your budget, and the speakers' or entertainers' preference (always ask ahead of time). A formal presentation or performance on stage to a large audience usually dictates a microphone on a podium or the use of one or more wireless lavaliere mics. An emcee or master of ceremonies may use a wireless, handheld mic. Speakers for smaller presentations and breakouts may prefer wireless or hardwired (with long cords) lavaliere mics, especially if they need to handle slides, transparencies, or other materials. For panel discussions in which the presenters are seated at a head table, consider using one table mic for every two people.

> **Meeting Speak**
>
> A cordless or wireless **lavaliere** microphone is a small microphone that can be attached to clothing, leaving the speaker's hands free and allowing for movement throughout the room.

> **Food for Thought**
>
> Sometimes speakers choose not to use a microphone. If you are recording their sessions, remind them to use one and to repeat all audience questions and comments.

When selecting handheld or lavaliere mics, it is preferable to use wireless. The wired types (a cable leads from the mic to the sound system) are cumbersome and have a limited range due to the cable length. Naturally, the wireless mics cost more. If you don't have the budget for wireless mics for each speaker, at least provide wireless for your main speaker(s) if appropriate.

As you increase the number of mics in a room, you will need to have sound mixers. Be sure to budget for this and let the experts guide you.

Audiotaping

An option to extend the life of your meeting or event is to provide an audiotape or CD for purchase. There are companies that specialize in onsite recording and duplication. The process usually goes like this: the recording company, contracted by the meeting host, provides the labor, equipment, and supplies needed to record the desired sessions. The company then duplicates and sells the tapes or CDs to your attendees during the meeting. These companies usually rebate the client (the meeting host) a percentage of each tape or CD sold after a certain sales figure has been reached. If that sales figure is not reached, the client pays the difference between the amount sold and the minimum sales figure required by contract.

As the meeting host, you should get or ask for a complimentary copy of each session recording from the taping company. In addition, each speaker should receive a free tape or CD of his or her session. Make sure you obtain signed consent forms from each speaker prior to taping. It is important to market these items during the meeting. Make frequent announcements and make it easy for attendees to find the vendor during and after the meeting (usually via a website). Tapes and CDs should be available for at least a few weeks after the meeting.

Media Options: Satellite, Video, Audio, and Web Conferencing

Reaching an audience beyond the confines of your meeting room in real-time has become more prevalent with the advances made in video and audio technologies. Now you are able to invite team members and guests all over the world to join your meeting in person through a variety of media options—at an accompanying variety of costs. Here's a brief rundown of the popular options available, which comes to us through the tried and true expertise of JW Lampert, Executive Events in Detroit:

◆ **Satellite conferences** are like television shows: They allow audiences in remote places to view the meeting as though they were watching a news or talk show. Satellite gives you the highest degree of visual and audio clarity of any medium by utilizing satellite uplinks or fiber optic lines to send the signal. It also requires the most technical support (usually) at the highest cost of any medium. Satellite broadcasts can be sent directly to a single receiver or played on a specific television channel at any number of locations, and are usually one-way broadcasts—sender to receiver.

- **Video conferences** also allow audiences in remote locations to view the meeting, with the added capability of cost-effectively interacting with the host site both visibly and audibly. Video conferencing uses telephone or Internet technology to send video and audio signals back and forth, to and from multiple sites, allowing a true dialogue to occur at much slower speeds and with less visual clarity than satellite, but also at a lower cost.

  Satellite and video conferencing are labor- and technology-intensive. Both require video cameras, audio equipment, video production equipment, and technical staff that are not always standard in most venues. If you decide that you want your extended audience to see, hear, and interact during your meeting, you will need to consult a video production company or in-house producer far in advance of your meeting. If, however, you decide that your audience only needs to hear the meeting or see the presentation(s), you might consider one or both of the following.

- **Audio conferencing** is now available through most major telephone carriers and offers an inexpensive method of bringing the message to the masses—with the advantage of permitting audience feedback and questions. External attendees dial-in to a central number (either local or toll-free) and listen to the meeting, and can then be prompted to ask questions if desired. Audio meetings can also be "hosted" by a telephone carrier employee, freeing your staff from some of the more technical aspects of monitoring this type of meeting. Audio conferences require some technical staff and specialized equipment, but the cost is generally far less than either video or satellite.

- **Web meetings** have become very popular with the increased number of Internet-savvy attendees. Web meetings can incorporate some or all of the above media and broadcast your meeting directly over the web. Web meetings come in a variety of software options—from graphics-only packages to full-blown video, audio, graphics, chat, and survey packages. Consult an IT specialist for more information on the possibilities and associated costs. *Caution:* If your meeting contains sensitive information, such as financial data or marketing information, you may want to think twice about putting your meeting on the Internet.

Professional A/V Production

One of the biggest challenges when planning a meeting or event is how to present and produce the material for maximum impact. There are two options: produce it

in-house or hire a professional production company. How do you conceptualize your message,
package it, and deliver it? Do you have the
internal resources? Do you have the time? Most
organizations only hold a few meetings or a
single event each year and probably do not have
dedicated staff members who are experts in
presentation production. If you need to make a
strong, professional impression, consider getting bids and hiring a professional production
company.

There are many types of A/V companies with
different levels of sophistication. For some,
their primary focus is equipment rental, setup,
and technical support. Others provide state-of-
the-art presentations, slides, and videos. Still
others custom design a variety of presentation technologies that incorporate projection systems, audio systems, lighting, and remote controls. Some production companies prefer to concentrate on the logistics of staging and production; others will offer
more. Need an outdoor laser light show? Consult with an expert who can sort out
show design, logistics, and timing, and provide advice on power level considerations,
just for starters. Sorting out which type of company will meet your needs is a challenge, and you will need to do some research.

> **The Inside Scoop**
>
> Have your A/V production com-
> pany produce a "happy video"
> onsite. Throughout the confer-
> ence, under your direction,
> the company takes pictures of
> people meeting, eating, and
> having fun. The photos are set
> to music and shown at your last
> general session. People love to
> see themselves on the big screen.
> Then, once back at the office
> (with permission, of course), put
> some of these photos on your
> website, too!

In addition to content development, A/V production companies also provide video
presentations, animation, interactive multimedia, staging, production design, and execution. They provide speaker support and message enhancement. They are often
involved in new product launches, annual stockholder meetings, and national or
regional sales meetings. They bring new, fresh, cutting-edge ideas on how to maximize the impact of your message.

The Least You Need to Know

- Communicating your message using A/V technology is getting fancier, more
  fun, and more expensive.

- Review all A/V needs with an A/V provider early in the planning process.

- A/V rental is expensive and covers more than just equipment. Labor, power, and
  supplies quickly add up, so be sure to budget accordingly.

◆ Satellite and video conferencing are labor- and technology-intensive. Both require video cameras, audio equipment, video production equipment, and technical staff that are not always standard in most venues.

◆ Big shows require a lot of production. Talk to experienced, qualified, full-service production companies at the onset.

Chapter 21

Meeting Registration and Housing Reservations

In This Chapter

- ◆ Learn what a meeting registration form should include

- ◆ Discover some important tips for your attendee database

- ◆ Distinguish between a (meeting) registration list and a (facility) reservation list

- ◆ Understand online meeting registration and where it's going

- ◆ Find out why a meeting registration cancellation policy is a must

One of the most important aspects of meeting planning is collecting data on who is attending. Why? To enable you to communicate with your attendees in advance of the meeting, and to maintain a list of those to whom you might market in the future. More importantly, you need to know when they are arriving and departing, where they are staying, if they are bringing guests, what sessions and events they are interested in attending or plan to attend, their needs (disability-related, for example), and their emergency contact information. Knowing this type of information is critical when you have to make decisions regarding meeting space, capacity, amount of food and beverage to order, transportation, and so on.

Another key area is housing management. If you have contracted hotel room block commitments, you must be proactive in getting your attendees to reserve and stay in those rooms. Not meeting your contracted commitment (often called "performance" or "attrition") will impact your bottom line, and quite possibly the overall success of your meeting.

In this chapter, we delve into the world of meeting registration and housing reservations, and how the two are intricately related.

Designing Your Meeting Registration Form

The design of your attendee database is synonymous with the design of your registration form. What comes from one (the form) goes into the other (the database). Because they go hand in hand, we suggest you begin by drafting your registration form detail. To do that, you need to identify the information you want to track. The following table lists suggested items; you may need all or just some of this information.

Registration Information	Designations
Last or family name	Board of directors
First name	Committee member
Middle initial	Conference committee
Title	Exhibitor
Company/organization	Facilitator
Address (line 1)	Faculty
Address (line 2)	Guest
Address (line 3)	Host
City	Press
State/territory/province	Speaker
ZIP code/postal code	Sponsor
Country	Staff
Phone/TDD number	Student
Fax number	Volunteer
E-mail address	
Website	

Badge Information	Guest Badge Information
First name for badge	First name
Attendee organization	Guest city/state
Attendee city/state/territory/ province	Guest country
Attendee country	Guest of

In Case of Emergency	Special Needs (including disabilities which need to be accommodated)
First name	Diabetic
Last or family name	Vegetarian
Daytime phone	Vegan
Evening phone	Low salt
Cell phone	Kosher
Relationship	Food allergies (please list)

Session Selections	
Customize to your meeting	
A note should be added to your form stating that selections are first-come, first-served or they cannot be guaranteed (use whichever wording works best for you).	

Conference Events	Registration Fees
(Will they be attending …)	(Early bird/regular/onsite)
Breakfasts	Member
Lunches	Nonmember
Receptions	Student or other special membership category
Banquets	Guest
Workplace tours	One day
Customize to your meeting	Banquet only

continues

continued

Additional Events/Fees	Payment Information
Conference outings	Check
Pre-conference tours	Money order
Post-conference tours	Purchase order #
Pre-conference workshops	Credit card #/expiration date
	Signature line

Let's elaborate on a few categories, starting with the designation category. With large conferences, you may want to call attention to some of the different classifications your attendees fall into. This is where name badge ribbons come in. You can identify people by broad classification such as speaker or exhibitor, or you can customize titles for your attendees such as butcher, baker, or candlestick maker. For a geographically diverse crowd, you can give them a ribbon identifying their state, territory, province, or country. (More on name badges and ribbons in Chapter 16.)

With respect to the special-needs category, a registration form cannot possibly list all the questions that could pertain to every attendee's needs. Therefore, the best thing to do is make a statement similar to the following on the form: Pursuant to the Americans with Disabilities Act, please specify below, or check here *[box]* if you wish to be contacted about disabilities for which you require accommodation. Once you have a request in writing, you are obligated to follow up.

The Inside Scoop

There are tons of registration forms to use as examples, especially on the web. To get a first-hand look at how they operate, complete a few online forms, but don't hit the submit button! You can get some good ideas about what to do and what not to do by looking at other meeting registration forms.

Payment information is another category people frequently have questions about. Incorporate your policies about who pays, how they pay, when payment is due and how (check, credit card, purchase order), cancellation or substitution polices, and other issues that are specific to your meeting.

You will have major headaches if you don't get the payment information right from the start. If your instructions are not clear, attendees will pay the wrong amount, and you will either have to bill them for the amount owed or refund an overpayment. On your form, be sure to address the following payment criteria:

- Is payment required at the time registration is received?

- Make the check payable to what organization?

- Must check be in U.S. dollars only?

- If funds are received in a currency other than U.S. dollars, will they be rejected or will a conversion fee be assessed?

- Ask that the attendee's name be put on the check in the memo section, especially if it is a company check.

- Is there a cancellation or substitution [of another participant] fee? Under what conditions? Are substitutions allowed?

- After what date will refunds not be granted?

- Identify what the registration fee includes (refreshment breaks, reception, registration materials, and so on).

- Spell out all additional fees (meals, outings, etc.).

- Provide complete contact information for the registration office (phone, fax, e-mail) for questions, hours of operation, and time zone.

Don't forget to include detailed instructions on how to register. If you are using online registration, also provide options for faxing and mailing the registration form. It is a good idea to state that a letter of confirmation will be sent within x number of days and that, if no confirmation is received, the attendee should contact the registration office, and how to do it. Be sure letters of confirmation include a confirmation number. Remember that it's an extra verification to help you identify your attendees, and it does come in handy if there are discrepancies.

In some cases, you may wish to waive or reduce a registration fee for an attendee. Don't put this information on the standard registration form. Either create a separate form (called fee waived) for these unique cases, or send a cover letter with the standard form explaining that the fee is waived or reduced.

Developing Your Registration Database

The kind of database software you choose depends on what you may already be using for other applications, or on the kind of meeting software package you decide to invest in.

Once you have your registration form ready to go, the next step is to set up your registration database. One very important consideration is to create a unique identification tion number for each entry or *data record*. What if you have two Bob Smiths in your database? Bob Smith from New York may call and say he thinks he has registered twice and wants to correct the situation. Do you have two records for the same Bob Smith, or are there actually two different Bob Smiths, both from New York City? A unique data record number (which can also serve as your confirmation number) helps you sort out problems like this.

Meeting Speak

A **data record** is the unique collection of information about a specific object (in this case, an individual registering for your meeting).

This leads us to another tip. Design your registration database so it can distinguish possible duplicate entries. Sometimes an individual will register and then his or her assistant will also send in the registration form. If you test for duplicate names at the input process, you might avoid duplicate entries. Going through your database to cull out duplicates is a time-consuming, but necessary, process.

The Inside Scoop

Determining conference registration fees is extremely important when planning nonprofit meetings, as the fees (considered income) are used to offset costs. This is rarely a consideration when planning a corporate meeting, as the host company would not charge its employees to attend a mandatory meeting. Refer to Chapter 9 for pointers on how to set fees to break even or turn a profit.

Create a unique field for each piece of information. You may not need it all, but you never know when you will want to print a report or sort on a specific field. The more unique fields you have, the better you can manipulate your data. For example, don't combine the first and last names into a field called Full Name. Separate them into two fields called First Name and Last Name. That way, you can sort and alphabetize on just the last name. It's much easier to input the data into many different fields from the beginning than it is to go back and separate this information after the fact.

After you have designed your registration form and database, do several trial runs. Ask people who are unfamiliar with your project to register. Listen to their feedback and improve the process.

Registration Made Easy

Now that you have created your registration form and your registration database is ready to go, you must make it easy for potential attendees to register.

Registration the Old-Fashioned Way

Some people still like the old way of filling out a paper registration form and mailing or faxing it in. Even if you want most of your attendees to submit their registrations electronically, you should still have a paper version for those who have difficulty registering electronically.

Try to keep your registration form to a single page, but if that's not possible, at least have a version that is printable in standard 8½ × 11-inch format. If someone requests a copy of the registration form, having one in an 8½ × 11-inch format makes it easier for the attendee to complete and for the registration staff to read if it is faxed back.

Some planners like to have a hard copy of each registration in a binder, alphabetized. That way, they can access registration info quickly. They also have the registration information as supplied by the attendee, if there are any questions onsite.

Online Meeting Registration

The technology to register people for meetings online is being used more frequently. If you are thinking about online registration, consider these points:

- Just about everyone has (at least limited) access to the Internet. Expect the number of Internet users to increase.

- Payment information via credit card is generally secure. Determine with your IT department what is needed to ensure the best possible encryption and safety for registrations sent electronically. Reassure those using your system about the security measures you have implemented.

- Online-registration websites are template driven, so you don't have to know or even understand website design. They make it super easy for you to enter your information and manage your data.

- Meeting attendees are becoming more sophisticated in their expectations of being able to go to the web to find current, accurate meeting information, to register, and to make housing and travel arrangements.

To decide which online-registration service would work best for you, think about your needs. How many meetings do you plan? How big are the meetings? Do you want just meeting registration capability, or do you want your participants to be able to make a room reservation and book an airline ticket?

The Inside Scoop

There are comprehensive online attendee management programs that do much more than just meeting registration. These programs take care of meeting/event registration (including signup for sessions and social events), housing reservations, flights, ground transportation, tours, printing name badges, confirmations, tickets, and other data management. They allow basic customization to your meeting specifications; generate up-to-date, accurate reports; offer password protection; and allow attendees to register 24/7.

Suggestions for online registration providers are provided in Chapter 5, but you will also want do some research on your own as new companies are coming online. Go to each of the online registration company websites and check them out. Most provide online demonstrations. Pay attention to what they provide versus what you really need. Rank the top three potential companies and get more information. Investigate how your data management fits into their system. If possible, as your top picks for recommendations and call them. Get feedback from other planners. Then make a decision based on your budget and what will work best for you.

Meeting Registration Cancellations

Clearly outline your cancellation policy on your registration form. A cancellation fee makes an attendee's commitment stronger and eliminates the tendency for people to register knowing they can cancel at the last minute with no financial penalty.

Food for Thought

An example of a meeting cancellation policy is as follows: "All cancellations are subject to a $25 cancellation fee. Cancellations 7 days or less prior to the meeting [insert date] will be assessed a $150 cancellation fee."

For example, if someone cancels the day before the meeting, but you have provided the meal guarantee to the facility two days before, you still pay for the meals. Of course, your guarantees have a fudge factor and you will have walk-ins onsite, but still be firm. You can always make exceptions for a family emergency or other major obstacle that prevented someone from attending. After all, we are all human.

Hotel Reservations: "Heads in Beds"

"Heads in beds" is lingo from the supplier side of the meetings industry, meaning they want guest rooms occupied. For meeting planners, keeping track of heads in beds and comparing it to meeting registrations is important, challenging, and time consuming. Why? Read on.

Your first concern is to make sure you are filling the contracted room block at the facility (or facilities). However, making housing reservations on behalf of each attendee is daunting, especially if individuals are paying their own charges. It's best to have each attendee make his or her own arrangements. You should contract for the hotel to provide you with a periodically updated *reservation list*, which is a list of names associated with reservations under a specific group's hotel room block, at least monthly before your meeting. As the meeting nears, weekly reports are critical to ensuring room block compliance. Here comes the time-consuming part. You must now compare the hotel's reservation list to your meeting registration list. That way, you can identify who has not made a hotel reservation. Because your meeting registration system is different than the hotel's, you must compare a hard-copy hotel reservation list with your registration list every time either is updated.

It is very important to track your attendees' housing status. If you are below your contracted room block, it may also stand to reason that fewer people than expected are registering for your conference. However, if your meeting attendance is good but your room block is low, possibly two things are happening: Either your attendees just haven't yet gotten around to making their housing reservations (and they need a reminder), they are staying elsewhere, or maybe both. Either way, you need to get the "heads in the (contracted) beds." Otherwise, you could miss your room-block commitments and end up paying attrition fees, as agreed to in the hotel contract. Paying attrition is never good to a meeting's bottom line.

If you have designed your database to capture attendees' housing status, you can easily identify which attendees do not have housing. At this point, you should generate an e-mail reminding them, gently, that they are not listed on the hotel's reservation list and should promptly make a reservation. You may also want to ask them if they have alternate housing (so you won't bother them again). This will generate some action, but be prepared to send out a second reminder, too.

You can also supply the hotel with your registration list and have them compare it with their reservations. This could catch some attendees

The Inside Scoop

It's getting harder to fill room blocks. Everyone has instant access to information online, including special rates at hotels near your meeting hotel. Attendees can find a bargain with a simple click of the mouse. You can't force attendees to stay in your room block, but consider providing incentives to do so (such as discounted meeting registration fees for those who book rooms in the official meeting hotel[s]).

that are registered outside your block. You should have a clause in your contract that states any reservations outside your block but on your attendee list will count toward your total room pick up regardless of their rate. See Chapter 5 for additional contract information.

Housing Reservation Forms

Regardless of who (meeting planner or individual meeting participant) is making the housing reservations, you will need to provide detailed housing reservation information in your meeting registration materials. Information you should provide:

- Hotel reservation phone numbers; local and toll-free (always provide toll numbers in addition to toll-free telephone numbers, particularly if you are dealing with international attendees), and TDD (telecommunications devices for the deaf)

- Hotel fax number and reservation email address (if applicable)

- Hotel URL for participants to learn more about the hotel

- Reservation cutoff date (last day that reservations will be accepted in the group block at the negotiated group rate)

- Room rate(s) (single, double, or multiple occupancy) and room types

- State and local taxes; resort fee or other taxes, if applicable

- Group identifier code

- Timeframe that rates are valid

- Hotel cancellation and substitution policies

- Early departure or extended stay fees, if any

- No-show charge, if any

- Reservation/payment information

- Description of guest rooms, décor, and amenities

- Parking information and fees

- Description of the hotel (pools, health clubs, grounds, nearby attractions, restaurants, room service, smoking or nonsmoking, and/or ADA-accessible rooms available)

- Check in/out times

- Extra person charge, if any

- Maximum occupancy per room

- Children (at what age) stay free

- Choice of hotel (first, second, third) where applicable

- How the reservation will be acknowledged

Earlier in this chapter, we discussed the attendee registration database as it pertains to capturing attendee registration information, and we described a scenario in which we needed to identify attendee housing information. Here is a list of the housing information you may wish to collect for each attendee and add to his or her registration data record:

- Arrival day, date, and estimated time

- Departure day, date, and estimated time

- Number of guests/children (names optional)

- Sharing with (may be another registered meeting attendee or an unregistered spouse or guest)

- Name reservation is in (primary person responsible for payment)

- Hotel name (if several to choose from)

- Hotel confirmation number

> **CAUTION**
>
> **Don't Drop the Ball**
>
> The arrival, departure, and guest information from the hotel's reservation list is almost always more accurate than what may be submitted on the registration form from the attendee. Update your database with the hotel's data.

You will get some of this information from the attendee registration form. You will get other info, such as a hotel confirmation number, from the hotel's reservation list. Update your registration database as frequently as you can with any and all pertinent information.

Housing Bureau

For city-wide meetings or conventions, a housing bureau is recommended. Either a convention and visitors bureau (CVB) or an outside company can provide hotel registration services. CVBs are now partnering with some of the online housing companies. Individuals who wish to make reservations rank their hotel preference and are assigned a hotel on a first-come, first-served basis. This is done either via a registration form or online.

Rooming List

You will usually submit staff and VIP room reservations to the hotel on a rooming list. Notify everyone for whom you are making a reservation and get a confirmation number from the hotel to give to each person. Make sure you keep your staff/VIP block separate from your regular block of rooms. You can even do this during the contracting stage, but the sooner the better! Ask the hotel to create two separate room blocks.

For one reason or another you may decide to collect attendee housing requests yourself and submit them to the hotel using a rooming list. For companies who are having a mandatory meeting, this is particularly helpful, to make sure there are no errors in hotel reservations. Attendees' special needs, roommate information, cancellations, and additions are communicated to the meeting planner who works directly with the hotel reservation agent. The housing charges are usually added to the meeting's master bill for those on the rooming list.

Call-in or Online Hotel Reservations

Attendees can also be instructed to call the hotel reservation line directly. In this case, they should identify themselves as part of your group or organization and, in return, will receive the negotiated rate. Make sure you provide both toll and toll-free numbers for the hotel, as well as a fax number. Some hotels also offer online registrations. Keep in mind that many hotels have eliminated their in-house reservation department. Calls are routed to a central reservation facility where personnel may or may not be able to answer destination questions such as transportation available to the facility from the airport.

The Least You Need to Know

◆ If you are using online registration, also provide options for faxing and mailing the registration form. This will assist those who choose not to be online.

◆ Always compare your meeting registration list with the hotel reservation list to identify people who have not made a hotel reservation, or have forgotten to register.

◆ Research a variety of online registration service providers before making a decision about which to use.

◆ A cancellation policy protects your budget and reduces the number of casual cancellations.

◆ Create a unique field for each piece of information. You may not need it all, but you never know when you will want to print a report or sort on a specific field.

Part 4

Center Stage and Beyond

Lights! Camera! Action! You are on stage, and this is your production. You are in charge, and these chapters will assist you with what to do once you arrive at the facility for your meeting or event. We'll walk you through the process, from checking in to organizing your onsite office to getting acquainted with the facility staff. You'll also learn about paying the bills, tipping, tabulating the evaluations, and obtaining final facility reports. We'll also show you how advance planning can prepare you for crisis management, so you'll be ready if disaster comes calling.

There is also a chapter for suppliers only (although planners can—*and should!*—take a peek) that provides the inside scoop on what planners really look for and need when booking a meeting or event. We'll also look at industry certifications and evaluate whether letters after your name are worth the time and money. Then, we'll leave you with a few tips for maintaining control in this crazy profession. After that, you are on your own. Good luck!

22

The Final Stretch: What to Expect Onsite

In This Chapter

- ◆ Learn what to do once you arrive at the meeting/event facility
- ◆ Identify the meeting/event facility players
- ◆ Understand the value of managing your rooming lists
- ◆ Understand your role and responsibilities onsite
- ◆ Distinguish between pre- and post-convention meetings

The day has finally arrived—you are going onsite. What exactly should you expect? What can you do to make things run smoothly? What exactly is your job onsite? In this chapter, we explore these issues to give you a good idea what happens from the minute you check in to the moment you leave.

We will also look at the convention resumé, meetings with the facility's staff, how to set up your conference office, and the lines of communication onsite. Going onsite can be one of the most fun parts of your job, but it is intimidating if you are not familiar with your role and the hotel staff's role in managing your meeting.

You're Here!

Upon your arrival, have your meeting boxes delivered to your onsite conference office. You should also check in to your hotel room and get settled. Ask for a room on a lower floor and if applicable, an early check-in. If the elevators are busy, you can take the stairs. Everyone has his or her own ritual, so getting comfortable first is a way of making your hotel room "home" for a while.

Setting Up Your Onsite Conference Office

Once you are settled in, let your meeting facility contact know you've arrived safely. If it is after hours, you may have to wait until morning, but at least leave a voicemail. When possible, go to the room designated as your office. By now, your boxes have arrived and you can start unpacking. If you shipped any boxes in advance, call and find out where they are and whether they can be brought to your office. Make sure you've been given a key for the office to lock up when you are done unpacking.

> **CAUTION**
>
> **Don't Drop the Ball**
>
> When packing to ship your materials to the meeting/event venue, label all boxes using this format: Box 1 out of 10, 2 out of 10, and so on. That way, if one is missing, you know exactly which one and what's in it. Bring your shipping list onsite. Include tracking and phone numbers of the carrier(s). Ask anyone who is shipping items to provide you with the same.

For one of our big meetings, we had flags from six countries shipped to the meeting site. Once onsite, they were nowhere to be found. It was a Sunday, and the flag company was closed. We ended up getting someone from the flag company (we were fortunate they were local) to bring us an extra set. Later, we found out they were shipped under a different name, and we were not looking for the right "ship from" information. We found the flags upon conclusion of the conference. The moral of the story is to make sure all items shipped to you are accounted for before you arrive onsite (and, if at all possible, plan to arrive onsite on a weekday). Call vendors to confirm that they have shipped and get all shipping info. Looking for missing items onsite is a huge time drain, but often a reality that can adversely impact your meeting.

Unpack, set up the office, and get organized. If you still have registration packets to stuff, now is the time to get started.

Exactly what do you need for your onsite office? Here's a checklist so you don't miss anything:

- **Registration materials.** Attendee packets, monitor packets, speaker packets, onsite registration forms, maps, blank receipts, nametags and badge stock, and brochures.

- **Office supplies.** Pack a complete assortment of paper, paper clips, note pads, a stapler, extra staples, transparent tape, masking tape, electrical tape, packing tape, overnight shipping envelopes/boxes, blades for opening boxes, pens, pencils, clipboards, flashlights and extra batteries, tools (such as a screwdriver and hammer), transparencies and pens, aspirin (seriously), and a first-aid kit. Bring preprinted overnight shipping labels to the meeting. These are very handy when you need to ship your leftover materials back to the office.

- **Office equipment as needed.** A computer, printer, copy machine, fax machine, paper shredder (remember you'll be handling payment and other classified information), and associated supplies.

- **A power strip and a few extension cords.** You may need them in the office, or a speaker may need one for a laptop. These can be expensive to rent onsite. (Check with the facility's union or labor steward to ensure you can set these up yourself.)

- **Snacks for the staff.** It's a nice touch, especially when things get busy and time gets short.

- **School bell or hand-held chimes.** You may need it for getting people's attention.

It's a good idea to keep an onsite meeting equipment and supplies checklist. Update it after (or during) each meeting for the next time.

Prior to arrival, prepare a staff assignment list including work schedules, times, and rules (such as no eating at the registration desk). You will need staff for a variety of tasks including working the registration desk, checking meeting rooms for setup accuracy, taking tickets at meal functions, and so on. Review staff assignments before you go onsite.

Another handy thing to have is a list of frequently asked questions (FAQs) by attendees. Brainstorm with staff and key volunteers in advance the questions you think attendees will ask your registration desk personnel. Here are some sample questions:

- Where are the restrooms?

- How can I pay for the conference? Can I pay by cash, check, or credit card? Which credit cards do you accept?

- Where is the nearest bank or ATM?

- Where are the meeting rooms? (Have your staff become familiar with the floor plan.)

- I need to cancel the last day. Can I get a refund?

- I have a special meal request. Who do I tell?

- Is Suzie Q. registered for the conference? Has she checked in yet? Can I leave a message for her?

- Where can I get breakfast, lunch, or dinner?

Also train your staff on the emergency procedures in the hotel. When do you call the hotel's security staff and when do you call 911? They all should know what to do in the event of any crisis. Make sure you know the facility's emergency procedures and communicate them to your entire staff. (More on this in Chapter 24.)

A Quick Tour

Once you have settled in, take a tour of the facilities. Bring your staff along because they need to see it, too. Reacquaint yourself with the property. Have a bite to eat in the restaurant. Get a feel for the property and what is going on there. Check out the meeting rooms and the reader boards to get an idea of other meetings onsite. Also, check the TV listings when you get back in your guest room to see if meetings and locations within the facility are listed—and whether yours are listed correctly.

Your Master List

Before the meeting, create a master to-do list that includes your detailed agenda (with times). The master list is different from your timeline and includes everything that you and your staff need to do throughout the meeting such as put signs out, speaker checks, meal and session counts, and so on. It also includes meetings you have scheduled with the hotel staff, when your speakers/entertainers are scheduled to arrive, rehearsal times, vendor setup times, staff training, and so on.

The Inside Scoop

The Accepted Practices Exchange Program (APEX) is an ongoing effort to provide meeting industry forms such as requests for proposals (RFPs), convention resumés, group history reporting forms, and more. To implement APEX accepted practices, the Convention Industry Council (CIC) has collected a toolset of more than 200 templates called APEX OfficeReady for Meeting and Event Planning. Check out their website for additional information and other products currently available at www.conventionindustry.org.

Convention or Meeting Resumé

Put your meeting and event details in writing. Too many times, verbal instructions are given to the convention services manager (CSM) at the hotel, and important details slip through the cracks. It is the planner's responsibility to provide clear directions as to what is needed for the program. Create a document including the agenda, set-up specifications for each meeting room including audio-visual needs, food and beverage requirements, and other pertinent details and give it to the CSM. This is done approximately 30 to 45 days prior to the meeting. The timeframe varies depending on the size of your meeting/event, and how far out it is booked.

Here is some information you need to give the CSM:

- A final rooming list indicating who pays for the room, tax, and incidentals for each individual (unless all attendees are making their own arrangements)

- Billing information—list what should be posted to your meeting/event master account

- Names of VIPs including arrival/departure days, dates, and times

- Who gets the earned comp (complimentary) rooms

- Authorized decision-makers and whether they can sign to the master account

- Security needs

- Registration desk hours of operation

- Expected attendee arrival/departure days, dates, times

- Details for each meal including setup and serving times

- Accounting requirements—ask to review and sign bills daily

- ◆ Amenity deliveries, if applicable

- ◆ Audio-visual requirements

- ◆ Computing, other technical requirements, if any

- ◆ Electrical needs

- ◆ Banners or signs that need to be hung (get prior approval)

- ◆ Shipping and receiving—provide number of boxes, shipper info, and airbill number if known

- ◆ Airport transportation needs

- ◆ Parking—ask about special valet passes

- ◆ Hospitality suites, including who is hosting and the hours

The convention services manager takes all of this information and creates the meeting or convention resumé, which includes the details for your entire meeting. Any memos to the hotel staff, special instructions, BEOs, function sheets, and information about VIPs are part of this report. The various departments in the hotel use this document to follow the needs of the group and to make sure everything the client ordered is provided uniformly.

You will have time to preview and approve the resumé prior to the pre-con (pre-convention) meeting with the hotel staff. Because the resumé also contains your agenda, make sure all the agenda information is correct. It will be posted on the in-house monitors and on internal documents used by the hotel staff. If you do not want something posted, such as a staff meeting, indicate that it is a "do not post" function. For example, your office is a "do not post" item. You do not necessarily want meeting attendees to know where it is. The registration desk is where they should go for answers to their questions.

The hotel will also carefully monitor when you do not have group meal functions. If you do not have a scheduled lunch planned on a certain day, then people are "on the loose" and may eat in the restaurants. The hotel will want to have adequate waitstaff available to accommodate the crowd. An accurate agenda is important.

Rooming List—Keep on Top of It!

Your rooming list is a document that outlines individuals for whom you want to make housing reservations directly with the hotel. It includes the individuals' names, their check-in and check-out dates, room type, roommates (if any), billing information, and any special needs. At a minimum, your rooming list should contain your staff, VIPs, and speakers. If your organization is paying for the housing of all your attendees, then your rooming list would contain all attendees.

There are three ways to pay for an attendee's room. Take a look at the following table and notice: 1) all charges to the master account; 2) room and tax (but not incidentals) to the master account; 3) all charges to the individual.

Name	Number of People	Check-In Date	Check-Out Date	Billing Information	Smoking/Room Type/Comments
John Q. Speaker	1	9-18-09	9-20-09	Room/tax to master, incidentals to individual	Nonsmoking King VIP/keynote speaker
Suzie Q. Banquet	2	9-18-09	9-20-09	All charges to individual	Smoking Two beds
Jane L. Meeting	1	9-18-09	9-21-09	All charges to master	Nonsmoking King

The rooming list should be finalized prior to the cutoff date. However, changes are inevitable, and even onsite you will have some revisions. Have on hand the file documenting every change you sent to the hotel and also a final list just in case there are some questions once onsite.

Make sure the hotel sends an alphabetized printout of all room reservations made under your group code. Compare your registration list against it to make sure everything was entered correctly. Sometimes one person could have a reservation under two different names, or one name might be spelled wrong in the system.

Every morning you are on site, meet with the front office staff to review your room pickup from the night before, any no-shows, *walks*, and cancellations. This is especially important in case a VIP or speaker was a no-show. Tell the

Meeting Speak

A **walk** (also called a dishonored reservation) is a term used for a person who has a guaranteed reservation but is moved to another hotel because the hotel is overbooked. If you are walked, the hotel will compensate you by taking you to another hotel and paying for the room and a phone call home.

hotel if you want any of these reservations reinstated for that evening. Otherwise, these people could show up and not have a reservation. You should also keep tabs on the current house count so you know if the hotel is oversold during your stay.

Another important reason to review this information on a daily basis is to keep track of any no-shows guaranteed by your organization that will be billed to your master account. Find out what the hotel occupancy was that evening; if it sold out, you shouldn't be charged. The front office staff will also appreciate your interest in helping them manage your group. It makes for a smoother meeting. Then, when you get the master bill, you know exactly what happened.

Your Role

Your role onsite should be like the conductor of the orchestra. Everyone knows his or her job, but someone is there to keep everyone in sync and moving forward.

You are also there to troubleshoot, make last-minute decisions, and act appropriately if there is an emergency.

Too Many Chiefs

Too many people directing the crew (both your staff and the hotel staff) is not a good thing. Establish a chain of command and communicate it to your staff and the convention services manager. Before you go onsite, establish who the decision-makers are. Once onsite, introduce those people to the CSM. At the very least, they should include you, an assistant who knows the meeting well, and possibly your boss or another individual authorized to make financial decisions on behalf of your organization. Make sure only people who can make informed decisions have this capability. In other words, do not assign someone who has had no involvement in the planning up to this point. This core group of people will be authorized to sign checks to the meeting's master bill and make operational decisions on the spot when a hotel staff person asks questions. The number of authorized decision-makers also depends on the size of the meeting. For very small meetings, it may be only one or two people. For larger 1,000+ person conferences, you may have four to five or more people who need that capability.

If you don't establish this chain of command, be prepared to deal with issues such as who changed the room set? Who ordered more cookies? Who made 1,000 copies and charged them to the master bill? Keep control. A good rule of thumb is the fewer decision-makers there are, the better.

You're Responsible

Even if the president of the company or association is in attendance at the meeting, you, the lead planner, are in charge. Accept the thanks for a job well done; accept the responsibility for problems. You will have cranky attendees, broken audio-visual equipment, monitors who do not show up, hot meeting rooms, cold meeting rooms, noise from the other meetings invading your space, late speakers, lost boxes, sick attendees, cold food, you name it—it happens. Do the best you can, use your best judgment, and keep your composure intact.

Don't Drop the Ball

No matter what happens, stay calm. If you are not sure how to handle an issue, explain to the person that you will get right back to him or her (unless it is an emergency, which you'll handle immediately!). Understand the meeting inside and out and get to know the hotel staff in charge of every area.

Meetings About Your Meeting

Before you get onsite, you may meet with the convention services manager (CSM) or catering manager (CM) or both. You may meet with them one time or a dozen times depending on the size, location, and scope of your meeting or event. You may also meet with the audio-visual personnel and the chef. This is when you finalize the details.

Once you are onsite, you are introduced to the rest of the staff responsible for the execution of your meeting. Each facility is run according to its own guidelines, but basically, there are seven departments you will work with onsite:

1. **Audio-visual.** Responsible for the sound, lighting, sometimes engineering, equipment, and labor for these.

2. **Banquets.** Serves the food and beverages to the attendees.

3. **Bell stand.** Helps the guests carry their belongings to their rooms; it is also a resource for directions and other general questions.

4. **Convention services.** Sets up the meeting and banquet rooms and oftentimes coordinates the overall flow of tasks between other departments.

5. **Front office.** Checks the guests in and out of the hotel; also oversees concierge.

6. **Housekeeping.** Cleans the guestrooms and public areas.

7. **Reservations.** Makes the guestroom reservations and helps you onsite with changes.

Pre-Convention Meeting

A pre-convention meeting (commonly known as a pre-con) is a meeting with the hotel staff about your meeting, usually a day or two before the start of the meeting. In this meeting, you meet most of the department heads; review the convention resumé, rooming list, and BEOs; and both sides ask questions to confirm or change all the details. You should also get a complete reservation report for your group.

> **The Inside Scoop**
>
> Even though your main contact is the convention services or catering manager, once you are onsite, you need to develop a good working relationship with the other staff members. The more proactive you are in learning their names, jobs, and a little bit about them, the better service you will receive. It really works!

The meeting begins with each hotel representative introducing him- or herself and giving an explanation of the department's role in your meeting. This is a good time to exchange business cards or get a list of the staff names, titles, departments and phone numbers. Then you give a brief overview of your organization and the purpose of the meeting and address any last-minute changes. Once that is done, everyone briefly reviews the resumé and then the chef and the convention services and/or catering manager, and A/V manager stay to review the BEOs in greater detail. This is also the time to provide guarantees if you haven't done so for the last few days of your meeting.

Daily Chats

Daily chats are something you should institute with most facility managers. It is good to touch base with the catering and/or convention services manager, front office, banquet manager, audio-visual manager, sales manager, and others who are handling your meeting. These are informal conversations to catch up on what has happened, what is going to happen, and any potential problems facing your meeting.

Post-Convention Meeting

A post-convention meeting (also known as a post-con) is also held with the hotel staff to review the meeting. This is your opportunity to hear from the hotel staff's point of view how things went behind the scene and provide constructive feedback on how things could have gone better from your perspective. This can be with all department heads or just the ones you select. You also can review the bill in detail one more time before you leave the hotel.

At this meeting, you should get your actual room pickup, number of no-shows, cancellations, and number of people served at each meal function. In some cases you will already have this information, but here is when you learn that you needed to order more vegetarian entrees, that your signage wasn't the best it could have been, and other useful things for next time.

The Three R's—Review, Review, Review

Keep a copy of the convention resumé, rooming list, BEOs, and function sheets on a clipboard that you can carry around with you throughout the meeting. You can reduce these on the copy machine for smaller copies, and then you don't even need a clipboard. At your fingertips, you can check room sets, meal information, start times, or whatever you need to know on the spot.

Give your key staff members copies of these documents and leave a copy in the home and onsite offices and at the registration desk.

Before each meeting, you should walk through every meeting room to verify that everything is set according to the BEO. If there are any discrepancies, immediately let the convention services and A/V managers know. It can be quite useful to rent walkie-talkies or radios, or even multi-use mobile phones, to contact the CSM quickly, because both of you will likely be on the run throughout the duration of the meeting.

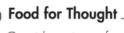 **Food for Thought**

Consider using a fanny pack onsite to carry paper, pens, radio or cell phone, and other needed items.

The Master Bill: Review Before You Go

At the pre-convention meeting, set a daily appointment with someone from the accounting office. Every day, while the information is fresh, review your master bill. Make sure you have signed every banquet check. Get copies of everything from the day before. If a charge is in dispute, sign the check and note what is in dispute.

Several weeks after the meeting, when you get the master bill, you will have already reviewed and approved most of the charges. It is a lot easier than trying to remember or reconstruct what exactly happened and why you are being charged weeks after your meeting.

The Least You Need to Know

◆ Bring plenty of office supplies for your conference office.

◆ Know how many and what is in each of the boxes you ship to the meeting site, including their airbill numbers for easy tracking, in case of loss or delay.

◆ Provide the meeting facility with your meeting details in a very thorough, dated, written document.

◆ Stay on top of your rooming list and room pickup situation by meeting with the front office every morning.

◆ Review the master bill before you leave the property at the conclusion of the meeting.

Chapter

23

Ready, Set, Show Time!

In This Chapter

- ◆ Discover how to set up an efficient onsite registration area
- ◆ Understand the importance of training your onsite staff
- ◆ Understand how the facility gets things done
- ◆ Identify common onsite problems and how to rectify them

You've unpacked, gotten settled, and it's show time—your meeting or event is about to begin. What do you do now? All of the behind-the-scenes work is done. Now it's time to sit back and relax because your meeting will run itself, right? We wish. Actually you still have lots of behind the scenes work to do. You have registration to manage; attendee, speaker, and VIP questions and needs to address; problems to solve; and decisions to make.

Even though you turn over the implementation of your event to the convention staff at the hotel or venue, what actually goes on behind the scenes to make sure your program is a success? Who is responsible to make sure every single detail is taken care of? Y-O-U! You still need to stay on top of all the details and make sure the facility does not drop the ball.

This chapter prepares you for what goes on onsite including what takes place in the "back of the house" in a meeting or event facility. It isn't magic (although sometimes it may look like it).

Registration Setup Considerations

One of the most important things you need to attend to is setting up and managing your meeting or event registration area. If you have a large registration area with booths, hundreds of registration packets, and so on, you should have everything set up and ready to go the day before registration opens. If your registration area is smaller, you can usually set up a few hours before the posted registration time. In any case, once you are set up, don't leave your registration area unattended. Most registration materials contain confidential information, such as detailed contact information for attendees and credit card numbers! Oftentimes you have expensive computer equipment that can go missing if not under watch. Lock down the registration area any way possible. If your registration is in an open area, post signage as to when you will reopen, or at the very least take down or cover up your registration signage and place tablecloths over your registration desks. People will understand that you're not open, plus it keeps their paws off of your registration materials. Remove computers and other valuable equipment to a secured storage area overnight or provide security staff to stay in the registration area when it is not otherwise staffed.

Food for Thought

If attendees show up before registration opens and you are ready, go ahead and register them. It helps reduce lines during registration hours, and grateful attendees are always good for PR!

How you set up registration depends on what kind of materials you provide. For example, assume all the registration packets are generic (they all contain the same info) and the only unique item is the attendee's name badge. In this case, you can place the name badges in alphabetical order on tables. As the attendees pick up their name badge, you check off their name and hand them a packet. Done.

If your packets contain name-specific information, such as name badges, receipts, letters, or other forms, it's important to make sure they get the correct personalized packet. The packets can be placed in alphabetical order behind the registration counter, and attendees can go to a specific table or booth where a staff member can assist them. If you have space, place several tables near the registration area so attendees have a place to review their packets and set their stuff down. In Chapter 16 we talked about the items that can go into the packets. Here are some items to consider:

- An attendee list (alphabetical)

- Conference *preprints*

- A meeting evaluation form and individual session evaluation forms

- A facility map, if not included in program

- Giveaways (conference gifts)

- Invitations

- Last-minute information not in the program

- Local maps, brochures, or magazines

- A name badge

- A program booklet or handout

- Receipts

- Ribbons

- Special handouts

- Tickets

Meeting Speak

Larger conferences sometimes provide a conference **preprint,** a bound copy of all the handouts and papers for every session. This is most typical at medical and scientific conferences where the sessions are quite technical.

When laying out your registration area, pretend you're an attendee and walk through the process. You want to make it easy and quick. Consider the following points:

- Is the registration area in a logical, central place?

- Which direction will people come from?

- Can they see the signage?

- Is there enough room for lines of people? Can people with disabilities easily register?

- Is there a place attendees can go if they have questions or need time to fill out forms away from the main lines?

- Can attendees pick up their materials from any of the registration staff, or must they go to a specific table/booth, based on their last name?

- Do you need a special registration area for exhibitors, VIPs, speakers, or sponsors?

- Will you have onsite registration for those who didn't register early? Paper forms or online?

- Do you need to collect payment? Do you need a phone line for credit card verification?

- Do you need Internet access?

- Do you need tables for displays, pamphlets, or handouts?

- Do you need tables for vendors or CVB staff? Hotel staff?

You need to answer these questions early in the planning process (you might even look during your site selection process) because you need to plan for location, space, signage, equipment rental, booth rental, additional furniture rental, packet preparation, and on and on.

The registration desk is where most attendees, exhibitors, vendors, speakers, and even facility staff will go to ask questions and get help. Therefore, it's very important to have someone there at all times while registration is listed as open, who can make decisions and answer questions. Remember that your registration staff will be busy. Any questions your staff cannot answer should be referred quickly to someone who can help. If you cannot have the "answer person" stay in the registration area (maybe because it's you and you have to be everywhere), put your staff members on radios or cell phones so they can reach you instantly. Unless you have a very small program of fewer than 20 people, it's best to have at least two people working a meeting. One should be glued to the registration desk so the other can run around to check rooms, make on-the-spot decisions, and solve last-minute problems.

> **CAUTION**
>
> **Don't Drop the Ball**
>
> Take your staff on a walk through the facility and provide facility maps at registration. Prepare an easy-to-read agenda and a list of anticipated questions by attendees.

Staffing and Training

A big question is how much help you need onsite. It really depends on the number of attendees and the complexity of your meeting. A rule of thumb is one staff person per every 100 attendees—give or take. However, also factor in all the events in your meeting. If you have only general sessions and a few breakouts, you will need less staff than if you also have exhibits, offsite functions, tours, big-name VIPs or celebrities, numerous consecutive breakouts, and so on.

Before you leave your office, you should meet with your staff and develop a list of responsibilities. Make sure people understand what tasks they are responsible for, and what kinds of decisions they can and cannot make, and to whom to direct questions. Also make sure each staff member knows the roles of the other people on staff to avoid confusion. These responsibilities should be in writing.

If you hire temporary staff just for your onsite needs, you need to train them upon arrival. Because you may not know them and they have not been a part of your planning process, it is difficult to put them into positions that generate a lot of questions. Therefore, it's especially important that they are used efficiently and know the chain of command. They are great for registration support. They also need to know the venue, so they can assist with questions about the city and surroundings.

During your meeting, you should have a wind-up (or is it a wind-down?) meeting with your staff at the end of each day. Make it a short meeting, 15 to 30 minutes tops. The purpose is to get feedback, determine any problems or issues, and make adjustments. These feedback sessions are very useful and help everyone get some closure on the day and keep morale up when there are lots of tired feet among you. Listen to the negative feedback and give some positive feedback. It makes a big difference. Take notes so you can factor in these comments and suggestions at your next meeting.

Signage

Another thing you will need to do is place your signs strategically. Wait! Did we talk about signage? Whoops. Well, let's discuss it here. Signs are always important to direct attendees and provide pertinent information.

In many cases, the information on the signs won't or can't be known until several weeks or even days prior to your meeting. However, well before then, you need to decide what kind of signs you need, their style, their size, and approximately how many.

Here are some questions to consider:

- ◆ Do you want a logo or meeting theme on them?

- ◆ Do you have specific colors?

- ◆ Do you need directional signs with arrows?

- ◆ How will you display the signs? Easels? Stand-alone? Hanging? What are the facility's guidelines on signs: color, size, print, and placement?

Don't Drop the Ball

Hanging banners usually require special equipment and labor. You also may have to get special permission from the facility and may be assessed a fee.

◆ Will you need the ability to make signage onsite?

◆ Do you want to acknowledge sponsors? Vendors? In-kind contributors?

In addition, you may want a banner or large organization logo at registration or in a general session. During site selection and contract negotiation, talk to your facility about your options for displaying these items. Many facilities have restrictions about where signs and banners may be placed. Also, what kind of signage do you need at your registration area? If you have multiple registration booths, you will need to direct attendees to specific booths. In this case, the vendor that provides the booths can also create signage for them. Whatever signage you need, make sure they are large enough and are displayed high enough to be easily seen.

If you are able to go on a pre-meeting site visit, it's an excellent idea to walk through the facility and map out the placement of your signs, especially the directional ones. That way, you can determine the number, size, and style. If you can't, use a facility diagram and discuss your needs with your convention services manager or catering manager. For directional signs, consider the use of removable arrows that can be adhered using Velcro. Also bring along blank sign stock and slip-in sign holders, so you can make signs on the spot. Ask the facility if all signs have to be professionally printed or if some can be hand written.

Behind the Scenes

You may think you have a lot of meetings with the facility staff. Well, they have meetings about your meeting (without you), too. Before you arrive, each department completely reviews the needs of your group. Staff schedules are created and pertinent information is posted and distributed.

In addition, most hotels have a weekly staff or operations meeting to review all groups arriving within the next few weeks. They review the number of arrivals and departures, the occupancy percentage, VIPs, meal functions, special requests, and other important information.

It is quite an operation behind the scenes in preparation for your group. The facility has to schedule staff, order food and beverages, prepare the paperwork, create the daily in-house meeting agenda for the entire hotel, make sure the necessary equipment is available, and communicate all the information amongst themselves in preparation for your arrival.

Welcome to My (Early!) Morning

Because mornings come very early while onsite, it is a good idea to review the next day's BEOs and function sheets with the banquet or convention services manager the day before. Try to be one step ahead in terms of meeting execution.

The banquet and convention services department personnel get up very early and are usually at work before your attendees wake up. Typically, they are scheduled 24 hours a day to set your meeting rooms and to make sure things are ready to go at the agreed times.

> **The Inside Scoop**
>
> Make sure your sales and catering contacts understand the goals and objectives for your meeting. They should also have a good idea of the attendee profile and as much information as possible on arrival/departure patterns, eating habits, and so on. The more they know about you, the better they can serve you.

The staff uses the BEOs or function sheets to set your meeting rooms, so make sure they are 100 percent accurate when you sign off on them. Keep your contact updated on changes and do it in writing.

Sometimes your meeting rooms are set the night before so they will be ready when you are in the morning. If you can, check your meeting rooms the night before to make sure all is ready for your meeting the next day. In any case, always check the rooms 30 to 60 minutes prior to the meeting start times. If there are any discrepancies, report them immediately to the convention services or banquet staff. Most A/V equipment is *not* set at night because of security reasons.

Mid-Morning Relay Race

About mid-morning and mid-afternoon, your group will take a break. Make sure the facility staff can access the meeting rooms during the break to "refresh" (clear the unnecessary clutter and trash from) the meeting rooms. Don't assume this automatically happens. The facility has many meetings going at the same time and it literally becomes a race to get from room to room. Keep your contacts informed if you are running late or are still on schedule. If you are running late, lunch, afternoon breaks, or dinner may need to be pushed back a bit, but try to stay on time.

Meals: Come and Get It!

Meals are another busy time for the facility's staff. They need to be aware of the meeting's schedule (and any changes) so they can serve the meal at the designated time. They also need to make sure the banquet room is set and the staff is ready to go. You should check the room, too, just to make sure everything is ready according to your BEO.

If you have a program with a speaker during your meal, you probably don't want the banquet staff clearing tables, making noise, and otherwise distracting your attendees. Consider scripting your program to accommodate the needs of the facility, speakers, and attendees.

Bumps in the Road

You will always have a few bumps in the road during your meetings. Here's a list of potential problems and what to do to reduce or eliminate them:

- **Changes not communicated to staff.** Constantly have a dialogue going with staff. Don't assume that everything is taken care of.

- **Power outages.** Make sure you have flashlights available and know the hotel's evacuation procedure and backup power source(s).

- **Broken A/V equipment.** Make sure the A/V company has extra of everything in inventory. For critical presentations, have a spare in the room. (You'll probably have to pay for it, but consider it insurance.) This is one very good reason to use the in-house A/V company, where they keep everything available onsite 24/7.

- **Lost or missing items.** Did attendees leave items in the room yesterday? Check all rooms immediately following the last session, or you may have to go dumpster digging to retrieve lost items. Yuck!

- **It's too cold!** Rooms should be cool in the morning. Once the bodies pile in, the room warms up. Don't be too quick to turn up the heat (unless icicles are forming on your attendees). Warm rooms make people sleepy, inattentive, and can make them nauseous. Recommend in pre-conference materials that attendees bring sweaters as meeting room temperatures can fluctuate. Part of your job is to ensure the comfort of meeting participants.

♦ **Your mic is dead.** When doing your room checks, test the mics by speaking into them, not tapping them. Insist that new batteries be placed in all wireless microphones prior to using them—especially general session mics!

♦ **Your meeting room has changed.** Make sure your contract states that you must agree in writing prior to the facility changing your assigned meeting rooms. If rooms are changed anyway, make sure all the postings are correct. The facility staff should provide signs or people (as "human arrows") to direct participants to the new location.

♦ **An attendee was walked (assigned to another hotel due to lack of gue-stroom availability).** Try to negotiate a no-walk policy for your group. If you can, stay on top of the hotel's occupancy and work directly with the front office manager to bring the walked person back the next day.

Do some of these things sound like hotel staff responsibilities and not yours? Yes, it is true. However, meeting and event professionals must always look out for their meetings. Sometimes you will run into staff turnover, lack of staff, lack of motivation, or just plain sloppiness. Staying on top of the details prevents problems from occurring. Stay in tune with the facility and its staff.

Problem Solving

Even the best, most thorough planner will have some problem or issue to deal with onsite. What happens if a speaker changes his or her mind at the last minute and demands a piece of equipment that A/V doesn't have? What if your keynote speaker gets stuck in traffic or an attendee complains about his room and wants a refund? What if your shipping company loses the shipment with your registration materials or more people than you guaranteed show up for a meal function? What if someone becomes ill, requiring medical attention?

Once onsite, you have to make decisions—fast. And at this point, almost all problems have an effect on the facility and its staff, not to mention your staff, too. The key here is to anticipate what could happen and, when it does, discuss the problem with your onsite manager and others who are involved. They really do want your meeting to be a success and, with your help, will do whatever they can to make it work. Working with composed, committed, and creative people is one of the greatest things about this business.

The Home Stretch

Onsite can be fun if you are on top of things. A lot of the hard work is done in advance when preparing the paperwork and documents for the meeting. To end this chapter, we leave you with the following tips for survival while onsite:

- Catch up on your sleep before you arrive. You need to be at your best!

- Preprogram your cell phone with the number of all your vendors. This includes the hotel you are staying at.

- Always confirm your onsite deliveries with all of your vendors. In the event of problems, ask to see the package room where the boxes are kept. Check the incoming package log to see if any of the boxes belong to your group.

- Don't leave anything of value unattended in the meeting rooms, registration area, or other public areas.

- Have your office re-keyed if you plan to keep valuables in the room, such as computer equipment. For keycard locks, place a lockout on it. Access to the room is limited to the people to whom you give keys.

- For large meetings, get on the in-house radio system with the hotel staff. This gives you immediate access to help when you need it. Learn their radio lingo, and you will fit in just fine.

- Carry a small, retractable blade (on a keychain or in your fanny pack). You'll be amazed at how many boxes you'll open. Remember to pack it in your checked luggage if the Transportation Security Administration (TSA) continues to implement some of their policies.

- Use your plastic name badge holder as a pocket to store room keys, money, and business cards (behind the nametag).

- Wear comfortable shoes! And change your socks or shoes at least once daily to protect your feet.

- Have big bowls of chocolate in your office. Don't share.

- Get a massage at the spa when the meeting is over.

Going onsite should be the best part of the planning process. All your hard work is finally paying off, and there is light at the end of the tunnel! Once the meeting is over, stay an extra day, meet with the facility staff to review the meeting, and take a little time to relax. You deserve it.

The Least You Need to Know

◆ Develop your registration process and layout so that it makes sense in the facility's environment.

◆ A well-trained and fully informed conference staff makes the meeting flow much more smoothly.

◆ A lot of work and planning go on behind the scenes, and you probably aren't the only group in-house. Plan ahead so you don't have to make major changes to your program onsite.

◆ Enlist the help of the facility when problems arise, and *always* maintain your composure!

24

Safety and Security

In This Chapter

- ◆ Learn what defines a crisis
- ◆ See what kind of negative things can and do happen onsite
- ◆ Discover what professional security services provide
- ◆ Learn three strategies for dealing with challenging situations

Planners spend so much time getting every meeting detail right that it's easy to put planning for the unexpected on the back burner. Just because you don't expect bad things to happen doesn't mean you shouldn't be prepared.

As a planner, you need to understand the importance of protecting your attendees, organization, and its property, and reducing overall risk. You spend a lot of money planning a successful meeting, so don't watch your efforts go up in smoke by overlooking safety and security issues. At the very least, when onsite, you should have a first aid kit, have fast access to someone who is certified in CPR, know where the nearest hospital is, know where the automatic external defibrillators (AEDs) are and what staff can operate them, and know how to contact the facility emergency staff.

This chapter sheds some light on preventing and dealing with bumps in the road.

What Is a Crisis?

In the meetings industry, you will hear the term *crisis management*. Before you can begin to manage a crisis, however, shouldn't you know what one is? A crisis in the meetings industry could be defined as when things don't go as planned. It happens all the time. But come on, really, how do you define a *true* crisis? We think that the definition is subjective and is relative to the impact on your attendees and your meeting. For example, if you are allowing a choice of chicken or beef for a meal and run out of chicken (leaving only beef), that's not a crisis. It may be disappointing, annoying, or embarrassing, but it's not a crisis. If, however, your attendees come down with food poisoning, that's a crisis.

A specific definition of a crisis is difficult to pinpoint because people react and handle issues and stress differently. If your highly paid celebrity keynote speaker is flying over the city in a holding pattern and can't make the opening session, whether you have a crisis depends on how you and your decision-makers handle it. Here is a list of some of the things that can have a negative impact on your meeting:

How would you classify the following: a real crisis (C) or a mere paper cut (PC)?

- Bomb threats (C)
- Chemical spills (C)
- Crime (C)
- Assault (C or PC ... it depends)
- Theft (C or PC ... it depends)
- Fire (C)
- Lost materials (generally a PC)
- Lunch buffet ran out of food (PC)
- Medical emergencies (C)
  - Allergic reactions
  - Choking
  - Death
  - Disease

- ◆ Injuries from falls

- ◆ Food poisoning

- ◆ Heart attack

- ◆ Illness

- ◆ Other serious conditions or injuries

◆ Natural disasters (C)

- ◆ Earthquakes

- ◆ Floods

- ◆ Hurricanes

- ◆ Storms

- ◆ Tornadoes

◆ Personal crises (C or PC … it depends)

◆ Power outages (C or PC)

◆ Speaker no-shows (PC)

◆ Strikes (C or PC)

◆ Terrorism or threat thereof (C)

> **The Inside Scoop**
>
> If you have attendees from overseas, consider asking them to provide medical insurance documentation during registration. You don't want a situation in which they need medical treatment in the United States but have no means to pay for it.

Your Motto: Be Prepared

You are running an important training seminar that requires numerous handouts. One hour before the session, you find that all the handouts have been mistakenly thrown out. The seminar is useless without them. What do you do?

Your organization spent $80,000 creating a multimedia video rolling out its new logo to be presented at the opening general session. The night before, you find out it's back at the home office. What do you do?

A huge snowstorm up and down the East Coast is preventing 40 percent of your attendees from getting to your meeting. Many are calling to cancel altogether. What do you do?

When faced with a crisis or a paper-cut situation, follow these suggestions:

◆ First and foremost, have a contingency plan in place. That will help keep you from panicking. Panic serves no purpose. You must collect information, discuss options, and make fast decisions, and you can't do that very well if you are upset or let the situation get to you. Take a deep breath and know, if you prepared ahead of time, you'll get through it.

◆ You cannot anticipate every scenario, but it is very important that you plan for the ones with the largest impact. Before your meeting, take the time with your staff, the facility, and local emergency personnel to think through the "what-ifs" and come up with crisis management methods.

◆ Always get a reservation list (with room numbers) of attendees staying in the hotel. You never know when you may need to contact an attendee or attendees quickly. A patient and cooperative hotel operator can be your best friend at a time like this.

◆ At the start of your meeting/event, obtain the names, titles, and phone and pager numbers for all people responsible for a facility's emergency procedures. Meet them in person, if possible.

◆ Work with the facility, vendors, your staff, and all others who are involved. In any emergency, crisis, or bad situation, you must rely on the talents and experience of others. Get their feedback and let them help in areas in which they have expertise.

◆ In the event of a crisis, instruct your staff not to guess or speculate on potential outcomes and to only state facts. Otherwise, rumors and misinformation spread, and it will make your task that much harder.

Food for Thought

For natural disasters, an emergency plan includes moving people to a secure, safe location and providing medical attention and good communication.

The bottom line is to plan and prepare for the unexpected. As the lead planner, you will be expected not only to make decisions but to provide leadership. It's important to temper your emotions and provide clear and honest communication. As long as attendees know that solutions are forthcoming, they will be calmer and happier.

Written Contingency Plans

You can't remember every meeting detail, can you? You have to write things down, especially information that must be communicated to others. Therefore, there's no way you can develop backup plans and not put them in writing. You, your staff, the facility's staff, and many others need direction, and the written backup plan is the place to start.

When creating a contingency plan, one of the first things you should do is obtain a copy of the facility's or hotel's emergency procedures. Review it and ask questions. It is important for you to understand how the facility implements its plan and who is responsible in various categories. Post 9/11/01, most hotels will not provide their entire emergency plan to customers. Discuss what plans they have in place and ensure they will help you if a problem arises.

Ask yourself how your meeting fits in with their procedures. Understand the chain of command. You should take the important parts of the facility's procedures and create your own supplemental document for your meeting (and staff). This document should provide an outline of what to do under certain circumstances. Be as specific as possible. These procedures should also be easy to read. In an emergency, people don't have time (and won't) thumb through lengthy volumes of material.

Do you need a written backup plan for non-emergency procedures? Maybe. It's your call. Many circumstances develop fast, and you will have to work with a variety of people to solve them quickly. If a speaker does not show up, referring to a procedure won't do much. But consider the value of identifying some common problems, putting them in writing, and reviewing them with your staff. Written procedures provide a reference point on which people can base their decisions.

> **Food for Thought**
>
> Have emergency contact information for attendees printed separately from the program and on special colored cards so that the information stands out. Keep it secure and destroy it once the meeting concludes.

Professional Security Services

Depending on the needs of your meeting or event, you may choose to hire a security services company. These companies specialize in onsite event security and management. The following are some of the services they provide:

- Controlled access into and out of meeting/event areas
- Establishment of emergency action plans
- Onsite uniformed security staff
- Protection of proprietary information
- Protection of equipment, valuable items
- VIP and celebrity security

To decide whether you need a security firm, consider the following factors:

- Will your meeting have diplomats, celebrities, or VIPs? They may come with their own security, but you might consider hiring some additional people, especially to work with their security personnel.

- What is the location of your event? Will you be in an area where crime or political turmoil is a factor?

- Is there a scheduled event or deadline that might expose your meeting to risk? A strike deadline or a nearby major sporting or other event?

- What is your meeting's topic? Is it controversial? Is there a concern for the safety of speakers or attendees?

- Is there potential for theft of materials or intellectual property?

With meetings and events costing significant sums, it is worth considering the value that a professional security company offers. It only takes one incident or one unforeseen event to turn your entire meeting into a negative, and the financial cost could be great.

Educating Yourself

Another important area in safety and security is learning what is going on "out there." What do you know about luggage theft, hotel burglary, pickpockets, laptop theft, and general travel safety? Probably not much. People who travel—and you and your attendees do a lot of that—are at a very high risk for some kind of theft. Travelers are usually weary and distracted, a bad combination, and they often carry expensive items such as computers, PDAs, jewelry, and of course, cash and credit cards. Savvy thieves know this, too, and have figured out clever ways to part travelers with their treasures.

Fortunately, we have discovered a nifty resource called Corporate Travel Safety (CTS). CTS is owned by Kevin Coffey, a veteran police detective who is a pioneer in travel safety and crime avoidance. At his website, you can find a listing of over 130 travel safety links ranging from Aircraft Emergency Tips to Women Safety Tips (from a female cop) and everything in between. These tips and more can be found at www.kevincoffee.com/safety_tips_index.htm.

Other Minor Frustrations

Frustrations may not fall into the category of emergencies or crises (although sometimes attendees make you feel like you are in a crisis); they still need to be anticipated and addressed. You are much more likely to spend much more time dealing with little frustrations than with big dilemmas.

Last-Minute Requests

There are last-minute requests and then there are last-minute requests. When you are onsite, you need to be responsive to the needs of your meeting and your attendees. You don't have the time or the resources to honor everyone's requests. When considering whether to honor someone's request, ask yourself what's the worst thing that will happen if you don't. You don't want to do or say the wrong thing and run the risk of turning a minor issue into a battle.

Here are some examples of things you may be asked to consider doing:

- Mail an attendee's registration materials home (at your expense).

- Modify a speaker's evaluation form right before he begins speaking. (You can do this during his talk, can't you?)

- Leave the staff office open after hours.

- Change the banquet lunch menu the day before because one of the organizers doesn't like it.

- Add a data projector but not pay for it. Instead, take it from an existing room and return it later.

- Change an attendee's return airline reservation.

- Deliver something to someone's room.

♦ Watch someone's briefcase or suitcase for the day.

♦ Loan an attendee money.

This list could go on and on. You want to be helpful, but where do you draw the line? Sometimes you can't honor a request (like changing the menu). Other times, it's unethical (like not paying for the data projector). Still other times, it's just plain not your job (like mailing the materials—you've got enough to do). In some cases, however, there are good reasons to help (like making airline reservations for an attendee from overseas because his English is poor or he does not understand U.S. customs).

What you do is up to you. You should take each request on a case-by-case basis. Sometimes you'll have to bite the bullet and do things you think are silly or wasteful of your time; other times, you'll have to put your foot down. Use your judgment.

Oh, Puleese!

Some people get up in arms about very minor issues—they just like to complain. It's too hot; it's too cold. The food was terrible. I can't read the speaker's slides from the back of the room. Sometimes the requests (or complaints) border on the ridiculous. A veteran planner gave us a great piece of advice years ago: She said to listen with empathy. Many times, people just want to be heard. They have a problem and want someone to do something. Many times you can't solve it, but tell the person you'll try. Sometimes the problem solves itself. Sometimes it doesn't matter. Take heart and take notes. You just might want to write about it someday.

The Least You Need to Know

♦ Plan ahead for emergencies with written procedures.

♦ Review all procedures with your staff.

♦ Professional security services can provide a full range of pre-event and onsite assistance.

♦ It's okay to say no to last-minute requests.

Chapter 25

It's Not Over 'Til It's Over

In This Chapter

- ◆ Discover why you must always double-check your master bill
- ◆ Learn some tips on tipping
- ◆ Learn what goes into your meeting's final report
- ◆ Understand some of the ethical dilemmas planners face

Just when you think the meeting is over and you're done, you realize there's still quite a bit of wrap-up to do.

In this chapter, we focus on tying up the loose ends, paying bills, tabulating evaluations, tipping, and generating reports. We also talk about ethics. Ethics defines behavior, and it influences many of the planning decisions we make.

Paying the Bills

We recommend that you sign off on your *banquet checks* and review all charges to your meeting or event master account every day. You should also review, one more time, your master bill charges with accounting before you leave and keep a copy of all documentation. Now comes the easy part (or at least the fairly easy part).

Meeting Speak

A **banquet check** is the standard document used to break down the charges for a specific event, usually food and beverage.

In many cases, you will not receive the master bill for three to six weeks after your meeting, sometimes longer. Why? Well, it takes a few days for all the charges to get posted. Then someone from accounting needs to collect the charges, review your contract to make sure you've met your contractual obligations with respect to revenue, and start calculating. Plus, yours isn't the only meeting invoice accounting is working on. Consider stipulating in the contract that you will have a final bill in hand within two to three weeks of your meeting.

Eventually, you will receive your master bill with the associated backup. If you reviewed your charges daily and again before you left the facility, reviewing the bill should be easy. Be prepared to spend some time reviewing the bill in detail. Be on the lookout for last-minute additions such as shipping and additional food and beverage or A/V charges. Sometimes you'll find a charge for an attendee that gets put on your account by mistake. No matter how confident you are that you've approved everything, review each charge carefully. It's our experience that there are always errors on the master bill, mostly minor. The sooner you call errors to the facility's attention, the sooner they can revise the bill and get paid.

In addition, make sure all concessions or conditions outlined in your contract are met. Make sure your final bill reflects the following:

♦ Correct calculation of complimentary rooms

♦ Any food and beverage discounts

♦ Any A/V discounts

♦ Removal of state or local sales tax, if you are tax exempt

♦ Deposits

♦ All charges billed correctly

Tipping ... Didn't We Do That?

Yes and no. When onsite, a number of people work on your behalf to get things done. Your convention services manager (CSM) or catering manager (CM) is responsible for communicating your needs to the facility staff, which includes the following:

- ◆ Audio-visual staff
- ◆ Banquet staff
- ◆ Bell staff
- ◆ Concierge
- ◆ Front desk staff
- ◆ Housekeeping
- ◆ Recreation director(s)
- ◆ Setup crew
- ◆ Shipping/receiving staff

Food for Thought

If you forget to bring thank you notes, ask your sales contact or convention services manager for blank note cards. He or she usually will have some on hand and will gladly give you some, especially if you specify that they are for individual facility staff tips!

These people are the backbone of the facility and are the ones who make everything happen. Sadly, sometimes they go unnoticed and unthanked. Should you thank them by giving them a tip? Isn't that what the food-and-beverage service charge/gratuity was for? Let's shed some light on this.

The terms "service charge," "gratuity," and "tip" are frequently used interchangeably by meeting facilities, but they can mean different things. Ask a facility what service charges/gratuities you are paying for and to whom they are distributed. Many people contribute to the success of your meeting but are not included in the distribution of the service charges or mandatory gratuities. The bottom line is, be sure to ask and understand who is covered and who is not in both the service charge and gratuity categories. In most cases, gratuity or service charges are taxable.

Individual tipping is always very much appreciated but is not expected. We do it at each meeting because we want to recognize the people who have provided great service (and they *will* remember your kindness when you return for your next meeting).

If tipping is important to you, at the start of your meeting, begin a "tip list." Throughout the meeting, write down the names and departments of people who help you. Ask the convention services manager for a list of facility staff who worked on your program. On the last day of your meeting, compare your list to that of the convention services manager (it may get lengthy) and assign dollar amounts. It's a nice touch to put the tips in individual handwritten thank you notes.

If you want to thank a group, like the banquet staff, housekeepers, or bellstaff, and don't know their names, put some money in an envelope with a thank you note and ask the convention services manager or group's supervisor to distribute.

One big question is how much to tip. You might decide to give a banquet staffer $10, your A/V technician $30, and your convention services manager $50. It really depends on the amount and level of service you received and your budget. If your A/V person ran around nonstop for four days and worked miracles, $30 may not be nearly enough; in fact, $100 may not even seem like enough! A quick way to get cash onsite for tipping is to request a cash advance or "payout" against your master bill. Ask your onsite contact if this is possible.

The Inside Scoop

Tips don't have to be in cash, especially if you have a large group and many people were involved. Flowers, chocolates, candy, and other treats for "the crew" are always welcome and go a long way. Others may appreciate T-shirts or conference tote bags with the meeting logo. Be sure to ask your contact what the facility's rules are before distributing any of these items or cash. In some cases, the employees will need permission to take these items out of the building or accept money.

When the time comes to distribute tips, it's best to do it in person with a verbal thank you. When you can't do that, ask your convention services manager or catering manager to do the honors. If you need a record for accounting purposes, ask that individual to sign your distribution list and get a copy of the payout slip from accounting.

Tabulating the Evaluations

Evaluations are one of the last important meeting details to handle. Before you leave the facility, make sure you have collected all your evaluations, especially if they were left in various locations. Once you leave, poof—they're gone.

Depending on the complexity of your evaluation form, it may take a few days or weeks to get them tabulated. When you return to your office, it's a good idea to get started tabulating evaluations quickly. We know from experience that the longer it takes to get to them, the harder they are to finish. This is because your body and mind move on to the next project, and it's so hard to go back. If possible, assign the tabulation to one or more administrative staff and get it finished.

Once they are completed, you should prepare a cohesive synopsis. The synopsis may include your interpretations and recommendations for the next meeting. Send them to all of the decision-makers as well as the people who were involved in planning the meeting. Also consider sending a copy to your sponsors and exhibitors so that the value of your meeting is reinforced. Send the facility a copy of the evaluations that pertain to the facility and service. They want to know, too!

You should also provide all of your speakers with a copy of their evaluations(s). Speakers probably are not interested in the full synopsis of the meeting, just their portion. However, if your overall evaluations contain pertinent speaker-related information, send that along, too.

You may want to consider an online evaluation service. These companies send an e-mail to your attendees and ask them to respond online. This takes a lot less time than tabulating individual paper responses.

Final Facility Reports

Make sure you receive a final report from the facility. The report should include a recap of everything you contracted for (rooms, food and beverage, A/V, and so on) and final comments, if possible, about how the meeting attendees used the facilities.

CAUTION

Don't Drop the Ball

Make it a part of your contract that the facility agrees to provide detailed information about your meeting in a recap report.

For future meeting negotiations, it is also helpful to know if the attendees used airport transportation, ate and drank in the restaurants and bars, used room service, and so on.

Your Final Report

After you have received all of the bills, tabulated your evaluations, and received your facility reports, it's time to put them all together in one final meeting report. Don't worry; it's not a huge project. You just need to consolidate the useful info into a report that outlines your meeting or event. The final report should have the info described in the history report form as well as the following:

- Meeting/event name and dates
- Location

- ◆ Goal(s)

- ◆ Objectives

- ◆ Registration summary including the number of registrants (paid) and number of complimentary registrants, VIPs, sponsors, exhibitors, cancellations, no-shows, etc.

- ◆ Comments

- ◆ Evaluation summaries

- ◆ Conclusions

- ◆ Any other information you deem relevant

The final report is valuable because it contains your meeting/event history. Chances are someone, probably you, will do this meeting/event or a similar one again in the future. The decision-makers, planning committee, and facility sales staff will ask a lot of questions. You won't remember all the details, and in the early planning process, you will be able to refer to this document. The great thing is that all the important information you need to get the next program going will be in one place! Check the APEX tools at conventionindustry.org for some good ideas and formats for final reports.

Ethics

Ethics is an important topic in any industry and is always a hot topic in meeting and event industry circles. Planners must make many decisions, some having large financial implications. It's quite common for vendors to "sweeten the pot" with personal incentives, gifts, and deals. The full range of temptations is enough for an entire chapter; unfortunately, we don't have room for this discourse. However, we want to highlight a few of the ethical discussions that meeting and event planners (and suppliers) are having. As you will see, there are two sides to every story.

To Fam or Not to Fam

Familiarization (fam) trips are usually multi-day, all-expense-paid trips to a location for the purpose of showcasing specific hotels, restaurants, other facilities, and attractions. Often a planner can bring a guest for a nominal fee and/or the cost of their airfare. Because the venues are marketing themselves, they fly you in, limo you around, wine you, dine you, lavish you with nice gifts, and house you in upgraded accommodations. Sounds like tremendous fun, huh? But you also get tours of many facilities, meet upper management, see a lot of the area, get tons of pertinent information, and get to ask a lot of questions. (It is always important to keep in mind while on a fam trip the level of VIP service and upgraded accommodations you receive are not necessarily going to be the same caliber as that which your average attendee will get. Fam trips are a sales effort.)

If you are asked to go on a fam trip, what would you do? (Hint: Not all are appropriate.) Here are some considerations:

- Go because you are seriously considering the location.

- Go because you've never been there and you want to check it out and are sure your employer is considering or could consider the destination.

- Go because you can take your family and make a vacation out of it.

- Go some other time when you can pay for it yourself.

The Debate on the Rebate

Almost all hotels will pay a commission or a rebate on the sleeping room revenue if negotiated prior to contract signing. Asking for a commission or rebate on sleeping room revenue may or may not increase the cost of the sleeping rooms. It depends on whom you talk to. Commissions are paid primarily to third-party planners or to travel agents, and rebates are paid back to the meeting host.

There are two considerations here, both about disclosure. The first centers on whether the third party should disclose to the client (the meeting sponsor) that they are receiving a commission from the hotel. In many cases, the hotel will insist that it be disclosed and put into the contract. The second consideration centers on whether any rebate or commission, no matter who gets it, should be disclosed to the attendees. If it does not affect the room rate, what difference does it make? Do attendees really care? If you do tell them, will it open up a can of worms? So, now you've booked a meeting and are getting a nice rebate for your organization (let's say $7 per room night). What would you do? (Before you answer these questions, talk with your attorney and tax advisor—some of these fees have other implications.)

- Take the rebate because it really helps your bottom line.

- Take the rebate but disclose it to your attendees.

- Only get net (non-rebated) rates.

Other Ethical Issues

Other ethical dilemmas that planners face include receiving gifts from vendors, using someone else's creative theme or meeting design ideas from a proposal, receiving a free weekend vacation from a hotel as a thank you, and receiving tickets, dinners, or other perks from vendors.

Another interesting "reward" is awarding hotel points. Some major hotel chains offer hotel points, which are like frequent flyer miles, to planners who book meetings at their property. Planners can redeem these points for free stays and other things. You get the idea. Depending on the size of your meeting, these points can be substantial.

Many of the industry's associations have codes of ethics or guidelines for professional behavior. If you are not sure about a specific situation, you can always check these guidelines for help in making your decision. Another good test is to determine how you'd feel if your name with this action were on the front page of your local paper.

It's not enough for planners to make decisions about meeting-related details; some decisions require a reflection on what is ethical. Ethics are always being debated in the meetings industry and that's good. It's not okay to look the other way or to do something just because the industry allows it. When faced with an ethical quandary, ask yourself, "Is it the right thing to do?"

The Least You Need to Know

- Your master bill needs to be reviewed carefully and compared to your contract. Resolve discrepancies immediately while the meeting is fresh in your mind.

- Tipping facility staff is not expected, but it's fairly common and is always appreciated.

- Your final meeting report is one of your most important resources for the next time.

- When making important decisions, consider the ethics behind them. You are your reputation and in this industry with its great networking opportunities, the word spreads quickly.

26

For Suppliers Only (Planners May Take a Peek)

In This Chapter

◆ Learn the six ways to lose a customer

◆ Discover six steps to a great partnership

◆ Learn the number one mistake a hotel salesperson makes on a site visit

◆ Understand how to educate your customers

◆ See what kinds of information a planner wants to see in a post-meeting report

This chapter will give meeting and event industry suppliers an inside look at what planners are looking for when purchasing goods and services. It also will help suppliers foster positive, mutually beneficial business relationships with meeting and event planners.

For planners, this chapter provides a glimpse of what other planners look for when working with suppliers. It is always helpful to have a frame of reference to help you determine your best course of action. It's nice to know you are not alone!

Of course, the best relationships are honest and open, and you both learn from one another. In these changing times, we all need to work together to maximize the benefits of our business relationships.

Six Ways to Lose a Customer

We start with this topic not to be negative but to send a wake-up call to all suppliers that many times you will never know the real reason for the loss of business. It is true that the meetings industry is cyclical; it is either a suppliers' or buyers' market. The point is that things change, and treating your customers consistently well, regardless of market conditions, is a tried and true way to keep them in good times and in bad.

Here are the top six ways to lose (or not win) a customer:

1. Send a contract with items that are different than what was discussed or send a contract omitting the items a planner will be charged for onsite.

2. Don't return phone, fax, or e-mail inquiries promptly.

3. Don't show genuine interest in the client and his or her business (for example, by serving cookie-cutter proposals and contracts).

4. Underestimate the value of a small meeting. Keep in mind that your client may represent large and small opportunities at different times. Paying attention to today's small meeting may lead to a huge convention next year.

5. Leave messages like "Hi. I am calling to find out if you plan meetings. Please call me at …." If you make cold calls, then do your homework in advance and plan your approach.

6. Be inflexible. There is a difference between being inflexible and genuinely not being able to honor a request. It comes down to educating your clients. Inflexibility is often perceived when, in reality, there is a real business reason behind not taking a piece of business. Explain why.

Six Steps to a Great Partnership

On the flip side, there are ways to be a true partner to meeting and event planners. These may sound too simple, and you may already think you do them. The real question is "Do you?"

1. Ask questions and listen to what meeting planners say.

2. Return phone, fax, and e-mail inquiries promptly.

3. Understand client needs before responding. Read the request for proposals (RFPs) and ask a lot of questions if needed. Provide solutions.

4. Know your product or services.

5. Know your competition and your competitive advantages.

6. Be sincere.

Know Your Property/Product/Service

One of the most frustrating experiences a planner has with a supplier is when a supplier does not know his or her product or service inside and out. For example, things like freight elevators, electrical outlets, loading docks, and how many people fit into meeting rooms are just some examples of things suppliers often do not know. If you are not sure, conduct site inspections when there are different groups in house to see how your facility works best. Take a tour with a facility engineer, A/V personnel, and the convention services manager. Be able to answer questions with confidence. Check out the APEX Site Profiles Panel (conventionindustry.org) and become familiar with the areas noted.

> **Don't Drop the Ball**
>
> The number one mistake made by salespeople on a hotel site visit is not doing their homework. Understand the meeting's needs and how your facility can accommodate them.

Site Visits

When a planner conducts a site visit, he or she is there to determine whether the facility is a good match for a particular meeting. (Don't underestimate the possibility that they may also have a future meeting or event in the back of their mind, as they review the facilities capabilities.) If you have done your homework prior to the site visit, you know the program and other ancillary needs of the group. You should first talk with the planner and, with convention services staff, map out a plan as to how you can accommodate the group. Come up with some ideas and present them to the planner. All too often, the planner is left to map out the program in a facility without expert advice. Explain how exhibitors will load in and out, where the stage might best be placed in the ballroom, and how the breakouts could fit into the allotted space. Tell the planner what tends to work best in your facility. After all, you've seen many more programs in your facility than the planner has.

Show the planner what he or she wants and needs to see. Go the extra mile. Explain where you envision the meetings, meals, and other activities taking place. Paint a picture for the planner and help the person place his or her meeting in your facility.

Know These Things, Too

Planners want to know that their business—today and tomorrow—is important. If you understand their business, they will see that you are a valuable resource, and the relationship will start out strong. Here are some other things meeting planners ask about that salespeople should know:

- The location of meeting room light switches and thermostats
- A/V equipment basics
- Food and beverage basics
- Food and beverage outlet hours of operation
- Area attractions
- Offsite dinner/reception venues
- Directions to the airport
- Facility emergency procedures

In addition, know your competition and your competitive advantages. Also update the planner on changes such as personnel, property name or management changes, special promotions, policy changes, renovations, and construction dates. These could impact planner decisions.

Prepare to Solicit

Your goal is to build rapport, analyze needs, show how your facility can meet those needs, and build a trust-based relationship. Soliciting for customers isn't the same as it used to be. Planners, just like everyone else, have too much on their plate and really don't want to be bothered with calls, faxes, and e-mails from organizations they will never do business with.

Find out where you can go online to market your property and where to find clients looking for space. Here's a hint: Start by surfing the websites we have highlighted in the book. Take a look at all the marketing opportunities on these sites.

Food for Thought

Make sure your collateral material is relevant and easy to read. Your website should be user-friendly and should address the most frequently asked questions. Get rid of "canned" solicitation letters.

Participate in some of the meeting industry online discussions. Get your name out there! Networking still works in the new century—particularly in this industry. If you are not good at using e-mail and getting on the web, take a class or ask someone for help.

Exactly how do you reach planners who need your products and services? If we knew the exact answer, we'd be relaxing on a beach in Kauai. You will have to figure out which methods work best for you and create some of your own, too!

Here are some of the rules for finding customers:

- Plan your strategy.

- Determine your target market.

- Hang out at meetings and other places your target market frequents. Attend educational sessions—you'll meet the smartest planners there and learn more yourself.

- Do your homework. If you call a prospective client, know why you are calling and make a connection.

- Work hard for referrals and follow up.

- Use technology efficiently. Find out where you can find potential customers online.

- Always carry business cards and never be timid about striking up conversations with strangers.

Random, cold solicitations are obsolete. By networking, garnering referrals, and personalizing solicitations based on needs, you'll see a bigger bang for your marketing buck.

Food for Thought

Keep on top of the meetings industry. Subscribe to trade publications and read about the issues and challenges planners face on a daily basis.

You are better off spending $3,000 to attend a meeting and tradeshow and sit alongside meeting planners in sessions while you both learn, than by sending unsolicited marketing materials via mail, fax, or e-mail. Heck, you are better off attending conferences and spending time just to network in the hallways!

It comes down to providing a solution to the customer's problem. When responding to an RFP or other lead, sales managers need to find out very specific details about the piece of business. Nine times out of ten, planners receive canned proposals because the sales manager didn't read the RFP and failed to qualify the business. Guess who has the best chance to book the meeting? The one who paid attention. We had a client that was so impressed at how a facility customized their proposal to a meeting, the client used that as the deciding factor to give the facility the business.

Educate the Customer

Educating the customer is an important and often overlooked role of every supplier. We all know that supply and demand drives availability and rates. We also know there are great pieces of business and not-so-great pieces of business. Educate your customers on the value of their business. If a customer is aware that there are ways to make his or her business better for a property, you both win.

Educating customers means being honest and telling them exactly why you can't book their business. On the flip side, it means telling them why you want their business. Maybe it fills a hole for you, but they think it is great because there are a lot of food functions. Level with them. Be open and honest to begin with, and long-term relationships can develop.

Inquiry Calls

The inquiry call, from a potential customer, is the first opportunity to educate him or her. To begin with, you do not know the experience level of the person making the inquiry. To respond properly, the first thing you should find out is the caller's level of understanding of the meetings industry. Determine at the beginning of an inquiry whether you have a first-time planner on your hands or a 25-year veteran. Then you will know better how to approach the business.

You do this by asking a few open-ended questions about the meeting, the organization, and where you might have met before. You'll know in a few minutes where the person stands in the experience department. If he or she has read this book, you're in trouble!

Once you have evaluated the person's business, explain in detail why you are submitting a proposal or declining it. Explain what would make it good business. Do you need more food and beverage revenue? Do you need a higher room rate? Exactly what are the criteria?

Don't Drop the Ball

Be up front on items such as setup fees, labor charges, comp rooms, upgrades, surcharges, and delivery charges. Explain what a "tentative hold" is and how long you will hold space, if at all, before a contract is signed.

Preparing a Proposal

The next opportunity to educate the customer is in the proposal. The inquiry determines how you structure your proposal, but you now have the occasion to be very detailed as to how the business fits into your facility. Make sure to include all costs associated with doing business with your facility or business. All too often, planners get onsite and find unforeseen details turning into budget busters. For example, what is the cost of copies? Internet connections? Valet parking? Service charges and taxes? At what percentage do attrition charges kick in? Newer meeting planners may not anticipate these charges and may not realize it until too late simply because they have little or no experience.

Some suppliers will argue that if planners don't ask, you don't tell. If this is your philosophy, you may have a one-time customer. Forget repeat business.

Proposals should ...

- Be customized.

- Be concise and to the point.

- Be on time.

- Respond to customer's requests.

- Be creative and demonstrate your understanding of the business.

Contracts

Once the proposal goes to a contract stage, review and explain it to the planner. Especially pay attention to the cancellation, attrition, and insurance sections. You should also tell planners who will be their contact for planning the meeting, and you should review their deadlines as specified in the contract. Next, explain your accounting and billing process. An informed customer is a happy customer.

Anticipate Needs

This is where you can really help newer meeting planners use your facility to their benefit. Until a planner is actually onsite for the meeting, there are many things that can get overlooked. By asking the right questions, you can figure out all of his or her needs in advance and eliminate unnecessary frustrations onsite.

Here are some important questions to ask planners:

- **Where will your attendees eat when there are no food functions planned?** This will clue you in to when and if to staff the F&B outlets.

- **When and how do you expect your attendees to arrive?** This will clue you in to those motor coaches about to pull up to the front door.

- **Tell me about the most successful part of the meeting last year.** This will clue you in to specific things that you should make sure work well.

- **Tell me what you would change about last year's meeting site and service.** This will clue you in to how you can become the hero.

- **Explain how you envision the general session setup.** This will clue you in to space and setup issues like 24-hour meeting space holds.

- **Tell me about your attendees.** This will clue you in to the types of services you need to offer during the meeting. Will your health club be busy?

- **Tell me about your exhibitors. What kinds of products and services do they exhibit?** This will give you a heads up on the elephant they plan on bringing in the front doors of the lobby entrance.

You get the idea. This is where you ask pointed questions and let planners describe their meeting and their needs. We are sure you can come up with a hundred other questions.

Provide Their Meeting History

Suppliers always want to know about a group's past meeting history during the early contracting stages. It is important that the planner tracks this information for each meeting. To make it easier, after every meeting, suppliers should provide detailed information to the planner in a timely manner, so planners can update their records and maintain an accurate history prior to the next round of contract negotiations.

Statistics

Statistics include guestrooms picked up per day compared to the room block, guestrooms picked up at certain intervals prior to arrival, food-and-beverage revenues, *covers* and guarantees by food function, revenue generated in the outlets, A/V revenue, rental fees, and general statistics about the meeting.

Meeting Speak

A **cover** is a meal served to one attendee. If you serve 200 people for dinner, you serve 200 covers.

Observations

Observations, in addition to statistics, are very helpful to planners when planning future meetings. Provide comments from the various department heads on how the group was serviced. Break it down by department and create a report for all to complete. Include the following:

- ◆ **Reservations.** Room pickup, suite usage.

- ◆ **Bell stand.** Self-parking and valet usage, comments about bell staff usage.

- ◆ **Front desk.** Arrival and departure patterns, late check-outs, no-shows.

- ◆ **Housekeeping.** Rollaway beds and refrigerator usage.

- ◆ **Switchboard.** Number of additional lines, wake-up call usage, phone call traffic in general.

- ◆ **Food and beverage outlets.** Number of covers and revenue in each outlet for the group.

- ◆ **Security.** List calls from attendees and if there were any problems.

- ◆ **Accounting.** Deposit received, any special billing issues.

- ◆ **Banquets.** Number of covers served versus guarantees. Total revenue by function. Note any special meal requests.

- ◆ **Audio-visual.** List any last-minute requests and the total amount billed.

Indicate whether the final numbers are inclusive of service charges and taxes. Even go so far as to include the final calculations. Planners will appreciate detailed information when they refer to the report in the future.

Ask all departments to contribute to post-meeting reports. This is a program you can institute in the hotel by asking all departments to provide a report within a few days of every group's departure. Include statistics as well as general comments and even suggestions for improvement. This process also forces the staff to pay closer attention to the details—an added bonus!

This report should be sent to the client within a few weeks of departure. There are some major chains already doing this, but more could jump on the bandwagon.

The Least You Need to Know

- ◆ Know your property, product, or service inside and out. Enough said.

- ◆ Do your homework prior to writing a proposal and conducting a site inspection. Know exactly how the meeting fits in to your property and be prepared to discuss it.

- ◆ Be up front on all charges associated with doing business with your facility.

- ◆ Provide all meeting and event groups with a post-meeting report.

Chapter 27

Meeting Industry Certification

In This Chapter

- ♦ Learn the certification designations available in the meetings industry
- ♦ Find out what colleges and universities offer degrees or certificates in meeting management
- ♦ Learn what kind of education you need to become a meeting planner
- ♦ Discover some resources for finding a job in the meetings industry

The meetings industry, like most industries, has its own educational process and certifications. If you are serious about the meetings industry as a career path, you may want to work toward obtaining professional certification. Many of the associations listed in this book offer certification programs for their specific discipline. This chapter will help you sort out your options.

We'll tell you about resources for finding positions within the meetings industry. We'll also tell you about college degrees and how to find schools that offer meeting planning programs. Finally, we'll address how associations are stepping up to the plate to provide cutting-edge education via distance learning, seminars, and conferences.

Education is a lifelong process, and keeping up with the industry takes time and effort to maintain the knowledge base necessary for future success.

Certification: Is It for You?

Okay, so you think your name would look good with a few initials behind it? Many people do. We know many talented certified planners and suppliers. We also know many meeting and event planners and suppliers who do not have any certifications, and they, too, are excellent in their field. Whether or not you decide to obtain certification depends on your particular situation and what type of education you need to do your job. Within the meetings industry, certification is quite visible and can lead to higher salaries.

> **The Inside Scoop**
>
> A certification designation demonstrates your dedication to your profession. It is not a reason to stop learning once you have achieved it, nor is it a piece of paper that says you are better qualified than people who are not certified.

Currently, there are two main certification designations for meeting planners:

- **Certified Meeting Professional (CMP).** Founded and organized through the Convention Industry Council (CIC). You can find more information at www.conventionindustry.org.

- **Certificate in Meeting Management (CMM).** It is awarded by Meeting Professionals International (MPI). You can find more information at www.mpiweb.org.

There are many other professional certifications within the meetings industry that apply to either planners, suppliers, or both. Here's a partial list, including the association that confers the designations:

Educational Institute of the American Hotel & Lodging Association (www. ei-ahla.org/certification.asp)

Certified Hospitality Sales Professional (CHSP)

Certified Hotel Administrator (CHA)

Certified Lodging Manager (CLM)

Certified Hospitality Educator (CHE)

Certified Food & Beverage Executive (CFBE)

Certified Rooms Division Executive (CRDE)

Certified Hospitality Housekeeping Executive (CHHE)

Certified Human Resources Executive (CHRE)

Certified Engineering Operations Executive (CEOE)

Certified Hospitality Supervisor (CHS)

American Society of Association Executives (www.asaenet.org)

Certified Association Executive (CAE)

Hospitality Sales and Marketing Association International (www.hsmai.org)

Certified Hospitality Marketing Executive (CHME)

International Association of Assembly Managers (www.iaam.org)

Certified Facilities Executive (CFE)

International Association of Exhibition Management (www.iaem.org)

Certified in Exhibition Management (CEM)

International Special Events Society (www.ises.com)

Certified Special Events Professional (CSEP)

National Association of Catering Executives (www.nace.net)

Certified Professional Catering Executive (CPCE)

National Speakers Association (www.nsaspeaker.org)

Certified Speaking Professional (CSP)

Society of Incentive and Travel Executives (www.SITE-intl.org)

Certified Incentive Travel Executive (CITE)

For a lot of people, years of experience are worth their weight in gold. A planner who plans multiple meetings and is active in the industry gets more education on the job than a planner who plans one or two small meetings a year. Only you can determine the areas in which you need more education and training.

Food for Thought

When you investigate a certification designation, find out for how long the designation is valid and what the requirements are for recertification.

Higher Education

You may want to consider a degree or certificate program from a college or university. Four-year hospitality degree programs are currently available from a variety of locations such as Arizona State University, Columbia College (MO), Appalachian State University (NC), and Baylor University (TX). As well, degrees in tourism and hotel and restaurant management can lead to some pretty exciting careers!

Degrees/Certificates

Many colleges and universities offer certificates or degrees in meeting, event, convention, exhibition, tourism, hotel, and restaurant management. The exact courses vary by institution. Here is a sampling:

California State University
Fullerton, CA
www.takethelead.fullerton.edu

Cornell University
Ithaca, NY
www.hotelschool.cornell.edu

George Washington University
Washington, DC
www.gwu.edu/emp/main.html

Indiana University Purdue University Indianapolis
Indianapolis, IN
www.iupui.edu/~indyhper/tcem_courses.htm

Madison Area Technical College
Madison, WI
matcmadison.edu

Michigan State University
East Lansing, MI
www.bus.msu.edu/shb

New York University
New York, NY
www.scps.nyu.edu/chtta

Northeastern University
Tahlequah, OK
www.nsuok.edu

Roosevelt University
Chicago, IL
www.roosevelt.edu/tourismstudies

University of Nevada—Harrah Hotel College
Las Vegas, NV
hotel.unlv.edu/departTour.html

University of Wisconsin—Stout
Menomonie, WI
www.uwstout.edu/programs/bshrtm

You also should check with local community colleges in your area. Many offer certificates in meeting planning. If you are not sure where to call, check with your state chapter of the industry associations. They will send you in the right direction.

Distance Learning

Distance learning no longer lets your hectic schedule preclude you from pursuing a degree. Taking classes online allows you to learn from the comfort of your own computer in your pajamas if need be. Most colleges and universities are beginning to offer courses online, so be sure to check. Some of the ones in the preceding list offer online courses, too.

Professional Associations

It's no big surprise that associations are great places to further your professional educational needs. Most offer seminars, conferences, and conventions featuring the newest trends, the latest technology, and cutting-edge speakers. This is another great reason to be a member of at least one professional industry association. Associations also offer distance-learning programs. Check out their websites for opportunities in this area. If you can't attend their meetings, at least you may be able to take advantage of their educational offerings.

Continuing Education Units (CEUs)

When you join an association that offers a certificate program, you will more than likely have to earn continuing education credits (CEUs) to qualify for the certification and recertification process. Each certification designation will have its own rules and stipulations for the program. In some instances, you will have to qualify to sit for the exam. For example, you may be required to have five years of employment experience in the field before you can apply for certification.

Conferences and Seminars

Attending conferences and seminars is one of the best ways to learn a lot in a small amount of time. The networking allows time to problem-solve, and that by itself is worth the registration fee. The opportunity to meet colleagues face-to-face provides the motivation and energy to do a better job back at the office. Connecting and sharing with your peers is powerful. Sharing what works and how to do things better will never be replaced by a computer screen or a textbook.

Get a Job! Get a Life!

People who want to become meeting planners often ask us what degree or education they need to get a job. This is a very good question and is one that has many different answers and perspectives.

First of all, if you ask planners today how they became meeting planners you will hear the following top five reasons:

1. By accident.

2. It fit into their current duties.

3. Their boss volunteered them to plan a meeting.

4. They were good at organizing parties and events.

5. They love people and the challenge of getting things done under pressure.

These days, it is not as easy to "fall into" a meeting-planning job as it used to be. With employers realizing that they need strategic thinkers and leaders, the planner positions are taken more seriously and are categorized at higher levels. In some companies, being a CMP or CMM is a requirement.

So in answer to the question of what you need in the way of education, we offer the following advice:

- ◆ Obtain a certification, degree, or certificate in the meetings industry.

- ◆ Be willing to start out in a support role in a meeting-planning department.

- ◆ Don't limit your job possibilities to a "meeting planner" or "assistant" title. Look at hotels, Convention and Visitor Bureaus (CVBs), destination management companies (DMCs), and event-planning companies for other opportunities. Working in other capacities, such as a sales assistant in a hotel, can also give you valuable experience and you can meet all the clients who need planners!

- ◆ Get an internship at a hotel or CVB.

- ◆ Be persistent.

Networking is still a great way to find a job in the meetings industry. Attend industry functions, talk to both planners and suppliers, and in general, be active in the industry!

There are also some very good websites you can visit to peruse the job opportunities and submit your resume. For starters, take a look at these:

- ◆ www.meetingjobs.com and www.meetingtempjobs.com

- ◆ www.hotel-jobs.com

- ◆ www.hoteljobsnetwork.com

- ◆ www.hcareers.com

- ◆ www.searchwide.com

Most of the industry associations listed in this book also have job boards on their websites. Just by surfing the websites mentioned in this book, you will find many places to look for a job.

The Least You Need to Know

- ◆ A professional industry certification is a stepping-stone to professional excellence.

- ◆ It is never too late to earn a certificate or degree in meeting management.

- Investigate colleges, universities, and local community colleges for certificate and degree programs in meeting management.

- There are many online job boards on which you can post a resumé or search through job listings.

Chapter 28

Keeping Cool Under Pressure

In This Chapter

◆ Learn a four-step process for standing firm on meeting planning decisions

◆ Discover ways to look out for number one—*you!*

◆ See how being too busy takes you away from the really important things in your life

◆ Learn some simple tricks to keep control of the information flow in and out of your office

Today's lifestyles demand our full attention. We are constantly exposed to new technology, higher stress levels, increased job responsibility, a nonstop business climate, the need for more education, family commitments, and that nagging feeling of always being "behind" in whatever we are supposed to do.

Meeting and event planning can really stress you out. You are responsible for tons of details including budgets, goals, objectives, negotiating contracts, marketing, brochure development, travel plans, speakers, VIPs, registration, meeting supplies, and pulling it all together within a finite amount of time to create the perfect onsite experience for a multitude of people, who may or may not appreciate your efforts. The real kicker is that meeting and event planning is all based on deadlines, and there are real consequences for missing those deadlines. Meeting and event planning is a huge responsibility.

This chapter is for you, the planner. Who really knows what you do besides you? We do. We can help by sharing with you some thoughts and ideas we have come up with during our tenure in the meetings business.

How Much More Can I Take?

Planning revolves around details, and it's always amazing how much time the little things take up. Your best bet is to get and stay organized. Here are a few good, quick tips that we use:

◆ Assign each task a priority: low, medium, high, or urgent.

◆ Every day, do at least three items more than you add to your list. Start with the highest priority.

◆ Let voicemail answer the phone when you are concentrating on urgent matters. Respond to low- or mid-level e-mails and voicemails after hours if possible.

◆ Create a "waiting for" response list so you can see at a glance who or what you are waiting for.

◆ Don't let things pile up. File at the end of every day.

◆ Review and modify your next day's list before you leave the office.

◆ When you need information, make phone calls or send out e-mails early in the day.

◆ Use caller ID or e-mail filters to screen calls or e-mails.

◆ Review and discard redundant information.

◆ Take some time each day to relax.

Don't Drop the Ball

When things get tense (and even before they do), rally the troops. If you have support staff, take care of them. Buy lunch, tell jokes, provide snacks and toys in the office—make it fun.

Taking some time out also helps keep things in perspective. There will be times when a problem develops and you have to answer to people who don't understand the situation or what you need to do to rectify it. They get upset, your staff gets upset, and you get upset. Situations can escalate to the point that even the littlest deals turn into big deals. Slow down, take a deep breath, and most of all, don't take it personally. Maintaining your composure is the name of the game.

Who's Clueless?

Meeting and event planning is just now becoming recognized as a profession. Planners should be involved in the strategic part of meetings, not just logistics. All too often, the planner role is considered administrative in nature, and that can be a huge mistake. Don't get stuck in the dirt. Think big picture.

One word of caution: You will run into folks who think they know more than you when it comes to planning your meetings and events. If you run into a situation in which your organization or managers want to do something you know will not work, stand up for what you know. Act professionally and state your viewpoint based on experience. What is your recourse, however, if you are asked to do something that you know will not work and that could possibly have a negative impact on your meeting? Consider using this four-step process:

1. Go to the person/group making the request and explain why you think the idea won't work. Back up your explanation with facts and provide an alternative solution.

2. Garner support from within your organization or from seasoned veterans in the meeting and event industry. Make sure you clearly state your case and your alternative solution.

> **Food for Thought**
>
> Continue your professional education and stay current on industry trends. Go to meeting planning educational seminars and conferences; read trade, business, and training magazines; and consider certification.

3. If you are still asked to implement the request, make sure you document your recommendation in writing and give a copy to all decision-makers prior to the event or meeting. Then, if your predictions come true, you cannot be held responsible.

4. Follow up after the event or meeting and evaluate the outcome. Learn from your experience.

As an example, consider the company executive who does not consider the meeting/event planner an integral part of the company's strategic-planning process. The planner has no strategic role and is told to just plan the meeting logistics. In this scenario, if the planner has no idea about goals, objectives, and the reasons for the meeting/event, how can this person communicate needs to a potential vendor? How can he or she determine the right site for the meeting/event? How can he or she negotiate a contract that meets the needs of the program? The answer is he or she can't. The planner can only plod along and check off one detail after another.

Consider another company in which the meeting planner is part of the organization's strategic-planning advisory group and is well versed in why meetings are held within the organization. This person is in a much better position to select the right site, set the meeting rooms, internally market the meeting to the attendees, and negotiate contracts. The meeting planning process is more strategic in nature, and as a result, contracts are negotiated to meet those needs. The right sites are selected to support the meetings' goals and objectives, and attendees understand why they are attending the meetings.

To reach a strategic position in your organization, you need to constantly educate your superiors as to how you bring value to the organization. Document how and when you saved the company money, and how much, because of your negotiation skills or how you leveraged your buying power by signing a multiyear meeting/event contract. It is very easy to spend a lot of money on meetings and special events. It takes a talented planner to keep tabs on the purse strings and be recognized for it.

> **Food for Thought**
>
> When you get recognition for a job well done, take it and don't be afraid to toot your own horn.

What's So Hard About That?

Then there are the people who think your job is nothing but fun, fun, fun and can't believe you get paid for it. We have not come across any other industry in which so much responsibility is placed on individuals who have little or no experience and have to learn the hard way—by doing. Think about the awesome responsibility you have and how it can really affect your organization. For example, if your contracts are not negotiated effectively because you have no idea about your history and the company ends up paying huge attrition fees, that affects the company. The flip side is that a well-negotiated contract can avoid attrition fees altogether.

> **The Inside Scoop**
>
> The good news is we can have better control of our time if we take the time (no pun intended) to sort through and prioritize our efforts by focusing on the really important stuff.

We know of one meeting planner who got sick and tired of not making what her peers made in other departments so she researched the skill sets, documented that she has huge responsibilities that can make or break budgets in her company, and won a well-deserved pay raise.

Look Out for #1

Ever notice how busy everyone is? Doesn't it seem that everyone's response to "How are you?" is "I'm busy"? How did this happen? We remember a time when work was more manageable and people went home each night feeling good about the workload in their office, without bringing work home. The "B" word (balance) is affecting us all. These days you are lucky if you are ever caught up.

Planners are constantly under deadline pressures and have a lot of last-minute tasks to accomplish. These things tend to get in the way of accomplishing your goals and objectives.

Would you like to take back your life and maintain some sense of balance? If so, make a list of things you do that are not really important and stop doing them. Your list might look like this:

- Making too many volunteer commitments, both professional and personal
- Making too many business commitments
- Watching too much television
- Attending business-related social gatherings
- Stacking unread mail or magazines, hoping to get to them later

Make a list of the really important things you need to do and do them! This list could include the following:

- Be home to tuck the kids into bed every night, or scratch the dog's ears.
- Make more home-cooked dinners and eat at least one meal a day with family or friends.
- Upgrade your technology and your knowledge of it to make your life easier.
- Go for a walk or a bike ride; smell the roses.
- Have lunch with your favorite person.
- Take a vacation every year and leave your pager and cell phone at home.

Here are some additional tips to take control:

- **Delegate at home and at work.** Delegate when you can. If you are a volunteer, make sure you are not doing the majority of the work.

- **Look at your to-do list and do the "worst" thing first.** Once the hard part is over, the rest of your day is much easier.

- **Listen to your body.** If you are a morning person, try to accomplish the most important things when you are at your best. If you are a night person, work at night. Do not fight your body's internal clock.

- **Hire outside help.** Hire help to clean your house, mow your grass, or even run errands. You can find professional services or perhaps even neighborhood teenagers. Your time is important and has value.

- **Simplify your life.** Get rid of things you don't use and throw out excess stuff.

- **Accept that it's okay to do less.** In fact, sometimes it's okay to do nothing.

Many people find validation in crossing items off a to-do list. This is not living; it is just accomplishing tasks. Think about it. Is this how you measure your success? What do you really want to do? How do you really want to spend your time?

Meeting planners tend to carry over their *big* checklists into their personal lives. Before you know it, you are running your life like you run a meeting. Sometimes our kids have to say, "Mom, you are not at a meeting." Understand this and your life will be less stressful.

Get a Coach

Ready to make some changes? Ever heard of having a *coach?* A life coach? A career coach? A family coach? Yes, they exist and can be a valuable part of helping you make changes. Not only have you committed to make changes, you now have to report progress to someone with the experience and leadership to guide and help you achieve your goals and ambitions. Talk about motivation!

A coach brings a different perspective to your life. Sometimes just knowing that other people are going through the same thing is comforting. Plus, a coach is less expensive than a psychiatrist. Check out www.coachfederation.com for more information and to find a coach.

Friends and Family

Make time for friends and family. Do you eat dinner with them? Do you celebrate events such as birthdays and holidays? Make sure family is a top priority and carries more weight than work does. Try not to miss important events because you are too busy. Establish family traditions. This is especially important if you have young children or elderly parents. The worst thing that can happen is you go through life on a huge racetrack, and one day you wake up and realize you didn't spend enough time with your family and friends. Don't let it happen.

When the Going Gets Tough

When the going really gets tough, write your obituary. Sit down and write about who you are or what you want to be remembered for. It really puts things into perspective. You will find out very quickly that being busy all the time and accumulating a million frequent flyer miles is not something people will remember you for. You will also find that whatever is creating havoc in your life really doesn't matter much in the whole scheme of things.

The Office Never Closes

With technology racing faster than the speed of sound, you may never catch up. Get over it. In fact, when you are onsite at one meeting, you may have several other meetings and events piling up at the office! Or, at the very least, your other work is piling up, too. Not to mention the voice and e-mail messages waiting for your attention.

E-mail is one big game of "gotcha!" You are helpless and are tagged "it" with the click of a mouse—unless, of course, you program one of those handy little e-mail messages that says you are out of the country for the next several months. You can also program your voicemail not to accept messages. We really like that one.

> **CAUTION**
>
> **Don't Drop the Ball**
>
> In these high-tech days, many people are using hand held PDAs (personal digital assistants). They allow you to keep a large number of contacts handy, record calendar information, and send and receive e-mail. They can really increase your productivity.

All kidding aside, the reality is you need to be reachable and need to control the flow of information in and out of your office. Here are some ideas for helping you manage this flow:

- Delegate time-consuming tasks, such as mailings, to other staff members or out-source this work if possible.

- Network with other meeting-industry professionals to find out how they do things. If you belong to any industry associations, these are perfect places to find other people with similar job responsibilities. If you do not belong to any associations, join one now! Didn't we say that already?

- Say no to time wasters such as extended lunches or seminars offering content with little or no value to you.

- Understand your job and ask the question, "Is this task really important to the bottom line?" If the answer is no, don't do it. You may be surprised how effective this is.

Juggling Multiple Meetings

It would be great if you could plan one meeting or event at a time, but more than likely, you will be responsible for several at any given time. Here are some ideas to make it easier to manage them and to save time in the booking process:

- Book multiple meetings at the same hotel or with the same hotel chain.
- Schedule site visits together. Piggyback meetings in the same city.
- Create a standard RFP for all your meetings.
- Hire an industry attorney to create a meetings contract or at least an addendum that addresses your needs.
- Keep good meeting history records.

Staying Ahead

In our line of work, the key to staying ahead in this fast-paced world is to stay focused on a defined set of issues. For example, a meeting planner has a defined role—simply put, to plan meetings. A supplier's role is to meet the planner's needs within the scope of the meeting. To succeed, we need to organize ourselves, as well as our meetings and events, in a way that progress can be monitored and improved upon. Good luck!

The Least You Need to Know

- Solid organization is necessary to stay in control of the details.

- In any dispute over meeting decisions, state your viewpoint and stand up for what you know.

- Each day, tackle the least desirable tasks first. The rest of the day will seem much easier.

- Keep a good balance in your work and life.

Appendix A

Sample Forms and Checklists

Here are some handy forms for you to copy and use. You can customize them for your needs or use them the way they are. Make your own forms along the way, too. Meeting planners just love forms and checklists!

Breakout Evaluation

1. Name of breakout session: _____

   Date: _____

2. Presenter name: _____

3. The information presented is useful to my work: Yes ❏   No ❏

4. The delivery method was appropriate: Yes ❏   No ❏

5. The handouts were relevant and covered the subject: Yes ❏   No ❏

6. Please rate each of the following:

	Excellent	Good	Fair	Poor
Speaker knowledge of topic	❏	❏	❏	❏
Delivery style	❏	❏	❏	❏

Suggestions for improvement:

_____

_____

_____

_____

Return form to: <add your contact information here>

Conference Evaluation

	Excellent	Good	Fair	Poor

1. Please rate each of the following:

   Educational value of overall conference: ❏ ❏ ❏ ❏

2. How would you rate the conference logistics?

   Schedule ❏ ❏ ❏ ❏

   Registration process ❏ ❏ ❏ ❏

3. Please rate the hotel:

   Service ❏ ❏ ❏ ❏

   Food and beverage ❏ ❏ ❏ ❏

   Meeting rooms ❏ ❏ ❏ ❏

   Audio-visual ❏ ❏ ❏ ❏

4. Do you have suggestions for next year's conference?

   Keynote speakers: _____

   Breakout topics: _____

   Activities: _____

   Schedule: _____

5. Were your professional goals and objectives met during the conference?
   Yes ❏   No ❏

6. What did you learn that you will put into use once you return to the office?

   _____

   _____

7. What didn't you learn that you thought you would?

   _____

   _____

8. Did the promotional material adequately describe the educational value of the conference?   Yes ❑   No ❑

If not, do you have any suggestions for improvement?

_____

_____

9. How do you rate the conference fee?
   High ❑   Just right ❑   Low ❑

10. Do you plan on attending the conference next year?
    Yes ❑   No ❑   Maybe ❑

11. Are you a member?   Yes ❑   No ❑

12. What is your title? _____

13. Name/phone number (optional): _____

Return form to: <add your contact information here>

Exhibitor Evaluation

Please share your comments on the value of being an exhibitor. Your feedback will be extremely helpful in planning future conferences.

	Excellent	**Good**	**Fair**	**Poor**
1. Please rate each of the following:				
Overall exhibit experience	❑	❑	❑	❑
Overall schedule	❑	❑	❑	❑
Networking with attendees	❑	❑	❑	❑
Booth registration process	❑	❑	❑	❑
Pre-conference info	❑	❑	❑	❑
Cost of booth	❑	❑	❑	❑
Meeting facility overall	❑	❑	❑	❑
2. Please rate exhibitor services company:				
Service	❑	❑	❑	❑
Pre-conference information	❑	❑	❑	❑
Pricing	❑	❑	❑	❑
Package handling	❑	❑	❑	❑

3. List suggestion(s) for improvement:

_____

_____

4. How did you first learn about this conference?

❑ Word of mouth

❑ Info mailed to you

❑ Website

Other: _____

5. Will you return again next year as an exhibitor?

❑ Yes—please send information

❑ No

If not, why: _____

6. Include your name and affiliation (optional).

Name: _____

Affiliation: _____

Return form to: <add your contact information here>

Room Pick-Up Report

Meeting name: _____

Meeting dates: _____

	Hotel Information	Meeting Sponsor
Name	_____	_____
Address	_____	_____
City	_____	_____
State/ZIP	_____	_____
Contact name	_____	_____
Phone	_____	_____
Fax	_____	_____
E-mail	_____	_____
Website	_____	

Total Days to Arrival	Date	Date	Date	Total Pick-Up	Revenue
Contracted block	_____	_____	_____	_____	$_____
Pick-up 6 weeks out	_____	_____	_____	_____	$_____
Pick-up 5 weeks out	_____	_____	_____	_____	$_____
Pick-up 4 weeks out	_____	_____	_____	_____	$_____
Pick-up 3 weeks out	_____	_____	_____	_____	$_____
Pick-up 2 weeks out	_____	_____	_____	_____	$_____
Pick-up 1 week out	_____	_____	_____	_____	$_____
Pick-up 1 day out	_____	_____	_____	_____	$_____
Pick-up day of	_____	_____	_____	_____	$_____
Actual pick-up	_____	_____	_____	_____	$_____

Room rate(s): $_____   Total room revenue: $_____

Suite rate(s): $_____   Number of suites used: _____

Complimentary policy: _____   Number of comps: _____

Number of no-shows: _____   No-show percentage: _____

Number of cancellations: _____   Cancellation percentage: _____

Room tax percentage: _____

Additional information: _____

Food and Beverage Pick-Up Report

Meeting name: _____

Meeting dates: _____

Contact name: _____

Phone/fax/e-mail: _____

Meal Function	Guarantee	Actual Served	Cost/Person	Total Cost
Date: _____				
Continental breakfast	_____	_____	_____	_____
A.M. break	_____	_____	_____	_____
Lunch	_____	_____	_____	_____
P.M. break	_____	_____	_____	_____
Reception	_____	_____	_____	_____
Dinner	_____	_____	_____	_____
Date: _____				
Continental breakfast	_____	_____	_____	_____
A.M. break	_____	_____	_____	_____
Lunch	_____	_____	_____	_____
P.M. break	_____	_____	_____	_____
Reception	_____	_____	_____	_____
Dinner	_____	_____	_____	_____

Total Food and Beverage Cost* $_____

*not including taxes and gratuity

Gratuity Percentage: _____   Gratuity taxed? yes/no ×_____% Gratuity

F&B Tax Percentage: _____ $_____

Entertainment Group(s) and Cost(s): _____   ×_____% Tax

Decorations and Costs: _____

TOTAL $_____

Observations about food functions: _____

Site Visit Checklist

Property name: _____

Contact person: _____ **Phone:** _____

  Distance from airport:

      Miles: _____

      Minutes: _____

  Transportation available: _____

  Nearby restaurants: _____

  Nearby shopping: _____

  Arrival Experience (list comments)

  Check-in: _____

  Check-out: _____

  Lobby area: _____

  Bell stand service: _____

  Front desk service: _____

  Guest Rooms

  No. of guest rooms:

      Kings: _____

      Dbl/Dbl: _____

      Suites: _____

  Amenities in rooms: _____

  Condition: _____

  No. of phone lines: _____ Data port? Yes No

  Food and Beverage Outlets

  No. of outlets: _____

  Names: _____

  Hours of operation: _____

  Meeting Space

  Condition: _____

  Square footage: _____

  No. of breakout rooms/size: _____

  _____

  _____

Are walls soundproof?   Yes   No

Temperature controls in rooms?   Yes   No

Lighting quality: _____

Sound system(s): _____

List any obstructions: _____

Room signage clear?   Yes   No

AV company onsite?   Yes   No

   Name: _____

Restrooms nearby?   Yes   No

Questions

Is the hotel unionized?   Yes   No

   Which departments? _____

Are there any renovation or construction plans?   Yes   No

What other groups are in-house over these dates? _____

Is the hotel ADA compliant?   Yes   No

   Issues: _____

Are there any big events in town over these dates?   Yes   No

Will the hotel likely be sold out during meeting dates?   Yes   No

Call reservations. Rate quoted during meeting dates: _____

What is the guest emergency procedure?

   Medical: _____

   Fire: _____

   Other: _____

Breakout Session Speaker Agreement

<Date>

<Name>   <Title>

<Organization>   <Address>

<City, State, ZIP>

Title of Session: _____   Start Time: _____

Date: _____   End Time: _____

Thank you for agreeing to be a presenter at our conference. In exchange for your time, you will receive a complimentary registration to the conference. Although we are unable to cover your expenses related to the conference, we will copy your handouts if you provide an original at least fourteen days in advance of your presentation.

Please send us the following information as soon as possible:

1. A brief resumé of your education and experience for your introduction.

2. Audio-visual requirements for your breakout session. <Please note that all rooms will be set crescent style with a podium and table for the speaker's use.>

   ___ Overhead projector and screen   ___ Flipchart

   ___ VCR and monitor   ___ LCD projector

   ___ Slide projector   ___ Wireless microphone

Please note you are responsible for making your own housing reservation. Please call <000-000-0000>. Enclosed is a tentative conference agenda for your planning purposes.

I hereby agree to present at the <name of conference>. I affirm that, to my knowledge, none of the material presented, either verbally or in written materials, infringes upon any copyright or any person's right of privacy. I will not libel or slander any other person, facility, company, product, or service during my presentation. If such affirmation is breached, I indemnify and hold harmless <insert your organization here> and all contracted service providers.

I also understand I cannot make a "sales pitch" for any specific firm, publication, or service during my presentation. I can provide participants with an opportunity to purchase publications or materials at the conclusion of my session.

_____ I agree to have my session audiotaped and the tapes reproduced for sale with the proceeds going to <insert designee of proceeds>.

Accepted: _____

Date: _____

Print Name: _____

Please fax or mail this agreement along with your brief resumé to: <add your information here>

B

Meeting-Related Websites

This appendix lists all the websites referenced in this book. It represents just a very small sampling of the wide variety of meeting-related websites. To find the latest, most comprehensive, hyperlinked list of hundreds of websites, go to www.corbinball.com.

Associations and Organizations

www.acomonline.org	Association for Convention Operations Management
www.adme.org	Association of Destination Management Executives
www.ahiattorneys.org	Academy of Hospitality Industry Attorneys
www.ahla.com	American Hotel & Lodging Association
www.ammc.org	Alliance of Meeting Management Companies
www.asaenet.org	American Society of Association Executives
www.ascap.com	American Society of Composers, Authors, and Publishers
www.bmi.com	Broadcast Music, Inc.
www.conventionindustry.org	Convention Industry Council
www.hsmai.org	Hospitality Sales and Marketing Association International
www.iaam.org	International Association of Assembly Managers
www.iacconline.org	International Association of Conference Centers
www.iacvb.org	International Association of Convention and Visitors Bureaus
www.iaem.org	International Association for Exhibition Management
www.iasbweb.org	International Association of Speakers Bureaus
www.ifea.com	International Festivals and Events Association
www.ises.com	International Special Events Society
www.mpiweb.org	Meeting Professionals International
www.nace.net	National Association of Catering Executives
www.nbta.org	National Business Travel Association
www.nsaspeaker.org	National Speakers Association
www.nsfre.org	National Society of Fund Raising Executives
www.officialtravelguide.com	Official Travel Guide
www.officialtravelinfo.com	Official Travel Guide
www.pcma.org	Professional Convention Management Association
www.sesac.com	Society of European Stage Authors and Composers
www.tsea.org	Trade Show Exhibitors Association

Certifications

www.asaenet.org	Certified Association Executive (CAE)
www.conventionindustry.org	Certified Meeting Professional (CMP)
www.hsmai.org	Certified Hospitality Marketing Executive (CHME)
www.iaam.org	Certified Facilities Executive (CFE)
www.ises.com	Certified Special Events Professional (CSEP)
www.mpiweb.org	Certification in Meeting Management (CMM)
www.nace.net	Certified Professional Catering Executive (CPCE)
www.nsaspeaker.org	Certified Speaking Professional (CSP)
	CPAE—Council of Peers Award for Excellence (Speaker Hall of Fame)
www.site-intl.org	Certified Incentive and Travel Executive (CITE)

Gifts, Giveaways, and Meeting Supplies

www.4imprint.com	4imprint
www.awards.com	Awards.com
www.branders.com	Branders
www.events.seton.com	Seton
www.landsend.com	Lands' End
www.marcomeetings.com	Marco
www.nambe.com	Nambe
www.pcnametag.com	*pc/nametag*
www.tiffany.com	Tiffany

Industry Jobs

www.coachfederation.com	International Coach Federation
www.hcareers.com	Hospitality Careers Online
www.hotel-jobs.com	Hospitality Jobs Online
www.hoteljobsnetwork.com	Hotel Jobs Network
www.meetingjobs.com	Meeting Candidate Network
www.searchwide.com	SearchWide Hospitality Recruitment Experts

Meeting and Event Management Resources

www.ada.gov	American Disabilities Act
www.aglobalworld.com	AGlobalWorld
www.all-hotels.com	All-hotels
www.conferencedirect.com	ConferenceDirect
www.conferon.com	Conferon
www.convert-me.com	Convert-me
www.corbinball.com	Corbin Ball Associates
www.fjglaw.net	Foster, Jensen & Gulley, LLC. (Attorney John Foster)
www.fusionproductions.com/tools/roi	Fusion Productions (ROI program)
www.helmsbriscoe.com	HelmsBriscoe
www.hotrateshotdates.com	HotRatesHotDates
www.meetingsnet.com	Meeting Planners Information and Resources
www.meetingnews.com	MIMList, a hospitality industry listserv
www.mpoint.com	mpoint.com by OnVantage
www.starcite.com	StarCite
www.tradeshowresearch.com	Successful Exhibiting
www.uniquevenues.com	Unique Meeting and Event Facilities

Meeting Technology Software

www.badgepro.com	BadgePro
www.cardscan.com	CardScan
www.certain.com	Register123 and Meeting Planner Plus
www.cvent.com	cvent.com
www.dea.com	Event Management Systems
www.expocad.com	Expocad
www.exposoft.com	Exposoft Solutions
www.getthere.com	Get There
www.gomembers.com	Go Members

Meeting Technology Software

www.meetingmatrix.com	MeetingMatrix
www.mpoint.com	mpoint.com by OnVantage
www.netsimplicity.com	Meeting Room Manager
www.newmarketinc.com	Delphi Diagrams
www.onvantage.com	OnVantage
www.passkey.com	Passkey.com
www.pcnametag.com	pc/nametag
www.peopleware.com	PeoplewarePro
www.senada.com	Senada.com
www.starcite.com	RegWeb
www.timesaversoftware.com	Room Viewer
www.viewcentral.com	ViewCentral

Trade Publications

www.btnonline.com	*Business Travel News*
www.corbinball.com	*Corbin Ball Associates*
www.corporate-inc-travel.com	*Corporate & Incentive Travel*
www.event-solutions.com	*Event Solutions*
www.meetings411.com	*Meetings West, Meetings South, Meetings East*
www.meetings-conventions.com	*Meetings and Conventions*
www.meetingsnet.com	*Primedia Business Magazines & Media*
www.meetingnews.com	*MeetingNews*
www.midwestmeetings.com	*Midwest Meetings*
www.smallmarketmeetings.com	*Small Market Meetings*
www.successmtgs.com	*Successful Meetings*
www.tradeshowresearch.com	*Successful Exhibiting*
www.wheremagazine.com	*Where Magazine*

Trade Shows and Expositions

www.expochange.com	ExpoExchange
www.freemanco.com	Freeman Decorating
www.gesexpo.com	GES Exposition Services
www.tradeshowresearch.com	*Successful Exhibiting*
www.tradeshowstore.com	Trade Show Store
www.tsea.org	Trade Show Exhibitors Association

Web Blogs

http://blog.meetingsnet.com/face2face	Face2Face
www.hotelchatter.com	Hotel Chatter
www.misoapbox.com	Meetings Industry Soapbox
www.tech3partners.com/blog	Tech3Partners
www.tradeshowstartup.com	Tradeshow Startup

Web Conference Services

www.gotomeeting.com	GoToMeeting
www.imconferencing.com	IMConferencing
www.saveonconferences.com	SaveonConferences
www.webex.com	WebEx

Index

D

N

T

U-V

W–X–Y–Z

Check Out These
Best-Sellers

Read by millions!

Grammar and Style
SECOND EDITION
Laurie E. Rozakis, Ph.D.

1-59257-115-8 • $16.95

Buying and Selling a Home
FOURTH EDITION
Shelley O'Hara and Nancy D. Lewis

1-59257-120-4 • $18.95

Being a Groom
SECOND EDITION
Jennifer Lata Rung and Mark Rung

0-02-864456-5 • $9.95

Learning Spanish
THIRD EDITION
Gail Stein

0-02-864451-4 • $18.95

Personal Finance in Your 20s & 30s
SECOND EDITION
Sarah Young Fisher and Susan Shelly

0-02-864374-7 • $19.95

Organizing Your Life
FOURTH EDITION
Georgene Lockwood

1-59257-413-0 • $16.95

Total Nutrition
FOURTH EDITION
Joy Bauer, M.S., R.D., C.D.N.

1-59257-439-4 • $18.95

Positive Dog Training
Pamela Dennison

0-02-864463-8 • $14.95

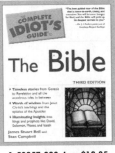
The Bible
THIRD EDITION
James Stuart Bell and Stan Campbell

1-59257-389-4 • $18.95

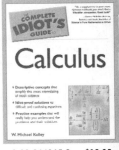
Calculus
W. Michael Kelley

0-02-864365-8 • $18.95

Music Theory
SECOND EDITION
Michael Miller

1-59257-437-8 • $19.95

The Perfect Resume
THIRD EDITION
Susan Ireland

0-02-864440-9 • $14.95

Playing the Guitar
SECOND EDITION
Frederick Noad

0-02-864244-9 • $21.95

Manga Illustrated

1-59257-335-5 • $19.95

Knitting and Crocheting
SECOND EDITION
Illustrated
Barbara Breiter and Gail Diven

1-59257-089-5 • $16.95

More than *450 titles* available at
booksellers and online retailers everywhere

www.idiotsguides.com

Λ
ALPHA